On the History
and Method of Economics

FRANK H. KNIGHT

On the History and Method of Economics

SELECTED ESSAYS

Phoenix Books

THE UNIVERSITY OF CHICAGO PRESS

This book is also available in a clothbound edition from
THE UNIVERSITY OF CHICAGO PRESS

Library of Congress Catalog Card Number: 56-6632

THE UNIVERSITY OF CHICAGO PRESS, CHICAGO & LONDON
The University of Toronto Press, Toronto 5, Canada

© *1956 by The University of Chicago. All rights reserved*
Published 1956. Third Impression 1963. First Phoenix
Edition 1963. Composed and printed by THE UNIVERSITY
OF CHICAGO PRESS, *Chicago, Illinois, U.S.A.*

PROFESSOR KNIGHT's writings on the history and method of economics illuminate not only their immediate subjects but also the connection, which he has persistently emphasized, between economics and ethics. From the extensive list of his publications, we have selected these essays as characteristic and particularly striking expressions of his views in a field he has made peculiarly his own. This collection, like two previous volumes—*The Ethics of Competition* (1935) and *Freedom and Reform* (1947)—has been gathered with Professor Knight's consent but without his participation. He has neither questioned the choice of essays nor altered their form, and they appear as originally printed, except for minor editorial changes. We are greatly indebted to Milton Friedman and Aaron Director for their advice and to various publishers for their generous permission to reprint. All royalties from the volume are assigned to the Frank H. Knight Scholarship Fund of the University of Chicago. We are especially pleased to be able to bring the book to press during the year of Professor Knight's seventieth birthday.

WILLIAM L. LETWIN
ALEXANDER J. MORIN

Contents

Contents

I

I

Economics[1]

THE term "economics" has come into general use since the early years of the present century, replacing the older "political economy" as the name of a somewhat vaguely defined branch of social science. The change of name reflected changes in the discipline itself, which had become subdivided into a number of specialties. A separation had been made between a pure science and the treatment of public—and to some extent of private—problems of policy, more or less explicitly "application"; another separation has been made between empirical fact—historical or statistical—and theory. The word "economy" comes from two Greek roots referring to the management of a household or estate. But in the past two centuries or so, the meaning has become generalized to cover all use of means in such a way as to "husband" them, to make them go as far as possible. "Political economy" itself is a modern term. It was introduced about the beginning of the seventeenth century (in French—corresponding to the German *Kameralwissenschaft*) to describe the study of the problems of the princely states which at the close of the Middle Ages in Europe replaced the feudal-ecclesiastical political order. It referred to the "economic" affairs of the state or principality—the raising and use of revenue and increase of resources—treating the state as the estate of the ruler. But this study never was generally known by this name. After the nationalistic epoch gave way to individualism or liberalism, at the time of the Enlightenment in the late eighteenth century, "political economy" was adopted as the name of a science based on the new moral and political world view, and the older literature came to be designated as "mercantilism."

EPOCHS IN THE DEVELOPMENT OF ECONOMIC THOUGHT

The sketch above suggests four main periods or epochs in the evolution of modern economics, corresponding to those usually recognized in European history. They are the Greek (or "classical" in the meaning of general history, but the Roman contribution was

1. Reprinted by permission from *Encyclopaedia Britannica* (1951).

[3]

minor), the medieval, the early modern (sixteenth to late eighteenth century), and the modern, roughly the nineteenth century. Each corresponds to a distinctive political order and to distinctive conceptions of man and society; and it is an important fact that books were written by and for different social classes in the different periods. The Greek literature was written by aristocratic philosophers and publicists and related to the problems of the city-state, nominally democratic but based on slave labor and with further exclusion of the merchant and financier from civic life. Such writers as Plato and Aristotle commented on many of the obvious facts and principles, such as the importance of division of labor and the use of money. But their interest centered in such moralistic and metaphysical notions as the condemnation of lending at interest as unnatural. Modern knowledge of the economic and industrial life of ancient Greece is derived mainly from other sources, incidental references in literature and archeological remains. Many of the ideas were in fact survivals of primitive attitudes; they are found also in the older parts of the Bible and survive as a strong influence even today.

Medieval economic thought is still more moralistic and alien to the modern outlook. The literature was produced chiefly by and for monks, at a time when the monastic life was accepted as the ideal, when worldly interests were denounced in favor of salvation in a future world as the one serious concern of man. The dominant social organization was the Church, and recorded thought was more of the nature of preaching than of science, as words are now used. For this world, the accepted ideal was a static or customary society and civilization, every man working out his lot in the situation to which he had been "called." Trade was frowned upon, beyond limited routine exchange at "fair"—meaning customary—prices, corresponding with a customary standard of living for each social class, and interest-taking was condemned outright. In the later Middle Ages, however, the canon law and the Church courts played a large role in everyday affairs, and the monasteries themselves were the spearhead in great advances in both industry and trade. Numerous evasions of the prohibition against interest-taking, achieving the same result through other contractual arrangements, came into use and were recognized as legitimate. Men's interests were shifting to the concerns of earthly life, cultural, aesthetic, and scientific, as well as material, i.e., political and economic. The evolution of economics must be seen as integral with that of economic life and of European civilization as a whole.

The third period is best designated as that of economic nationalism, but the economic thought is usually called mercantilism. It dealt with the economic policies of the national monarchic states which displaced the feudal order at the close of the Middle Ages and in general dominated the Church, whether or not the states established national churches following the Reformation. Vast changes came over social life and men's conceptions and interests. A great cultural renaissance spread from Italy to northern Europe, and technological advances were made in all fields. Paper and printing, and especially the modern Arabic system of notation, the foundation of both science and business, were even more important than gunpowder and the compass and greatly improved methods in mining and metallurgy. The distinctive writings on economic matters were produced by political pamphleteers. It was the age of the "commercial revolution"; the monarchical states saw wealth through foreign trade as the basis of their power and money as the embodiment of wealth (*pecunia nervus belli*). Europe was flooded with silver and gold (especially from the New World) which came in chiefly by way of Spain and the northern countries. These countries having no mines at home or in the colonies centered attention on sharing the treasure through a favorable balance of trade, an excess of exports over imports. A quasi-alliance was formed between the governments and the wealthy merchant and financier class against the ecclesiastical power and the higher nobility. Meanwhile, social, moral, and intellectual as well as economic forces had tended, especially in the towns, to the emancipation of labor from slavery and serfdom. But men were not ready for the ideal of individual freedom; the state took the place of the Church and the town oligarchies that grew out of the guilds as the supreme regulative authority, and its aggrandizement became the accepted end of policy, with control over economic life as the means.

Mercantilism flourished from the sixteenth century down to the nineteenth century and was exemplified in innumerable writings and in the restrictive and regulative policies of such statesmen and rulers as Colbert, Burleigh, Cromwell, and Frederick the Great. Besides attempting to secure a favorable balance of trade (an excess of exports, bringing in money or bullion), other aims were low interest rates, low wages, encouragement of population growth and colonies. It has been interpreted as "nation-building" and as an advance toward free trade, which was promoted within the national domain, in contrast with the application of similar policies by smaller units in the medieval towns. Whether the measures advocated met the immediate needs of the times is still a disputed question. In economic terms the fallacies have long since been exposed, but the general attitude survives today, as the reader will observe in "protectionism." Contrary to the admitted advantages of international specialization, this is favored and practiced not only by the national states but by smaller units, such as the American states and municipalities.

TRANSITION TO MODERN POLITICAL ECONOMY OR ECONOMICS

Modern economics is an aspect of modern thought and of the individualistic or "liberal" outlook on life, of which "capitalism," or the competitive system, or free business enterprise, is the expression on the economic side, as democracy is on the political. Our fourth epoch takes its rise in a second great cultural revolution in western Europe, in which the period of the Renaissance moved into that of the Enlightenment or Age of Reason. In this development leadership shifted, in the early modern period, from Mediterranean Europe to the northern countries, and especially to England, with the British colonies in North America playing an important role. England escaped the wars of religion which devastated western continental Europe for over a century after the Reformation, and here especially religious toleration eased the tension between Church and State. England was predominant in the great scientific movement of the seventeenth century and the great Civil War and the Revolution of 1688 established representative government at the same time that the treaties ending the Thirty Years War fastened political absolutism on the major Continental states. In England, science was inspired with a "practical" philosophy, formulated by Francis Bacon, a contemporary of Galileo, the heir of Copernicus. This movement led naturally to the technological revolution of the later eighteenth and the early nineteenth century, which involved the triumph of free enterprise; and modern economics is essentially the theory of free enterprise. It is interesting to observe that the great mercantilist writers of the later seventeenth century in England (contemporaries of John Locke in political philosophy) were in substance free traders, as Sir William Ashley has pointed out in detail. Thomas Mun's famous booklet, *England's Treasure by Forraign Trade* (published posthumously in 1664 but in circulation earlier) sophistically used the balance of trade argument in favor of freedom to export specie. Other writers, such as D'Avenant, Barbon, Child, and especially Sir

Dudley North, worked out the theoretical argument for freedom in foreign trade about as explicitly and clearly as did Adam Smith himself, nearly a century later. North argued that the wealth of a nation is that of its citizens and that the businessmen, traders, and producers are the best judges of when trade involves a net gain. It remained for someone to apply the same reasoning to internal policy, against the surviving guild restrictions or national control of apprenticeship, wages and interest, grants of monopolies, and the like.

All through the later mercantilist period, economic relations were gradually becoming more free, controls were falling into disuse, particularly in England. The process, like the earlier disappearance of serfdom, is one of social development, to be explained by the sociologist and culture historian; the formulation of a general theory lagged behind the factual change, at least until the latter was far along. In notable respects the statement of free-trade doctrine came earlier in France, where the movement itself was much slower. It was here, of course, that the phrase laissez faire (earlier associated with *laissez passer*) originated, in the first half of the eighteenth century. The kingdom of France was subdivided into many districts with customs frontiers until the Great Revolution. About the same time appeared one of the most notable of the books anticipating the liberal point of view, the somewhat mysterious *Essai sur la nature du commerce en général* by Richard Cantillon. It is apparently a translation, perhaps by the author himself, of an English manuscript which has disappeared. Cantillon showed a fairly clear insight into the mechanism by which a free market will direct resources into the production of the goods in most demand. Similar insights were conspicuous in the nearly contemporary essays of David Hume, though he wrote no systematic treatise. Early in the second half of the century much attention was attracted by the writings of a French school, who called themselves *les économistes* but are now referred to as the Physiocrats. The word is practically equivalent to law (or rule) of nature. The leader was the court physician François Quesnay. Like many of the mercantilists, these writers used rather absurd if ingenious arguments; and it has been pointed out that the position was connected with the self-interest of certain groups that had achieved wealth and power in the disturbed conditions in France after the death of Louis XIV, especially in consequence of the ambitious schemes of John Law and the famous "Mississippi Bubble." (A similar wave of speculative fury in England at the same time is known as the South Sea Bubble, from the name of the most spectacular of many companies that were organized.) But the Physiocrats are to be credited with an attempt to see and analyze a national economy as a whole. Their most characteristic doctrine was the view that only agriculture yields a "surplus" beyond what is required for the support of the workers; hence land rent alone is available for the support of the state or the increase of wealth and is the only proper subject for taxation. These ideas survived in the work of Adam Smith and the British "classical" economists. The pre-Revolutionary statesman, A. R. J. Turgot, renowned for his courageous but abortive economic and fiscal reforms, was to some extent a disciple; his work, *Reflexions sur la formation et la distribution des richesses* (1766) is an exceedingly able treatise.

CLASSICAL POLITICAL ECONOMY

In 1776 Adam Smith published *An Inquiry into the Nature and the Causes of the Wealth of Nations,* a work in which wisdom, learning, and the power of analysis are joined to an extraordinary degree. As already noted, Smith shared many of the popular prejudices that were evident in the writings of the Physiocrats. He held that "in agriculture nature works with man"—as though this were not true of all other pursuits—and that only labor is productive, and indeed only that labor is productive which at least reproduces the capital which supports it. Also that the interests of businessmen, as a class, are more often opposed to the interests of the community than are those of landowners. Nevertheless, Smith gave the world a new view of the advantages of trade as a mechanism for working out the "division of labor" and a new "philosophy of commerce." But he saw in commerce, as well as internal trade, a means to welfare, not merely to the aggrandizement of the state. His book was, in one leading aspect, a formidable tract directed against mercantilism. Money, from the communal point of view, he held to be merely an instrument, a "wheel of trade." The real source of a country's wealth, he said, is its "annual labor," and its wealth or well-being could be increased only by making its labor more effective, particularly by extending specialization and accumulating product in the form of capital. (For "labor" we should now say "productive resources.") That "the division of labor is limited by the extent of the market" is one of his most famous sayings.

These were Adam Smith's fundamental principles. He elaborated them with great skill in relation to concrete problems, showing unusual powers of fresh observation in his selection and use of illustrative material, and passing large sections of economic history and the whole range of the contemporary commercial and fiscal problems of Britain under survey. Although the book is the most influential brief ever formulated for unimpeded trade, neither hampered nor coddled by governments, its greatest importance lies not in that circumstance but in the general picture, at once simple and comprehensive, which it gives of the economic life of a nation. The apparent chaos of competition, the welter of buying and selling, are resolved or transmuted into an orderly system of economic co-operation by means of which, under individual freedom in contrast with central direction, the community's wants are supplied and its wealth increased. This general picture has been in the minds of economists ever since, whatever their opinions with respect to the efficiency or morality of the competitive system, and its general outline is admitted even by collectivists to be valid for their systems. Despite some sweeping phrases which invite another interpretation, Smith was no doctinaire advocate of a hands-off policy by governments in respect of economic matters. His treatment must be understood against the background of conditions of his day, in which so much was a holdover from the period of mercantilism and even the Middle Ages. He was opposed to monopoly, exclusive combinations, and special privileges of all kinds quite as much as to the type of legislation which aims at fostering a country's prosperity by restricting its trade. He is often styled the "apostle of self-interest," but he took no pains to conceal his dislike for some of the forms in which self-interest manifests itself in trade and industry, and he had no aversion to legal measures wherever they actually promised to be beneficial. What his attitude would have been under the later conditions of the nineteenth and twentieth centuries toward the factory acts, social insurance, and particularly measures intended to foster equality of opportunity, we cannot tell. But there is nothing in the aims of these newer types of legislation which runs counter to his principal contentions or is inconsistent with his general economic philosophy.

Adam Smith's work had a profound influence, not in Britain alone, but in almost every part of the western world. It was partly responsible for some radical changes in the commercial policies of governments, though its influence cannot be measured since the current of the times was moving in the direction of his contentions. Its effect upon scientific thought and upon the character and quality of public discussions of economic questions cannot be questioned. Men like J. B. Say in France and K. H. Rau in Germany based their work very largely on Smith's and helped to diffuse his influence. Say, however, was more than a mere popularizer. He had some clear-cut views of his own and developed Smith's work in directions other than those it took in the hands of Smith's British successors. In the United States, Say's work came to be about as widely read as Smith's.

The particular trend which the development of economics took in Great Britain after Smith was largely determined by the character of the economic problems which confronted the nation, partly by reason of rapid changes in its own industrial structure (the Industrial Revolution) and partly in consequence of the French Revolutionary and Napoleonic Wars. Population increased rapidly, and in particular there was a "mushroom" growth of new industrial towns; foreign trade expanded, especially the export of industrial products and import of agricultural, reversing the previous situation; yet agricultural cultivation was extended with the commercialization of farming and vast improvements of methods both of tillage and of stock-breeding. The changes were accentuated by interference with trade through the wars and governmental effort to maintain self-sufficiency in food) or to benefit the landed interest which controlled the government); land rents rose with the increase in agricultural prices relative to industrial; the currency was depreciated (a practically universal accompaniment of a major war); rates of interest and of profits were disturbed, and, after the peace, both industry and agriculture experienced depression conditions. Some of these conspicuous and important phenomena engaged the attention of Parliamentary committees; all of them attracted the interest of thoughtful men who, with Adam Smith's picture of the mechanism of organized economic life in their minds, thought of them as interrelated and attempted to explain them in some consistent and comparatively simple way. Out of the discussions of the period, in pamphlets and controversial tracts, there emerged a formal system of political economy. It owed much to Smith, but it stressed matters to which he had given little or no attention and emended his views at a number of important points. This newer political economy was concerned more largely with abstract general relations, but it dealt with real problems and dealt with them in what was intended to be a practical way. There is an appearance of paradox, but only an appearance, in the fact that the type of economics which grew out of attempts to deal intelligently with the problems of a period of economic storm and stress was one which gave particular attention to "normal tendencies" and to the conditions of "economic equilibrium" rather than to the immediate causes of economic maladjustments. A parallel may be found in the way in which the study of pathology has contributed to men's knowledge of normal physiology.

For convenience, the period of which we are now speaking may be taken as definitely beginning with the publication of David Ricardo's *Principles of Political Economy and Taxation* in 1817 and as culminating with the publication of John Stuart Mill's *Principles of Political Economy* in 1848. One who compares the economic tracts and the systematic treatises of that period with *The Wealth of Nations* will be impressed with the increased importance given to a group of problems which have continued to be principal concerns of economics—problems now commonly grouped under the head of "theory of value and distribution." These problems of price-mechanics unfortunately tend to get separated from the real issues of the way in which the price system organizes production and distributes the result. The theory of value, of course, attempts to explain why goods exchange at particular ratios, why some are relatively expensive and others cheap. (Absolute money prices are, of course, a matter of the value or purchasing-power of money, a distinct problem.) The modern theory of distribution is really a part of value theory, dealing with the prices of "productive services," with a view to explaining the sharing of the national income or "social dividend." But the classical economists (from Smith to J. S. Mill) did not look at the problem in this way; they held a more metaphysical theory of the division of the total product into the three traditional shares: wages of labor, profits of capital, and rent of land. This theory will be considered presently. Later on, the conception of a fourth share, the profits of enterprise, or of the successful direction of production, was taken over from the French economists (Say and his followers); the earnings of capital, separated from the entrepreneurial functions of management and responsible risk-taking, were called interest (whether actually paid out for borrowed money or "imputed" to that of the owner, an individual, or a group). This has been more true in the United States than in Britain, where economists still rather typically speak of the "profits of capital" in the language of business and of everyday life. And the treatment of enterprise or risk-taking (better called uncertainty-bearing, since there can be no measurement of the risk as in gambling or insurance) raises problems on which there is no agreement among economists anywhere.

The threefold (or fourfold) classification of "factors" is clearly in part arbitrary. Some economists use a twofold classification, treating land as a particular form of capital; others point out that a logical classification would recognize many different kinds of capital, of labor, and of natural resources, with some kinds under one head economically less similar to others in the same class than to some in other classes. And it must also be recognized that in the long run, all productive agents largely represent a cost of production, an investment of resources in the past (with wide variation in the relation between such cost and present value because of "uncertainty") and that this investment is more or less subject to recovery and reinvestment in other types of productive agent. Yet the three forms of income are very real to ordinary thinking, which does not distinguish, for example, between the four or five elements obviously present in most personal earnings. One part is based on natural capacity, one on the "pain" or irksomeness of the work, one on the investment in training; and there is the factor of risk or imperfect foresight, which so profoundly affects the return on any investment for return in a fairly remote future; and, finally, non-economic motives affect in special ways the investment in human capacity. A somewhat similar analysis could be made of the payments for the use of what are commonly classed as either natural resources or capital goods.

The classical theory of value stressed chiefly the tendency for the prices of goods produced and sold under competitive conditions to be proportionate to the respective costs of producing them. However, costs meant not the money outlays of the producers (entrepreneurs) but the "real" costs, human sacrifice or pain. For Ricardo in particular this in turn meant "quantity of labor"; that labor alone is really productive, other "factors" only "assisting," was basic to the "labor theory of value," which was taken over and exploited for propaganda purposes by the various schools of socialists and economic radicals. Later, the notion that the "abstinence" involved in saving and accumulation of capital was also a pain cost was introduced by N. W. Senior (*An Outline of the Science of Political Economy* [1836]). The socialists of course scornfully rejected this innovation. The classical economists did not see, at least not at all clearly, that what is "economized" is the use of resources, both human and non-human, and that the ultimate meaning of the cost of any product is the non-use of resources for some other end. This fact is now known as the "alternative cost" principle. But the alternative end sacrificed is not always and entirely a quantity of another marketable product but may be the leisure use of time and labor or some direct (non-market) use of any other resource. Interpreted in this way, the notion of pain cost has some validity. It should be noted, as all modern economists have recognized, that the cost explanation of value applies only in a long-run view, over time sufficient to adjust production to demand. The classical economists freely recognized that over short periods price depends on "demand and supply," i.e., the demand for the existing supply already produced or for which irreversible commitments have been made.

A similar division between short- and long-run views was inevitable in connection with the theory of distribution. Neither theory has stood up well under later criticism, though many important facts and principles were recognized. In a general way, the short-run theory held that labor gets as wages its "means of subsistence" and the capitalist the excess of the product (of labor or labor-plus-capital) on "marginal" land—or at the "intensive" margin on better land, in any case where no rent was deducted—*after* payment of a subsistence wage. Land (of a quality above that barely worth using) received as rent the excess ("surplus") product above that of the same amount of labor-and-capital on no-rent land. The foundation of the position is the subsistence theory of wages; but it is hard to make out whether this limitation was due to the power of the employer over the worker (Adam Smith sometimes comes near to stating the exploitation theory of the later socialists) or to a tendency of the working population to multiply up to the means of subsistence. The latter view (more conspicuous in Smith's treatment) would clearly operate only in the long run. And somehow another theory must be fitted into the picture—that of the famous wages fund. In its simplest version, this meant that the capital (the annual product of an economy or some ill-defined part of it) was supposed to be advanced to laborers each year, making the average wage simply the total capital divided by the total working population. Ricardo and later members of the school recognized that the period of production or turnover is longer than a year in industries employing a fixed capital, but they failed to see that capital is never produced by labor alone but rather reproduces itself (unless it is disinvested) so that no determinate period or cycle in production can be found.

In the long-run theory of distribution, the notion of cost played a part—though not as large a one as it logically should have in view of the fact that all productive agents, human or other, are in a general sense products. In the long-run interpretation, the idea that the standard of living determines wages is in effect a cost-of-production theory of the price of labor. This doctrine rested upon the theory of population associated with the name of T. R. Malthus, though it was clearly stated in general terms by Adam Smith and by still earlier writers. In the later form, the notion of "subsistence," as a physiological minimum, was replaced by, or interpreted to mean, a "standard of living," a scale or level which laborers think of as necessary for family life. If wages fall below that level, it was thought, the rate of growth of the working population will be negative (births fewer than deaths) and the decline in the labor supply will raise wages. If wages are above this level, population will increase and wages will fall—unless a higher standard of living becomes effective. Somewhat similar reasoning was applied to profit, the rate of return on capital. The supply tends to increase as long as the return is above what savers generally consider sufficient to compensate for the abstinence required to save and will decrease when it is below such a level, hence the rate of profit "tends toward" this level as a position of equilibrium.

The rent of land, however, was held not to be affected by the principle of cost. Land was thought to be permanently fixed in supply; it was defined by Ricardo as "the original and indestructible powers of the soil." Hence a rise in rent will not tend to counteract itself by bringing forth an additional supply—or reciprocally for a decline. Correspondingly, as already noted, rent was not supposed to be a part of, or to influence the price of, its produce, which in this view is determined by production costs (wages plus profit) on land barely worth using and yielding no rent—or by the cost at the "intensive margin." Changes in rent were thus the effect, not the cause, of changes in product prices. This doctrine rested on a sharp separation between land and capital (capital goods) which later economists have tended to view as unrealistic. It also rested on an assumption that land is used only to produce a single distinctive product and hence is not, like labor and capital, transferred from one use to another in response to changes in relative prices. This view has also given place to recognition that raw produce is less a product than a stage in the production of all final products. But there is an important element of truth in the older views. In the classical system of distribution as a whole a very important place was ascribed to the "law of diminishing returns," in a particular long-run or historical interpretation. As the theory ran, the growth of population, itself dependent on growth of capital, requires resort to poorer land and also to more intensive cultivation of land already in use. In either case, the increase of product would not be proportionate to the increased amount of labor and capital. Manufactures, in contrast, were thought to be subject to increasing returns, because of larger opportunities for the economies of the division of labor and for invention and the application of the fruits of scientific progress to industry. Agriculture also benefits by technical progress, but here the possibility of improvement was thought to be smaller and to be more than counterbalanced by the increasingly disadvantageous proportioning of labor and capital to land. Since laborers must always get the same real wages—the means of subsistence—the profits of capital must decline, until the growth of population and wealth would come to an end in a "stationary economy." Taken as a prophecy, this doctrine has so far been disproved by the course of events. The possibilities of improvement in agricultural technique were underestimated; new lands of good quality have been brought under cultivation and their produce brought to market by cheap transportation; and the Malthusian "law" has been partly falsified by declining birth rates accompanying the general progress of civilization—the rise in the effective standard of living already referred to.

Any general system of value theory must have something to say about the measure of value, hence the "value of money" or the general price level in contrast with relative prices. This problem was of especial concern to Adam Smith because of the price revolution and of its startling effects which had swept over Europe after the discovery of America. And this interest was nourished by the monetary and price changes of the period of the great wars of the French Revolution and of Napoleon. On this point, the classical school held to the doctrine later known as the "quantity theory of money": other things being equal, the value of money (and reciprocally the price level) depends on its quantity in relation to the volume of production and trade. Allowance would also be made for the use of money substitutes, such as bank credit, already familiar in Europe. As a long-run view, this was supplemented by the notion that the quantity of money is determined by the costs of mining the precious metals. Among different countries, especially those with and those without mines, prices would tend to be equalized by a flow of money or bullion from countries in which it would buy less to those in which it would buy more. This part of classical value theory has in general stood up better than the views on values and distribution. It would be an error to think of these earlier economists as altogether preoccupied with abstract theories or not to recognize that their interest in these was born of an interest in practical problems. And in general, they were not such uncompromising opponents of any sort of interference by government in industry as some later critics and pretended expounders of their views have made them out to be.

Before reviewing the later progress of economics, especially the revolutionary developments of the later nineteenth century, it will be helpful to look at the principal types of criticism which have been directed against the older political economy, and in part are still maintained against the later developments, and at the conceptions which have been proposed as replacements. In the first place, "romanticists," like Adam Müller in Germany and John Ruskin in England, intensely disliked the new individualistic economic mechanism into the workings of which the economists were trying to probe. And, consequently, they particularly disliked the defense of this mechanism of economic laissez faire, which the economists in general did defend, by statement or implication. They preferred an ordered society, with economic subordinated to moral or religious or aesthetic values, such as they typically thought had been more or less fully embodied in the social structure of the Middle Ages. Work, they inclined to insist, is not merely a means to an end, particularly what are called economic ends, but good work is worth doing for its own sake and for its effect upon character. They did not impugn the fitness of economics as an instrument of attack upon its special problems but they belittled these problems.

Another group of writers, for whom there is no better descriptive name than "the critical school," come much closer to meeting the orthodox economists upon their own ground. One of the earliest, and much the most influential, of them was Sismonde de Sismondi (*Nouveaux principes d'économie politique* [1817] and other works). Other able writers, often without any conscious discipleship, have taken a similar position. These critics urge that more attenton be given to the defects of the competitive economic mechanism, even viewed merely as a means of providing for material needs. They contend that the economists, contemplating the long-run or normal tendencies and the theoretical beauties of the automatic processes by which the pursuit of individual economic interests becomes organized into a vast scheme of economic co-operation, forget how often the mechanism breaks down and normal economic life is interrupted by crises and depression; how unemployment, chronic as well as epidemic, is a disease of this economic order; how equally the aggregate product is distributed among individuals or families; and how many of the things men do for their own economic advantage are in fact inimical to the interests of the community. As later critics have put it, businessmen are interested primarily in making money, which does not always mean making more goods. The picture of the "economic harmonies" (the title of a mid-nineteenth century French apologetic work) requires, it is urged, rationalizing of the facts to an unwarranted degree. These criticisms also undoubtedly go too far. They unduly play down the role of the abstract principles stressed by the older economics, in the general view of the economic activities of the community. And no economist of the first rank has ever been a devotee of the pure automatism of the market. But the critical school has had a wholesome influence on the progress of economic science. It should be observed that this school occupies a position between that of the orthodox school and that of the socialists who denounce the works of the latter as mere apologetic, a product of the existing economic order and prompted by the interest of those who benefit by its iniquities.

Another line of attack was adopted by the "historical school," or more accurately, "schools," since the term covers several different groups. This position has been represented in all countries, but it has been most influential in Germany. The most important of its early exponents were Friedrich List (*Nationales System der politischen Ökonomie* [1841]) and Wilhelm Roscher (*Grundlagen der Nationalökonomie* [1854] and other works). The form of a nation's economic life, said these critics, is a "historical category," peculiar to a given nation at a given time, a product of its past and therefore only to be understood by a study of that past. The wisdom of particular economic policies is relative to conditions of a place and time, and the supposedly universal laws of abstract economics need to be supplemented by or even subordinated to study of concrete facts of the national situation. If they had gone no further, the "historicists" would have found many to agree with them. But they tended to make of the historical method something arbitrary and doctrinaire. (Karl Knies, whose work, *Die politische Ökonomie vom Standpunkte der geschichtlichen Methode,* appeared in 1853, is a notable exception.) Not content with looking to history for the causes of these concrete differences of economic structure in which they were interested, they proposed to derive from history itself universal and binding laws, akin to those of physical sciences. They were fond of schemes of "stages" of economic development through which they thought every nation must pass. In these speculations they were really elaborating suggestions found not in historical research but in the Greek speculative historians. They regarded the forms taken by economic life, past and present, as inevitable products of historical forces; and at the same time, unconscious of the inconsistency, they advocated a rather heavy-handed control of economic activities by the state.

The British and French economists had looked upon the organization of economic life as being shaped and determined by the interplay of the interests and rational activities of individual men and had viewed the state as an instrument of individual purposes—well-being as judged, in the main, by each person for himself. The spokesmen of the historical school, in contrast, were strongly influenced by the philosopher Hegel, who ascribed a prior and independent value to the state, with individuals somewhat in the role of means, on the analogy of cells or organs in the human body, a view related to that of the mercantilists though more sophisticated. Although they pushed their views to extremes, they gave a needed emphasis to what has come to be called the "institutional" view of economic activities, as contrasted with the individualistic or contractual aspect. But both the older historicists and the later institutionalists (largely an American movement of the early twentieth century) slurred over the contrast between two kinds or meanings of institution, i.e., patterns of action moving in predestined grooves under the influence of relatively unconscious social forces, versus those embodying deliberate organization and control, such as the political organs of the state. The state, in turn, was conceived by the older schools in what would now be called "totalitarian" terms, while the institutionalists, like the socialists (in contrast with the Communists), thought of it as democratic. Historical economists have also been more ready to think of change, as contrasted with finality, in the pattern of economic organization, and they gave a useful impulse to the study of economic history, which is valuable both in itself and as a complement to economic theory. Under the influence of historical study the old dogmatism of the historical economists gradually gave way to a realization of the variety and complexity of the fabric of economic history; and the newer schools of historical economics, under the leadership of such scholars as Gustav Schmoller in Germany and Ashley and Unwin in Great Britain (to name only men no longer living) are, as they should be, devoted to historical research. The movement has also broadened out, particularly in Germany, under such leaders as Max Weber and Werner Sombart, into what is often called sociological economics, a position also well presented in France (Simiand, Halbwachs, Bouglé).

THE PROGRESS OF ECONOMIC THEORY

"Economic theory" is the name now commonly given to the more general and abstract parts of economics, to the "principles." These parts are no less practical than concrete-descriptive or applied economics but are less directly related to immediate problems. The mechanics of price relations or of markets affords a general explanation of the organization of production and distribution in so far as this is actually worked out and controlled through competitive buying and selling—which would largely be true even in a planned or socialistic economy that stopped short of complete military regimentation. This branch of the study bears somewhat the same relation to economic politics that pure physics bears to the engineering sciences. Hence the problems of values and distribution have continued to hold their place among the central concerns of economists. However, there has been a notable—one might say revolutionary—change in the general character of the analysis. The older classical economists, as we have seen, centered their attention on the long-run relations between value and costs and were generally content to dispose of short-run variations of price by merely invoking the formula of demand and supply. This was used without careful analysis of the short-run situation, particularly of the role of demand. Work directed toward filling in this gap had important effects in changing the whole conceptual picture. Similar steps introducing the new analysis were taken independently and almost simultaneously, in the early seventies of the nineteenth century, by W. S. Jevons in England, Carl Menger in Austria, and Léon Walras in France and Switzerland. (It presently became known that they had been in part anticipated by earlier writers who were ignored and forgotten.)

Adam Smith, in a famous passage, had contrasted "value in use" with "value in exchange," noting that the former is high for water and low for diamonds, and conversely for the latter. The new discovery was that there is nonetheless a definite relation between value in use (or "utility") and exchange value, hence price. The value in use is not properly measured by the difference between having the normal supply of a good and having none at all, but by the difference it makes to have a little more or a little less; that is, things are actually valued by increments in consumption. Water, for example, has a wide variety of uses, all progressively satiable; and its exchange value at a particular time and place depends on its "marginal" use, the use and the degree of importance in that use which would have to be foregone if the supply were just a little smaller. From the standpoint of action, since a buyer has choice of how much he will take, all units are alike and the use value as well as the exchange value of any total supply is the product of the value of the unit (increment) in the least important use by the member of units. Thus where water is scarce its value—both use and exchange value —is exceedingly high because the marginal use is an intense desire or need; and if diamonds were abundant enough their value would be small. And goods, however important, that are superabundant, the supply unlimited by any cost, have no economic utility or economic value, though to common sense this seems a paradox. The earlier utility or subjective-value theorists tended to think of the consumption of any quantity of a particular good as representing or causing a definite quantity of pleasure and of rational economic behavior as that which yields a maximum of pleasure or happiness. It is now generally agreed that this is dubious psychology, and that the economic theories had better use the notion of a maximum without trying to say exactly what is maximized—much as the physicist speaks of matter or mass in terms of the way it is measured without trying to define its nature. Perhaps the most important feature of the new views, considered as theories of demand and of price, was not the psychological explanation but the clarification of the nature of what Adam Smith called the "effective demand." It was seen that the demand for a commodity by any consumer or in any market is not a definite magnitude but a functional relation (most commonly represented in textbooks by a descending curve) showing a whole schedule of decreasing amounts that will be purchased as the price is higher. The actual quantities depend on both the desires and tastes of the consumer or consumers, on their purchasing power and, in addition, on the availability of other products competing for the expenditure of income and the prices of these. This idea served to clarify the relation that Smith and his followers had crudely expounded between "market price" and "natural price," now more generally referred to as price in the short run versus the long run. In the former case, the supply is typically the amount aleady on the market, and the price is the "marginal demand price" for this amount. But in the longer run, production itself responds to price and price to supply, so that the long run or normal or "equilibrium" price is that at which the amount consumers will take is equal to the amount which producers find it profitable to produce. This advance is largely to be credited to Alfred Marshall (*Principles of Economics* [1890] and numerous later editions, considerably revised).

Still more important were indirect consequences of the new theories in connection with supply and cost. One such consequence was a gradual shift of emphasis from wealth to income as the primary fact in economic life and the center of attention in the science. With respect to price analysis, the earlier economists had recognized —though not clearly or consistently, with N. W. Senior an exception for clarity—that even in the long run, cost affects price only indirectly, by influencing production and supply, and hence, as it was now seen, "marginal utility," which is the direct determinant. But the cost of which producers take account is the payments they must make for the productive services they require, and the value of these is derived from, or merely reflects, the value of final products. But with respect to any single product, the costs that must be incurred reflect the value of resources in other uses, giving rise to the principle now generally known as "alternative cost," in contrast with the older theory of "real cost" or pain cost. Subjective sacrifices do play some role, but the correspondence between such cost and the money cost to the producer is very imperfect and the relation may be inverse. (J. S. Mill pointed out that higher-paid labor typically involves less pain than lower-paid, not more; but he proposed no satisfactory way of meeting this difficulty.) It was also gradually recognized that the costs of production consist of the payments which at the same time constitute the shares in the distribution of the product among the different "productive agents." Thus a rational conception of production in terms of the allocation of productive capacity among alternative modes of use, through the competitive bidding of business units (or their managers or entrepreneurs), explains at the same time the prices of final products, the costs of production, and "functional" distribution. "Personal" distribution depends in addition on the amount as well as the value of the productive services of all kinds that are owned or controlled by the various participants in economic activity.

Goods are typically produced by the co-operation of various kinds of productive services, and the special problem of distribution, in modern terms, is that of the division of this joint product among the different kinds of co-operating productive services or agents. If only one kind were employed, or even if a number of kinds were always used in fixed proportions, the problem would be simple; the value of the productive service (or combination) would obviously be the value of the product. But the fact that goods can be produced by combinations in variable proportions sets the problem and also affords the solution. One type of agent can be substituted for another, or the product can be increased or diminished a definite amount by varying the amount of one "factor," all others being held constant. This will be clear if one thinks of a farm producing, say, wheat, and assumes that the manager uses the three traditional factors, land, labor, and capital (embodied in capital goods). But using increasing amounts of any one factor involves "diminishing returns." It follows that under effective competition the joint product—of a whole economy as well as of each single enterprise—tends to be divided up in the proportions which measure the efficacy of each factor in increasing the product, when the available supplies of all the factors in the economy are used in the way that yields the maximum total product, measured by the economic demand. Around the end of the nineteenth century a number of writers (especially P. H. Wicksteed) pointed out that the principle of diminishing returns, previously applied only to the use of more labor and capital on a given amount of land, is reversible and quite general in application. It governs the competition of different industries and enterprises for given amounts of all the factors; and the historical question whether labor and capital really increase faster than the supply of land is a separate issue and is to be answered only by observing the facts. Hence, under given conditions, and under free and frictionless competition, the amount of product assigned (in technical terms "imputed") to any particular laborer or other agent or unit is the amount which really depends upon the use of that particular agent. A laborer or other agent counts for more and in effect produces more when there is a larger supply of other agents to work with him or it. The amount earned will of course depend on effort and skill and the quality of management; and the "real" wage or other share will also depend on the prices of the final products for which the laborer or property owner spends the money income he receives. The effort of managers (entrepreneurs) to secure maximum return for their expenditures for productive resources will lead them to buy these in such proportions that "at the margin" equal expenditures secure equal increments to total product. Any resource will tend to move toward employments where the yield—of a "dollar's worth"—is highest. And the tendency, again in so far as competition is free and frictionless, is to establish such prices that all dollars' worths of each are of the same value to all employers.

This theory or principle that every agent tends to get what it "produces" does not mean that each person gets what he deserves and in fact tells us little about the ethical quality or social desirability of the result. It must be remembered that differences in respect of training and of opportunity greatly affect men's productive capacities as workers and that institutions, especially inheritance, enter into this picture as well as into the ownership of property and the opportunity to accumulate. The swift process of change in technology and demand often robs men of the fruits of skill acquired at great cost and also of the fruits of investment committed to particular industries. In particular such innovative activities as invention and exploration for minerals may yield anything from zero to a reward quite disproportionate to the outlay in effort or money. These facts set the general problem of profit and its ethical significance. Finally, even when a venture is not undertaken on a gambling chance, various impediments, including the antisocial activities of monopolists, prevent the free mobility of capital and labor from uses of lower to those of higher yield. The doctrine that "rewards tend to be proportionate to products" is true only as a tendency, but it is highly important as a corrective to the belief that there is little or no connection, and "product" itself, to repeat, is no measure of moral desert. The social problems raised must be examined on their merits, in terms of ethical principles and the pros and cons of the expediency of political measures. Enforcement of equality may reduce incentive and production, most especially the incentive to take the large risks or chances that always affect innovations. With respect to profit in particular—properly separated analytically from both wages of management and the yield of investment in fairly safe forms—it must be remembered that a prospect of disproportionate gain if successful is necessary if men are to assume voluntarily the risks of loss. The final judgment as to ideal right and the balance between that and expediency, where they seem to conflict, must be left to "that insidious and crafty animal vulgarly called a statesman or politican," to use a famous phrase of Adam Smith. Experience seems to show, however, that considerable taxation of exceptional gains is possible without demonstrably affecting incentives. As just suggested, profit, in realistic business usage, is a mixed form of income, containing elements of interest and of wages for that vaguely distinguishable part of management activity which may be treated as labor; and both the amount of the owner's capital and the proper rate of interest to allow are also uncertain. The distinguishing mark of profit is that its amount is not stipulated in any agreement or fixed in an exchange but is contingent upon the success of an enterprise or undertaking. In general, profit arises from error, or imperfect foresight, on the part of the responsible entrepreneur, in making policy decisions or in delegating these to salaried managers as his agents (in a corporation, managers are the agents of the voting stockholders as a group). "Pure profit" is the amount left over after making all stipulated payments for productive services, raw materials, etc., and after deduction of the going rate of payment for the entrepreneur's own capital and services. It is as likely to be a negative as a positive sum, and it is impossible to say conclusively whether the gains are greater or less than the losses in the aggregate for a whole economy. Pure profit is of course increased in any individual case by greater accuracy in the ultimate managerial decisions and tends to be decreased in particular by excessive optimism.

The rate of interest has also received much attention in modern discussion. Controversy was stimulated in particular by the publication, in the 1880's, of two books by E. von Böhm-Bawerk, a disciple of Carl Menger. He propounded two views of interest, both adumbrated a half-century earlier in the work of N. W. Senior. One is a reworking of the abstinence theory into one of postponement or "waiting" or discount of the future. Interest is viewed as the reward or necessary inducement for waiting, as the measure of the superior attraction of near over remote enjoyment. The other view regards interest as the yield or productivity of investment due to the greater efficacy of more roundabout processes. Böhm-Bawerk followed the Ricardian notion that capital goods are produced by labor, or labor and land; it has been pointed out that co-operation of previously existing capital is also involved and that in terms of values capital reproduces itself and in addition yields a surplus for consumption or further investment. The interest rate on loans tends to equal the ratio of the yield obtainable on investments to their amount, i.e., the ratio of the net rental on capital goods (after provision for maintenance and eventual replacement) to their cost, and the cost is the value of consumable goods sacrificed in using productive capacity to create them. When conditions change after an investment is made, the capital which the good represents is the least cost of producing an item of the same earning power. The psychology of postponement operates by affecting the supply of savings for investment. Interest is a form in which the yield of a capital good (or some part of it) is paid and received, rather than a distinct share in distribution coming from a distinct source; the lease of a farm or building or other piece of property for a rental achieves the same general result as its sale coupled with a loan, and under perfect competition the choice would be a matter of indifference to both parties. The theory of interest is of the greatest importance in the general system of value theory, since the value of all durable goods bought and sold is immediately determined by the "capitalization" of the expected future income. This tends to be the same as their cost, since no such good will be produced unless it is expected to yield at least the going rate on its costs. But errors and unexpected changes in conditions often cause capital goods to be worth more or less than cost (to yield less or more than interest on cost), the difference being a profit or loss.

METHODS OF ECONOMICS

Reference has already been made to the controversy between the critics and the expounders of analytical or theoretical economics—allied in its methods and aims to the older political economy, even when different in content. It is essentially abstract and deductive, proceeding from a few general principles, such as those of diminishing returns and diminishing utility and the uniformity of price to all buyers and sellers in an effective or competitive market. Most of its conclusions can be viewed as "cases" under a general principle of economic behavior. The principle is that resources tend to be allocated among alternative modes of use in such a way that they will be equally remunerative in all and so will yield the maximum total return. In another form of statement, it posits an "economic man," whose behavior under given circumstances is completely rational. A free economic order must assume that men actually tend to be rational in the use of means, that they try to be and tend to succeed. The given circumstances include the wants to be satisfied, the resources themselves, and the modes of use or technology extant in the society at the time. These must be explained or treated mainly by other disciplines than economics. Any science which explains phenomena in terms of measured cause and effect must be abstract; economics (by this method) is often compared with theoretical mechanics based on "frictionless conditions"; and the concept of adaptive behavior in biology is a similar principle, since in fact adaptation is always more or less imperfect. The careful economic theorist does not confuse the abstraction of perfectly economic behavior, or the economic man, with the actual behavior of real men, any more than the physicist or engineer assumes that friction is absent in real machines. Applied economics must try to take account of the role in business life of error and of motives (good or bad), such as prejudice, curiosity, and the various forms of the play interest, which do not conform to the pattern of economic rationality. Competition itself, in the psychological meaning, is a non-economic interest. The economic interest is merely a striving for efficiency in the use of means, whatever means are available and whatever ends are pursued. It does operate, at least in modern civilization, in a peculiarly regular and predictable fashion, and a community whose policies disregard its principles will suffer loss if not disaster. But these principles alone do not make it possible to predict the course of real events or the results of action. They must be filled in with data secured by inductive investigation, as well as qualified to allow for various departures from the behavior pattern of economic rationality.

Hence it will be evident that the other methods or approaches to economic data, notably historical research and statistical investigation, are not to be thought of as substitutes for sound theory, along the traditional lines, but as complementary to it. This is true also of social sciences other than history and statistics, notably psychology, with or without such qualifiers as social, political, analytic, etc. All are needed to supply data and interpretation, to put content and definiteness into the valid but highly abstract "laws" of economic choice and of market phenomena. Without such supplementation economic laws have little value for prediction, since the essential factor of wants is not open to sense observation and any course of events that occurs can be fitted into the theoretical pattern. The growing accumulations of numerical information covering a wide variety of economic facts, coupled with the advance of statistical technique, has been working a notable change in the character and content of economics as a whole; without nullifying any of its established principles, it has given more knowledge of the actual degree of stability or variability in the relationships in real life. Interpretation of records covering averages and aggregates and their movements can add much to what can be inferred from common-sense principles or observation of particular cases. This does not mean, however, that economics will be or can be purely statistical, a new kind of "political arithmetic." The broader the average or aggregate, the more heterogeneous the data it covers, and these magnitudes become subject to limitations similar to those of abstract principles. If statistical magnitudes and correlations are to be understood and intelligently used—in guiding such measures as taxation and the regulation of business in the public interest—they must be understood through weaving them into the general structure of our knowledge and relating them to other things we know.

On the other hand, any brief statement of general principles is bound to make abstract economic theories appear thinner and more remote from the concrete facts of economic life than they are. There is a place and a need for all degrees of generality. In recent decades this need has found increasing expression in the developing and spreading study of mathematical economics, in which exposition is made accurate and compact by the use of graphs and of algebraic formulas. In the form of "econometrics" this movement also brings analytical theory into close alliance with concrete facts, statistically presented. Only by the use of mathematics is it possible to bring together into a single comprehensible picture the variety, the complexity, and most of all the interdependence, of the factors which determine prices, costs, output, and demand and the wages or hire of productive agents. The mathematical treatment of economic principles was the first successfully undertaken by the French economist, mathematician, and philosopher, A. A. Cournot (*Recherches sur les principles mathématiques de la théorie des richesses* [1838]). Elaborate mathematical formulations of the conditions of general economic equilibrium have been worked out, notably by Léon Walras (*Éléments d'économie politique pure* [1874 and later editions]) and his follower Vilfredo Pareto (*Manuel d'économie politique* [1909] and other works). The principal value of such elaborate and abstract systems lies in forcibly reminding the inquirer that a change in practically any economic variable has direct or indirect effects on innumerable other magnitudes, thus preventing him from fatally oversimplifying conceptions of economic cause and effect. Other writers, notably Alfred Marshall, have adopted an intermediate position. Marshall was a competent mathematician but used and advocated the "literary" form of exposition (contemptuously so named by Pareto), relegating the mathematics to footnotes and appendixes in his monumental work. He also emphasized the interdependence of economic phenomena but centered his attention on the relations between the more closely related factors, the relations of greatest practical import, in contrast with system-building. But his successors, of the Cambridge or "neoclassical" school (notably A. C. Pigou), were impelled to make more direct use of mathematics in their exposition, and the study and use of algebra has of late spread rapidly among economists in all countries. And, in line with the older classical tradition, the science places increasing emphasis upon factors which make for change and "disequilibrium," as well as those making for stability.

THE PROBLEMS OF PRESENT-DAY ECONOMICS

Since all general principles are necessarily abstract, the more theoretical parts of economics cannot be taken to be a complete and adequate account of the mechanism of modern economic life. They afford serviceable approximations to partial, but important, aspects of the truth; the study of history and factual data yields other true and important generalizations. Even in their present imperfect and incomplete state the generalizations an economist has at hand constitute an organon of proved effectiveness, an instrument by means of which some of the results of economic changes, whether planned or not planned, may be predicted with a fair degree of certainty. New problems constantly appear and challenge attention as facts change and new interests emerge, and different groups of problems have their special literature and engage the attention of corps of specialists. The most striking and possibly the most important characteristic of recent work in economics, as contrasted with the older, is its greater realism. It does not attempt to do without abstract conceptions, but it does attempt to take these from the world of affairs or bring them into line with facts.

This trait is conspicuous in the treatment of the two great practical problems or groups of problems which have particularly forced themselves on the attention of the public and of statesmen and economists in roughly the past two generations. These problems center respectively in the growth of large-scale corporate business and associations of firms which concentrate power and tend to exploit the public through monopoly and high finance (and labor problems are related to these) and in the mechanism of money and credit, commonly held responsible for the recurring phenomena of industrial fluctuations or business cycles, with their attendant wastes and hardships. Depressions and the measures taken by different countries for dealing with them, in connection with the impact of two world wars, have also intensified interest in international economic relations affecting money and capital movements and in trade in general and in tariff duties and other controlling devices. The depression of the

1930's and World War II generated a world-wide movement toward state control or planning of economic life, and particularly toward use of quotas on imports and strict control of foreign exchange, and even governmental conduct of foreign trade. In none of these fields is the ground completely explored or all the issues settled, but findings have been reached which appear to have permanent value. The outcome of the various fiscal and monetary measures to which governments have resorted, and the results of the restrictions imposed upon trade and industry, have in general been about what competent economists predicted, and this is true of the experience with reparations and monetary stabilization after World War I. The tendency has been to confirm long-established principles, though political considerations have made it difficult for governments to learn, or at least for them to apply, the lessons taught. This fact is especially prominent in connection with the perennial issues of protection in international trade and of inflation through cheap money or credit. Inflation is tempting as an easy way to finance a government at war, or under special financial stress from any cause, and as a way to achieve a bogus prosperity, not to mention the fallacy of making capital cheap and lightening the burdens of debtors through an abundance of money. (But inflationary measures may be justified to counteract deflation and relieve depression.)

The general form given to economics by the early classical writers was determined very largely by preoccupation with certain special types of problems, notably problems of national commercial policy. Recent events have brought this group of problems again to the fore and later experience and discussion, while confirming earlier views in a general way, have led to some modification. The older economists, in their efforts to dig beneath that surface view of economic life which had deceived the mercantilists, held that money is merely an instrument or tool. They carried this idea to extremes, though in some types of "pure economic theory" today it is found convenient to go still further and assume that trade is conducted by barter, without the use of any special medium of exchange (all commodities having equally the character of money). But the phenomena of inflation and deflation, and of boom and depression, have forced modern economists to recognize that the use of money and credit has important effects on the character of effective demand and on production and distribution. Quite naturally, the great depression of the 1930's gave a tremendous impetus to discussion in this field, and its importance was further enhanced by the fear of depression, or boom and then depression, which might follow World War II, and by measures taken or proposed in this connection. A landmark in this discussion was the publication, in 1936, of a book, *The General Theory of Employment, Interest and Money*, by J. M. Keynes, of Cambridge University. It must suffice here to note that the discussion has at least called attention to one fact: The famous "law of the market" (often called "Say's Law" from its formulation by the great French economist) stating that the demand for any good is the supply of other goods, and the supply of any one is the demand for others, while a truism for a barter system, is not valid in the short run in a complex monetary economy. And further, the short run may be both longer and more important than is likely to be inferred from the orthodox or neoclassical exposition of economic theory. In emphasizing the nature and conditions of a theoretical equilibrium, these writers have tended to undue neglect of changes in monetary circulation (hoarding and dishoarding, or changes in the quantity of money or its velocity of circulation) and their often serious and protracted consequences. In particular, it cannot be assumed that monetary saving will be followed automatically and immediately by investment. The "funds" need not be offered on the loan market, and if they are offered they may not cause a sufficient decline in the long-run interest rate to cause real investment, since this depends largely on speculative anticipations and these in turn often depend more on conjuncture and mass psychology than on definite knowledge and rational calculation of future prospects. In consequence, production of capital goods, particularly the more lasting forms, including durable consumption goods, may decline heavily; and unemployment in these industries will cause shrinkage even in the industries producing for immediate consumption.

Even if it is admitted, as it doubtless must be, that if all prices were immediately and uniformly responsive to monetary changes, unemployment could not occur, this is not what happens in reality. In particular, monetary wages are "sticky" and are especially resistant to downward movement. And wages are the largest factor in production costs and notably in the variable and "marginal" costs which are most influential in producers' planning. Thus wage policy becomes a crucial factor in the problem. There is a real danger, even a probability, that reduction of wage rates may reduce total disbursement of purchasing power in the field of consumption, which may react seriously on the effective investment demand.

Drastic action in the direction of inflation (or "reflation," a word that came into use in the early years of the great depression) may be the only feasible way of counteracting the tendency to a downward spiral. The appropriate methods and instruments of such action came to occupy a large place in the discussion and controversy set in motion by the distress of the thirties and particularly by Keynes and his followers and opponents. Accentuation of issues in international economic policy was another result, which can only be mentioned here; the need for any country to protect itself against economic repercussions abroad runs into measures open to the accusation of "exporting unemployment," and in the absence of wise concerted international action they certainly tend to aggravate the situation.

One of the conspicuous phenomena in recent economics has been intensified activity in the field of labor problems, already mentioned as a development consequent upon the labor movement of the nineteenth century and after and connected with the growth of large corporations and other forms of unified action among business interests. Up to the last quarter of that century there was little careful analysis of those problems, apart from discussion of the general theory of wages under some approximation to free competition. Now, however, there is hardly a field of economic inquiry which is more thoroughly cultivated or in which there is more controversy: it runs into the general problems of economic planning and socialism. The labor union movement and its significance, the pros and cons of collective bargaining, the length of the working day, factory legislation, profit-sharing, the organization of control within the enterprise, labor turnover, the legal minimum wage, the prevention and settlement of industrial disputes, compulsory arbitration, and social insurance in its various forms, as well as the causes of unemployment and its possible remedies, are all burning issues in both economic science and practical politics.

It is important to observe that all these practical problems have been brought into the scope of economics by the course of change in economic and business life; the attention now given to them does not mark a change of attitude or general social position among economists. The earlier thinkers, in response to the conditions and needs of their times, at the beginning of the modern industrial era, were primarily concerned with exploding popular fallacies with respect to the ways in which the prosperity of the community can best be secured and, with that end in view, in showing how the economic activities of individuals may work together, through the open market, and be so interrelated as to constitute a great communal economic mechanism. Under the circumstances, they were more concerned with what governments could not or should not do than with that they could wisely attempt. Thus they often gave the impression—an impression which careful study of the writings of the ablest of them will dispel—that they regarded that mechanism as all-sufficient, needing neither interference nor direction on the part of the community. While the need for a better understanding of the theory of the open-market organization and better appreciation of its merits is still present, modern economics tends to strike a different note. Its tone is less negative; it is more insistent in its search for and scrutiny of possible ways of altering for the better the organization of the community's economic life, while remaining on guard against the dangers of disaster from unforeseen results of wrong lines of action. Since almost every gain has its cost, most of the problems resolve themselves into a question of a balance of advantage. But the advantages and disadvantages are hardly ever purely economic, and therefore no analysis in terms of purely scientific economics can completely dispose of such questions. Political, social, and ethical ideals and issues must also be taken into account, and economists are showing an increased awareness of these broader considerations. The economist, however, may gauge the general character of the probable effects of a specific measure upon production and distribution and so make it possible to discuss the wisdom of any proposed action in the light of its probable consequences.

In connection with this shift of emphasis an important factor is the vast accumulation of more and more reliable factual data. Reliable records of economic activities, or at any rate of their results, are now brought together and published by governments and by business and other private organizations, on a scale which would have excited the envy of the older economists. A much wider range of economic experience is now available for study and analysis. In dealing with this new material—in a sense a by-product of the activities which it records—economics is impelled toward a more realistic and concrete view. It has to deal with economic events in the forms in which they actually occur and to search for the systematic relations which run through the mass of real events. But although the interests of economics have become more varied and concrete, and although its conceptions have become better adapted to handling the facts of economic life as those facts present themselves, economics remains a political or social science and also, in the old sense as well as new senses, a "theoretical" discipline. Particular findings or tenets have been discarded and replaced or fundamentally restated, and sweeping additions have been made. But the general picture of a scheme of communal economic life remains a picture sufficiently ordered to be useful for analysis and prediction, though imperfect enough to give point and purpose to its continued study, elaboration, and refinement, in spite of changes of viewpoint and of method.

II

II

The Ricardian Theory of Production and Distribution[1]

I. INTRODUCTORY: BASIC MISCONCEPTIONS

On the assumption that the primary interest in the "ancients" in such a field as economics is to learn from their mistakes, the principal theme of this discussion will be the contrast between the "classical" system and "correct" views. The system is taken in the sense indicated by the title, with little regard to other writers than Ricardo's own great master and the two successors most competent and closest to his own spirit, Senior and Mill. While our special interest is distribution theory, it is useful to have in the background clear views of essential doctrines or points of view in the authors' theory of value or price; for these are often closely connected with fallacies in the other field. It will be appropriate to give by way of introduction a kind of formal list of main deficiencies and sources of error in the system as a whole. At least seven such "aberrations" appear to have vital importance.

The first to be noticed is the unfortunate conception of value, in negative terms—cost, interpreted as pain—instead of positive terms —desire or utility. This fallacy occurs explicitly in the parts of the argument which have come to be referred to in the literature as the "philosophical" account of value. Specific discussion of the determination of value (price) as a quantity (the "empirical" account) runs, indeed, largely in other, more "correct" terms of the equalization of return from productive expenditure in different fields through correct allocation. But the negative view of the ultimate nature and causes of value clearly shows through in many places as a source of confusion. It is, of course, completely wrong. Speaking "philosophically," the basis of value in human life is the necessity of making choices among alternatives more or less preferred in a purely relative sense and, also, where there is an economic problem, more or less subject to combination in varying proportions under a principle

1. Reprinted by permission from the *Canadian Journal of Economic and Political Science* (February and May, 1935).

of diminishing value-effectiveness. For any one individual, all the alternatives chosen should theoretically be equally "pleasant" or "painful" (at the margin) depending upon his arbitrary zero point; but for purposes of economic analysis, they are simply points on a scale of preference. Thus the cost of any value is the alternative value given up in choosing it.[2] In general, the ground of the necessity of choice—at least in any case which gives rise to economic value—is limitation of resources of some kind, which are to be economized by correct allocation among the open alternatives of use. That maximum return from any resource is obtained by equalizing the increments of return from equal small increments of the resource in all the alternative modes of use is the axiom underlying all economic reasoning and may be called *the economic principle*.[3]

2. The classical cost theory is a strange and interesting mixture of theories based on two different assumptions as to the character of economic life. The pain-cost theory would fit a society in which productive resources are completely immobile or specialized as between different money income yielding uses, but in which each resource is employed in its income yielding use at the "cost" of sacrificing some "non-pecuniary" employment. The most familiar case, and the only one recognized at all clearly by the classical economists, is that of labor and irksomeness. Irksomeness reflects the possibility of using one's personal powers for some purpose other than that of creating exchange value. The same principles apply to all, or virtually all, resources. (Regarding the classical doctrine of abstinence as the pain cost involved in the use of capital, see p. 58.) On the other hand, there is a large bulk of discussion of valuation more or less explicitly in terms of the mobility of resources between industries producing different commodities and value determination through the equalization of yield of resources. Both views assume, though in different contexts and unconsciously, that value is determined by utility, which varies inversely with supply. But, in general, the argument runs in terms of equalization of reward for equal sacrifice rather than of yield on resources. Since in either case the sacrifices are generally made by different individuals, this doctrine is subject to sweeping limitations, and Mill even pointed out (p. 388) that, in fact, the values produced by laborers at different wage levels about as typically bear an inverse ratio as a direct one to the presumptive sacrifice (see next footnote).

3. In practice the individual makes a twofold apportionment of his productive resources: first, between money-earning uses and direct uses; and second, as regards the part used for money-making, among different industries or occupations. In consequence of specialization, especially the division of labor, an individual does not do much apportioning under the second head, and, in fact, the first is rather rigidly determined by circumstances. These and related facts—especially the fact that the principle and motive of economy applies in various degrees to different behavior, with no definite boundaries—set limits to the clarity and accuracy with which it is possible to formulate cost theory. This argument is briefly developed in the author's paper, "The Common Sense of Political Economy: Wicksteed Reprinted," *Journal of Political Economy*, October, 1934 (reprinted here, pp. 104–18) and more fully in two articles in the *Zeitschrift für Nationalökonomie*, the first in the issue for January, 1935.

The second main aberration is a false conception of production, another aspect of which is a fallacious view of the nature of wealth or capital. Production was defined as production of wealth. But in fact, primary production consists in the rendering of services. Wealth is an agency by which services are rendered, not a product in the primary sense. (As a quantity it is abstract capacity to render service, not a collection of concrete things.) Wealth axiomatically is produced either to replace some item which is used up in rendering its service or to add to the total stock of service-rendering agencies. Wealth replacement is properly a detail of maintenance, and (simultaneous) maintenance is an essential part of the production of the services of wealth which are consumed in any interval, however short. No consumption corresponds to the production of additional wealth in any period, either during that period or at any subsequent time—unless the wealth itself is consumed by disinvestment, which in a free market means a net decrease in total social wealth or capital through undermaintenance. The use of the new wealth increment (throughout future time or until it is used up without replacement in a general liquidation of the social plant) constitutes production of the services contemporaneously rendered; and the same services cannot be produced twice.

These two observations or fallacies are combined in the view that "labour produces all wealth" (meaning here "want satisfaction"). Obviously, individuals render enjoyable services to others either through personal activities or through the use of their property (usually both combined).[4] Social economic life is essentially a matter of exchange of services among individuals; it is only more or less accidentally that the exchange and consequent valuation of service-rendering things, or their production, in a technical economic sense, enters into the economic process under stationary conditions.

The economic theory of progress or growth in the total means of want satisfaction is rather a separate branch of inquiry, and the activities ministering to current satisfaction, and those leading to growth, interact in complicated ways. The failure to separate clearly

4. It is perhaps more than a fancy to find a source as well as a picture of these two basic misconceptions in the classical system in the "curse of Adam": "In the sweat of thy face shalt thou eat bread" (Gen. 3:19). This suggests that cost is pain rather than the sacrifice of an alternative; and again, bread is a false and misleading illustration of the nature of economic value or production. Because it has practically no durability, it invites the confusion of consumption of services and consumption of things rendering services.

and sharply these two branches of the study is so important as to merit listing as the third major aberration in the system.[5]

The fourth deficiency or aberration to be noted is a methodological one. The classical writers had no clear conception of causality in the mechanistic or "positive" sense of function and variable; or, in less technical language, the relation between a continuously varying cause and its effect varying (quantitatively) in some corresponding way. This failure is manifested in, or closely connected with, a number of more specific errors; perhaps most directly in the failure to apply the law of diminishing utility. (In a real sense they did see it, especially Senior.[6]) In connection with the principle of uniformity of price in a market and that of uniformity of significance of interchangeable units of a supply to an individual, this law is essental to value analysis, including the role of cost (which, as Senior also saw, functions through limiting supply).[7] The principle could not be understood without at least an elementary grasp of the notion of increments, if not of the refinement of this in the theory of rates of change.

Fifth in the list is ignorance of the principles of analysis, closely related to the elementary mathematical or logical conceptions suggested under the fourth aberration. Before Adam Smith was born, it was understood by students of physical science that causes and effects must be brought into relation through another application of the principle of small increments or rates of change. All causes and all effects in nature are complexes. The effect of any cause must be measured as a variation in a total effect associated with a small variation in that cause, other elements in the complex of which it is a part being held constant; and similarly, *mutatis mutandis*, for the cause of any element of effect. Only after the passing of the older classical economics and the rise of the "subjective value" school has the theory of imputation (really partial differentiation) gradually come to be more or less understood in connection with production and distribution;[8] it is only now fairly beginning to be understood that all valuation, including direct utility, involves the same process.

5. As to the meaning of wealth and its increase, and the other problems in connection with the second aberration and the third, see Part II below.

6. *Political Economy* (octavo ed.), p. 12.

7. *Op. cit.*, p. 24.

8. There is one remarkable partial exception to this general statement in the Ricardian theory of rent, which involves a rudimentary recognition of the notion of increments, and of imputations. See Part III below.

The sixth point is that, ignorant of mathematical concepts, the classical writers had no clear or definite conception of the meaning of economy as a process of maximizing a value return from given limited resources of whatever kind.

Of particularly direct and vital interest to our topic here is the seventh aberration. The problem of distribution, the sharing of a joint product among an indefinite number of agencies (owners) co-operating in its creation, not merely was not seen as a problem of imputation, but was not approached as a problem of valuation at all.[9] This is really mysterious, in view, first, of the unescapable fact that the shares in the social income are received by individuals as money payments for services rendered; and it is even more so because in some parts of the discussion of the value problem all the writers, but especially Smith, were on the very threshold of a correct general conception of the organization of production and distribution in society as a whole through price competition.

It may be listed as a corollary of this observation (and perhaps of that under number six) that the classical writers had no conception of the nature of the economic organization in which alone a pecuniary distribution problem arises, the system or order best called "enterprise economy." In an exchange economy, where individuals (families) secured their livelihood by the production and exchange of products (services or direct service-rendering goods), the categories of rent, wages, interest, and profits would have no existence. In an enterprise economy, the individual gets his livelihood by selling productive services to one or more enterprises, individual or corporate, for money, and with the money buying from enterprises the products consumed. The organization as a whole is worked out through two interacting systems of markets and prices, one for products, in which individuals are buyers and enterprises sellers, and one for productive services, in which the relation is reversed. The classical economists give no picture of a system of prices and practically no hint of a system of economic organization worked out and directed by price forces.[10] As noted under the first two aberrations, they

9. In this connection, see the remarkable statement by Ricardo in a letter to McCulloch: "After all, the great questions of Rent, Wages and Profits must be explained by the proportions in which the whole produce is divided between landlords, capitalists and labourers, and which are not essentially connected with the doctrine of value" (Hollander ed., letter XV), p. 72.

10. Let it be observed here, once for all, that general negative statements are to be taken subject to interpretation. They mean that the system expounded by the writers does not take account of the facts in question. To say that they

failed to see the relativity of all values and of all costs; still less did they grasp the identity of costs with distributive payments and the functional role of the two interacting sets of prices.

II. PRODUCTION: THE PRODUCT AND THE PRODUCTIVE AGENTS

The best approach to discussion of the classical system is afforded by the last of the aberrations noticed in the introductory section, the failure to give any picture of the social-economic process as a whole, especially from the standpoint of the organization of production. Economic theory is nothing, or is significant only as an intellectual curiosity, unless it shows how, in a price economy, the price system works out: (*a*) in the assignment of productive capacity in society to different uses or industries; (*b*) in the technical organization of productive agents within each industry; and (*c*) in the sharing of the joint product among the co-operating individual owners of productive capacity. What is called "distribution theory" has to do with the pricing of productive services. These prices are significant in connection with the division of the product, but their prior and even more fundamental function is the dual one of apportioning productive capacity in the various forms among industries and among financial and technical productive units within each industry. It is the competition between producers in the same industry which provides the pressure to increase technical efficiency as well as to keep prices down to the level of costs.

As a first step in discussing the theory of distribution in these functional aspects, it is necessary to devote considerable space to the logically prior question of the meaning of production itself, espe-

---

absolutely failed to see anything essential to a sound theory is generally too strong. One of the mysteries of economic theory is the fact that most of the essentials are things of which no fairly intelligent adult living in a world where exchange relations are at all developed could possibly be ignorant. The problem is to build these inescapable facts into a coherent system of relations. Such general negative statements are in no wise disproved by citing particular passages in which the fact or principle in question is, or seems to be, recognized. But it is sometimes a matter of interpretation whether they are taken into account where they need to be. In general, our discussion deals with the chapters treating systematically the problems under discussion, and passages from other chapters are doubtfully, if at all, in point.

References to authors by pages are to the following works, unless otherwise stated: Smith, *Wealth of Nations* (Cannan ed.), 2 vols., Vol. I unless specified; Ricardo, *Principles of Political Economy and Taxation* (Gonner ed.); Senior, *Political Economy* (octavo ed.); Mill, *Principles of Political Economy* (Ashley ed.). In a few cases I have used decimals in page references to indicate the approximate position of the statement in question on the page, where this seemed desirable.

cially the meaning of product and the conception of the agencies by which product is created. The classical writers viewed production as the creation of wealth by labor; other agencies (capital or stock and land) were recognized, but their role was auxiliary, not co-ordinate. On the other hand, labor which does not produce capital was explicitly and emphatically called "unproductive." Part III of this paper will deal with productive organization and distribution. In this part, we are concerned with the meaning of product and especially with the confusion involved in treating production as production of wealth.

What is in fact consumed[11] in economic life is exclusively services, and accordingly, the primary meaning of production is the rendering of service. A service is a magnitude of the nature of intensity. It inherently involves time, and care must be used in giving it a time dimension. The relation between quantity and rate of flow is here, to begin with, like that involved in light, in contrast with a stream of water. Water exists, and can be measured, apart from any flow in time; but with light and services this is not true. A quantity of service or of light is derivative from flow and is obtained by aggregating a rate of flow over some time interval. But the service has an additional and complicating peculiarity. In practice, we rarely care about the quantity of the service as such but rather about the value (in exchange) of a specified service over some interval of time, which is either in the future or in the past with reference to the point in time at which the value is struck. Streams of service—of some intensity, constant or variable, and over some interval, from zero to infinity as limits—are the things valued and exchanged in the market. The value of any service stream is affected by discounting if paid for in advance and by interest accumulation if paid for after it is rendered and consumed. (The problem of the rate of discount and of interest will be considered later.)

A service in the economic sense is physically defined by reference to some agency which renders it (and sometimes further by the

11. The classical writers had no theory of consumption, and Mill even excluded it from the province of the economist. See *Essays on Some Unsettled Questions:* Essay V, "On the Definition of Political Economy, etc.," p. 132, n. They took it for granted that it is wealth which is consumed as well as produced and that wages are paid out of past, not current, product.

In modern discussion we have, of course, the theory of diminishing utility, which was really implicit in the classical discussion, and was also given clear statement by Senior, although it was not explicitly built into his version of the classical system.

specification of a particular physical use or performance of the agency). But the value of the physical service (in comparison with any other service) depends in the first place on its relative subjective appeal or utility to some consumer. More accurately, since all similar units are valued alike, it depends on the appeal of a single unit or increment (of flow) considered as an addition to the total flow—for both of any two services being compared. In accord with the familiar law of diminishing utility, the relative utility of any increment of service (flow) decreases as the relative supply increases. Thus utility and value become a matter of the scarcity of services, which in turn involves the scarcity of the economic agencies rendering them. Immediately, this is a matter of the (limitation of) supply of some economic agency in the particular use of rendering the service whose value is in question. But from the economic standpoint, this scarcity is always a result of the competition of some other use, or uses, for the agency or agencies; otherwise, no economic problem arises, though a technical, or technological, problem may. In free society, economic agencies, or resources, include human beings and external things owned by human beings. Postponing detailed consideration of the relations between the two classes of resources, we are concerned at the moment with the owned things or what is ordinarily designated as "wealth."

Many (not all) of the owned economic agencies in use at any time have limited life, in various degrees and for various reasons. In consequence, provision for the continuity of the service or services which they render must include provision for the replacement of the agency at the end of its life. In fact, if the consumption of any product (service) during any interval, long or short, is not accompanied during that interval by the complete maintenance of any scarce agencies involved in rendering (producing) it, the service cannot be said to be produced during that interval; instead, it will represent, wholly or in part, the consumption of supply on hand at its beginning. It should also be evident without discussion that there is no difference in principle between maintenance in the routine sense of, say, the oiling and care of a machine, and replacement, either bit by bit, or as a whole at a particular time. In fact, no very definite meaning can be given for a "whole" agency, in distinction from a part, and replacement of parts is naturally included in routine maintenance.[12]

12. The necessity of providing for maintenance of capital before counting any result of its use as product was seen, if not understood, by the classical writers

The owned agencies of limited life which render directly consumed services are typically made with the aid of other indirect owned agencies, and these, of course, must also be replaced as fast as they lose for any reason their power to function economically, or the final service currently consumed is not currently produced. Thus a considerable part of actual productive activity, in the primary sense of rendering consumed services, comes to be, in a physical view, indirect; it takes the immediate form of making things, to be used either to render services or to make other things, in an almost infinitely complex sequence and interrelationship. In other words, a large part of production in its true, primary meaning does physically take the form of producing wealth. But the maintenance of an existing stock of wealth (including any necessary replacements) does not represent the creation of any economic value in addition to the value of the services simultaneously consumed but appears in their value; and hence, in the economic sense, replacements are not product.

In addition to maintenance (including replacements), the making of fairly regular and considerable additions to the total social stock of owned economic agencies, or "plant," has been typical of the period of history in which enterprise economy has prevailed and must be considered as a normal feature in the working of such a system. Moreover, the increase in the social plant is typically associated with considerable changes in the form and kind of agencies used, brought about through replacement of one kind by another, presumably embodying a more effective way of using the same productive capac-

---

(cf. above, p. 41, n. 10). In Smith it appears in the confused discussion of capital and revenue in Book II, chap. iii (cf. also Book I, chap. viii, on revenue and stock, p. 71). Ricardo refers to it more explicitly several times, and in his first edition (*op. cit.*, pp. 32–33) he even set up an annuity to provide for replacement. As to Senior, there are few more puzzling passages in all the literature than his argument as to how to classify the replacement fund (pp. 94–95). Strange to say, Mill seems hardly to refer to the point directly, though he mentions capital as a perpetual fund (p. 72) and discusses its "perpetual consumption and reproduction" (pp. 74–75), and his definition of production (productive labor) restricts this to additions to total wealth (p. 49).

The maintenance of social capital was of the profoundest concern to all the writers and this interest underlies the doctrine of productive and unproductive labor. This, however, involves the fallacy of failing to impute product. The laborer who does not directly produce capital produces whatever he does produce, which is presumably worth his wages to whoever pays them, and worth at least as much as any other possible product. Failure to maintain capital means non-productivity of capital, not of labor. The reasons for not deducting the maintenance of the labor from apparent gross product will be considered presently.

ity. This fact makes it practically impossible to distinguish sharply between the maintenance and the increase of the plant as a whole, though none the less necessary to make the distinction analytically. A further source of confusion is that the specialized producer who secures his income by making material agencies or equipment goods cannot know, and individually has no reason to care, whether they are destined for replacement or expansion.

For practical reasons, the creation of additions to the social plant is included in the economic production of a given time interval. But it is essential to understand that this is production only in an accounting sense. There is no consumption corresponding to such production, either in the interval in which it takes place or at any other time. The specialized producer receives what he consumes through abstinence on the part of some saver. An addition to plant will presumably be used in the future for production in the primary sense (i.e., to render consumed services). But unless the process of social growth is reversed, the plant itself is never consumed; its subsequent use to render services constitutes the production of those services simultaneously with their consumption, and the same service cannot be produced twice.[13] Moreover, even if the process of social growth is at some future time reversed, it will never be possible to say when or in what connection any particular increment of wealth, described by the time and process of its creation, is disinvested and there will be no definite correspondence between the consumption of plant and its production.

The notion of an addition to plant has no meaning, especially if associated with any change whatever in form, unless it is possible to measure plant. We must now consider this problem, and here we have to do with another fallacy, as egregious and as persistent as that of viewing production as production of wealth. Wealth must be a

13. Treating capital growth as income involves a serious theoretical confusion, for it represents double counting (as Professor Fisher in particular has emphasized and as we have indicated). The wealth as a quantity is a capitalized service value, the present worth of a future income stream; logically its production is the production of this income stream. Yet it is unquestionably necessary in practice to treat an addition to wealth made in any interval as product and the activity as production in that interval, and to treat the use of the wealth to produce consumed service as production in later time. This is especially because the wealth rarely, if ever, in an organized economy, either yields its return or maintains itself automatically but requires constant management. The student must simply be careful to recognize at all times that such product and income do not represent consumption and reflect accounting convenience rather than economic reality.

quantitative concept, and indeed it is always treated as such, but commonly without recognizing what is necessarily involved in its quantification, which is inconsistent with the notion of it as a collection of concrete things. It is certainly obvious (as in the case of most general economic principles) that an aggregate is measured, or viewed as a quantity, only in terms of some common quality or attribute. And it is likewise self-evident that an economic magnitude is based upon the quality or capacity of contributing to some end, rendering some service to some subject, an individual, or possibly a group. The notion of a quantity of service has already been mentioned; a service is measured, and so reduced to a common denominator with other services, by its relative marginal utility. It goes without saying that the consumed service may take various forms, including the utility of mere miserly possession; but the value which makes a thing "wealth" can only be the value of some anticipated use, which to the user is at least as important as any other service of equal market value, or he would exchange.[14]

Since the product of any agency in any interval is reckoned only after complete maintenance of the agency, including any eventual replacement (which may mean replacement by a physically similar or dissimilar agency), it follows that productive plant is measured by the perpetual service income which it can be counted upon to yield. In other words, plant itself, in its quantitative aspect, is perpetual (regardless of changes in physical form), except for a possible net disinvestment in society as a whole. Perpetual service income is the primary magnitude in economic analysis. (It is necessary to specify "service" income if the word "income" is used because an increase in wealth, or assets, is regularly considered as income.) Quantitatively speaking, any two pieces or items of wealth are to be compared as perpetual incomes in monetary units, say, dollars per year. But in this connection, two observations are necessary.

In the first place, a matter of relatively minor importance, it is unrealistic and impracticable to treat very short segments of service

14. The measurement of service income is subject to limitations of a theoretically serious nature, and accurate measurement is impossible practically. In fact, the very notion of a total of value, in connection with either service flow or capacity to render service, is subject to serious conceptual limitations, value being relative. But these difficulties cannot be gone into here. It is necessary to distinguish analytically between larger and smaller (perpetual) service income streams, whatever the margin of error in objective discrimination may be. The character of the problem may be suggested by noting that what is involved is the definition of money of unchanging purchasing power. (This does not necessarily imply "ideal" money in an ethical or practical sense.)

flow, or short-lived items of material wealth, in this way. Only relatively durable things, or contractual income streams, are treated as wealth by separating, in practice or in thought, the source of a flow of service from the service itself. The classical economists were practically right in treating food and similar forms of wealth as products; where they were wrong was in treating such products as the type of wealth or capital in general. Very short-lived material consumption goods are best viewed as representing the services of the (human beings and) more durable material agencies which produce them.

The second observation is fundamental. As already noted, relatively few items of concrete wealth directly yield perpetual service income, or money income, to the owner. A thing either wears out in some sense, in a more or less definitely foreknown period, or it is problematically liable to supersession in connection with shifts in demand or technological advance. In either case, the effect is that, in order to secure perpetuity in the return, provision must be made for replacement of the physical thing by another individual, of the same or different (physical) kind as the case may be. In accounting terms, the item must be depreciated, or written off, out of its gross yield. But the process or calculation of depreciation involves a rate of return on capital. Such a rate thus comes into the problem of capital quantity (value) in two ways, the determination of the perpetual income to be capitalized as well as the capitalization.

As to what this rate would mean and how it would be determined in a world of a different kind from that in which we live—one in which durable wealth could not actually be produced or could not be exchanged—we need not speculate here. In the actual world, income-yielding goods are freely and competitively produced by the use, in large part, of resources which would otherwise yield current service income; and they are freely exchanged. In consequence, the cost of perpetual income, in terms of current service value sacrificed, is carefully reckoned and is known for a given market at a given time more accurately than most economic magnitudes. Under such conditions, the value of income-bearing goods must equal their cost. That identical applications of resources create equal increments of value in alternative employments is an immediate consequence, or case, of the "economic principle."[15]

But there is a technical difficulty in carrying out this analysis,

15. See p. 38 in this article.

arising from the fact that the production of a durable agency requires time and in consequence must include an element of interest. Accumulation, as well as discounting, is involved. However, the difficulty is not serious. It is also a corollary of the economic principle that the rate of interest and the rate of discounting must be equal. It is, then, merely necessary to set up an equation expressing the equality of the two values of any wealth item, one the discounted value or present worth of the stream of services it will yield—reduced to a basis of perpetuity, if not originally perpetual—and the other the cost of producing any new item yielding an equal stream of perpetual money income. Both sides of the equation involve the rate, and the equation is to be solved for the rate as the unknown. The rate of interest being known, the quantity of wealth, represented by any source of a known money value, is then found by the operation of capitalization. ("Capital" is measured wealth, considered in relation to a measured income.)

The capitalization operation is a matter of very simple arithmetic (dividing the yield by the rate) when the capital good under consideration directly yields a perpetual income. It is not so simple when the good is one of limited life as is, of course, more usually true. In that case, the perpetual yield may be computed as suggested by depreciating the item, i.e., reducing its imputed income during life by an amount sufficient to accumulate to a sum equal to its cost and so provide for its replacement. Both in capitalizing and in the more complex calculation determining the rate, it happens to be somewhat simpler algebraically not to make this conversion formally but to express the present worth of the time-limited income stream directly. The two operations, however, are exactly equivalent, and either form of algebraic expression may be converted into the other by a few simple steps.[16]

Especially because of the simpler form of the direct calculation,

---

16. 1. *Discounting Method:* Total Cost = Present Worth of Yield

Let: Cost of Capital good be S per year for c years, and its yield be R per year for l years

Accumulation of \$1 per year for n years at $i\%$ = $\dfrac{(1+i)^n - 1}{i}$

Present worth of \$1 per year for n years at $i\%$ = $\dfrac{(1+i)^n - 1}{i(1+i)^n}$

Let $(1+i) = A$

Then: Total Cost = $\dfrac{S(A^c - 1)}{i}$

[Footnote continued on the following page

where income has limited duration, there is likely to be objection to the definition of capital as perpetual income. But certain facts seem decisive in favor of this view. The first is the universally understood meaning of interest in everyday usage, which is that of a net rate of return after maintaining the principal intact. The second is the fact of perpetuity. Unless society as a whole becomes decadent with respect to its stock of capital, no increment of capital viewed as a quantity ever is disinvested; the physical item worn out or superseded is always replaced by an equal item or quantity in items of some kind. If an individual owner wishes to liquidate, he does so by sale to another owner. Moreover, even if the individual owner of a concrete item plans to "eat it up" without replacement, he can only know what he is doing by separating the interest element in the imputed yield from the amortization element, which involves calculating depreciation.[17] And if individuals disinvest, society will have no capital or practically none.

$$\text{Present worth of yield} = \frac{(R A^l - 1)}{i A^l}$$

$$\frac{S (A^c - 1)}{i} = \frac{R (A^l - 1)}{i A^l} \quad \text{or} \quad S A^l (A^c - 1) = R (A^l - 1) \quad (1)$$

2. *Sinking Fund Method:* Interest = Perpetual Income ÷ Cost

$$i = \left\{ R - \left[\frac{S (A^c - 1)}{i} \cdot \frac{i}{A^l - 1} \right] \right\} \div \frac{S (A^c - 1)}{i}$$

$$= \frac{R (A^l - 1) - S (A^c - 1)}{A^l - 1} \div \frac{S (A^c - 1)}{i}$$

$$= \frac{i R (A^l - 1) - i S (A^c - 1)}{S (A^l - 1)(A^c - 1)}$$

or

$$S (A^l - 1)(A^c - 1) = R (A^l - 1) - S (A^c - 1)$$

$$S A^l (A^c - 1) - S (A^c - 1) = R (A^l - 1) - S (A^c - 1)$$

$$S A^l (A^c - 1) = R (A^l - 1) \qquad \text{2 same as 1}$$

For continuous compounding

Amount of \$1 for n years at $i\%$ = e^{in}

Then e^{in} replaces $(1 + i)^n$

Formula becomes: $S e^{il} (e^{ic} - 1) = R (e^{il} - 1)$.

17. This is not the place for any extended discussion of interest theory; but it is in order to note that it is not properly a part of distribution theory at all. The special problem of interest is that of the rate, which is entirely a matter of the valuation of the wealth item or its quantification as wealth. The yield, either in perpetuity or as a known duration (and, more generally, the shape) of income stream, is a *datum;* in other words, the distribution problem must be solved before the interest problem can be attacked. We shall later have occasion to notice

Summing up: The significance for the history of doctrine of this long discussion of the relation of material things to the concept of product is that in general they are not products but means of production. But two exceptions are to be allowed and carefully understood. When a material thing is so short-lived that it must practically be treated as the embodiment of a certain quantity of service, not appreciably affected by the distribution of the service in time, it should be regarded as product. The source in this case would be the more permanent productive agencies producing the perishable item whose service is considered as the service of these agencies. The second exception is that the creation of net additions to a total stock of wealth, or plant, must for accounting and managerial purposes be treated as production, and the wealth increment itself as product, in the time interval for which accounts are kept. But such production is logically double counting, as there is no corresponding consumption.

---

the peculiar fallacy of the classical theory, still generally persistent today, that rent and interest are different distributive shares arising from different sources or in connection with different economic functions.

The equality of the two expressions suggested above constitutes an explanation of the interest rate (and capital quantity) in the conditions obtaining in a capital market at a moment of time, assuming freedom of investment, perfect competition, and full knowledge of all circumstances and conditions affecting the prospective yield of investments to the infinite future, on the part of all parties interested in capital transactions. In such a market the rate of interest is simply the demand price for capital set by the productivity of the increment of investment about to be made. Further discussion of the problem of interest would deal with the possible changes in demand and supply conditions as investment goes forward. That analysis cannot, however, be given the form of demand and supply curves or functions in the ordinary sense, because the changes have a time dimension, which the curves for demand and supply of a commodity do not have. The situation at a moment can be represented by supply and demand curves, but they have practically no meaning; for, as further analysis would indicate, the demand for capital is indefinitely (at a moment, infinitely) elastic, and the supply, even over time, is practically inelastic—if there is any functional relation between saving and the interest rate, which is questionable. For a brief discussion of the matter, see the article, "Interest," in *The Encyclopaedia of the Social Sciences*. See also the author's article, "Capital, Time and the Interest Rate," in *Economica*, August, 1934. On abstinence as subjective or pain cost in relation to interest, see pp. 58 ff.

In viewing interest as the marginal productivity of capital, as above, it must be recognized that capital quantity itself involves the interest rate. But the rate can be derived very simply in terms of perpetual income without reference to capital quantity. Whether income is paid continuously (if that is conceivable) or in instalments on any plan, the rate of interest, per cent, per annum, is the ratio of the additional perpetual income creatable by investing a one-year segment of any given perpetual income to the given income itself. Of course, both incomes must be realized on the same plan in relation to accrual, and investment made instantly (presumably at the highest rate which available investment opportunities offer).

Further analysis of the concept of product confronts the question of other productive instruments, i.e., other than "artificial" owned things. The greatest difficulty arises in connection with the theoretical position of human beings. It is necessary to consider each human member of an economic society (non-producers are not members) in the three aspects of (*a*) a bundle of wants; (*b*) a bundle of capacities, his technical knowledge and skill, which the individual owns and uses to satisfy wants as he uses other physical agents; and (*c*) his (productive) property in the ordinary sense of external things which he owns. It is the "capacities" that we are concerned with here. From the standpoint of causality, the productive capacity in one's person is generally the result, more or less, of activity on his own part, which has, more or less, the character of investment, and, in addition, every human being is originally "created" by the use of "resources" belonging to other persons, most of whose resources might have been used in other ways, and whose use in this way represents, *prima facie*, an economic choice.

But all this does not mean that the human being as a source of economic services can be treated in theory as wealth or capital, or additions to human productive capacity treated as product, or the act of making them as production, as in the case of material wealth. There is a fundamental difference, in the form of a somewhat paradoxical limitation to the individual's ownership of himself. The principle of inalienable rights, recognized in all free societies means not merely that one cannot sell himself outright, but that one cannot so much as give a valid lien on his services or make an enforceable contract to deliver them for any considerable time in the future. In other words, he cannot capitalize his earning capacity. Having no economic value to anyone but himself, he has in effect none at all. He cannot keep a capital account with himself with any degree of accuracy and has little incentive to do so, and it would have little meaning if he could. And the same is true of parents in relation to their children. Because of these facts, the human being as a producer is in a different position from property or capital, and activity expended upon him, by himself or another, must be treated (in so far as it comes into the economic reckoning) as the rendering of services instantly and finally consumed. This we actually know to be partly false to the facts; much effort and expense laid out on human beings, by themselves and even by others, is clearly, in terms of motivation, investment for the sake of a future return, on a par with the construction of income-yielding implements and materials. Professional education—often carried out with borrowed money—is the typical example. But the exigencies of accounting, which embody the rationale of management, preclude analytical treatment in these terms.[18]

The third type of agency recognized in the classical writings in connection with production, namely land, was really defined as "unproduced," i.e., "the original and indestructible powers of the soil."[19] This is the difference between land and "stock" or capital goods. The view, though so largely followed even down to the present and by the best economists, is a tissue of fallacies. In the first place, the historical question is irrelevant to economic theory in the strict sense, because the economic point of view is forward-looking: "bygones are forever bygones." And the notion that what are called "natural agents" are not produced (in the sense in which any material agents are produced) is false and reflects a false conception of production. In so far as economic conditions have held good in the past, i.e., to the degree that people knew what they were doing and

18. It is true that at various points in the classical writings (not to mention modern expositors) we find explicit or implicit reference to a supply function for labor and a cost of production. It is also true that in recent history efforts have been made (cf. Fisher, Huebner, and many others) to define and measure the capital value of human beings. These notions cannot be given critical examination here. Our conclusion must be that it is impossible to separate in the expenditure upon human beings the elements which represent respectively (*a*) want-satisfaction or consumption proper, (*b*) maintenance, and (*c*) growth of productive capacity, hence that it is necessary to treat all such expenditure as representing current final consumption.

The question whether the creation of human productive capacity is to be treated as "production" is explicitly discussed only by Mill of the four writers considered here, and he takes both positions (cf. pp. 46 and 48 *vs.* 51–52). The kinship of labor capacity with capital is referred to by Smith in various connections (e.g., Vol. I, pp. 103, 123). In his general analysis of capital (Book II, chap. i, pp. 264–65) Smith explicitly includes in fixed capital "the acquired and useful abilities of all the inhabitants or members of the society." But these "abilities" are certainly not included in the "value" product which distinguishes productive labor in the definition with which chap. iii of Book II begins (p. 313). Senior makes much of the relation, analyzing nominal wages into "all three" types of return: wages proper (payment for direct sacrifice), profit (payment for training acquired at a cost), and rent (costless surplus) (see pp. 128 ff., also pp. 61, 69). Ricardo gives no discussion of production—in classical terms productive versus unproductive labor—but his allusions to the topic show that he accepts Smith's position (see especially chaps. vii and xx).

19. As to whether land "produces" or not, the writers take contradictory positions. The crucial point is that they had no clear notions of production or the (symmetrical) relations between agencies in production, because they had none of mechanical causality. See Part I on the fifth aberration and the argument of Part III, *passim*.

there was effective competition, the use of labor and property in pioneering and all exploration and development activities could not yield a return smaller or greater than that obtainable in any other use. That is, the result must be equal in value to its cost. This is true even if possession be obtained by a mere contest or fight, and not less so because such activity would not be socially necessary or useful.

As to the facts, economic conditions have obtained in a country like the United States in as high a degree as in other fields of activity, and the social utility of the activities challenges comparison with any whatever. It is no doubt true that in comparison with many other types of capital creation, the results of expenditure of productive capacity in the natural-resource field as a whole are less accurately foreseeable and in consequence may be expected to show a wider dispersion from the competitive norm of equality. In so far as the divergence follows the ordinary law of error, it will be equal in both directions. But, in fact, the well-known principles of gambling psychology may be expected to skew the distribution as a whole in the unfavorable direction. In the more highly aleatory subdivisions of the field, such as prospecting for precious metals, this result is a familiar and undisputed fact, and there is no reasonable question about it in the field as a whole. But, again, some other types of capital creation also present a high degree of uncertainty, and no general difference between natural resources and other types of capital goods can be defended. Land is capital merely; defined in any realistic way, it presents an infinite variety of conditions as to maintenance and replacement requirements, and possibilities of increase in supply, as does any other general class of capital instruments.[20]

There are numerous other forms or embodiments of capital besides material agencies, such as inventions of every sort and various special advantages in production. The relation of most of these to monopoly is fairly evident as a fact, but its precise character defies general formulation. The question whether their creation is production can only be mentioned. The same applies to other vital but difficult problems in the meaning and scope of production. It would

20. In a physical analysis, as we have seen, labor power is also produced at a cost, and it has to a considerable extent the other properties of capital. The classification of types of productive agents and of productive capacity is a technological problem and also a sociological and human one; but economic theory is concerned only with the fact that there are different kinds, which co-operate in production, and with general characteristics, not with descriptive classification. See pp. 58 ff.

be reasonable to restrict all *economic* production to the creation of salable value under "economic conditions," meaning that the activity is deliberate and is carried on in view of, and motivated exclusively by, a perfectly correct anticipation of its consequences, all measured in exchange value terms by a perfectly competitive market. In reality, the capacity of most economic resources is allocated in some vague way between the production of exchange value and other (non-pecuniary) uses, in infinitely complex variety, of which the leisure use of men's personal powers (the basis of the pain cost of labor) is the type. There are no definite boundaries, either: (*a*) to the activities organized through the price system; or (*b*) to those of an individual which it is realistic to regard in economic terms as involving the rational allocation of resources. The activities of government would also constitute a special problem. In general, the difficult problems of production and product arise largely in connection with economic growth—the production of productive capacity (so-called only for reasons of accounting necessity).[21] There is little of all this in the writings of the classical economists —and not much that seems to the writer very much to the point in any later economic literature with which he is familiar.

The question of the conception and classification of productive agencies, to which we now turn, overlaps extensively with that of the meaning of product, and relatively little need be added to what has already been set down. The historical problem is that of explaining the origin (and persistence) of the indefensible "trinity" of factors.[22] As a classification of agencies, the theory might have been derived by distinguishing first between human beings and non-human things and then dividing the non-human, but not the human,

21. It is common usage in economics to refer to phenomena of growth or change in the given general conditions of a stationary economy as dynamic and to this general branch of study as "economic dynamics," in contrast with "economic statics." This is misleading, because entirely different from the meaning of the terms "statics" and "dynamics" in the field of theoretical mechanics, from which they are taken. Dynamics deals with motion, and the working of a stationary economic system involves the analogue of motion. The process of establishing a moving equilibrium under stationary conditions might more reasonably be called economic dynamics. Changes in these given conditions (wants, resources, and technology), are analogous with nothing dealt with in the science of mechanics and should be designated by some other term, such as "historical" or "evolutionary" economics.

22. This term was not used by the British classical writers and is said to come from J. B. Say.

group into two subclasses, the unproduced or natural and the produced or artificial. Reasons which seem to justify the first dichotomy have already been given in the differences in ownership relations and facts which follow from these.[23] It may be added that because human beings are not property in the full sense of capital, and investment in them is not made under approximately economic conditions, there is no effective tendency for such investment to yield a return equal to the general market rate, i.e., for value to equal cost. But the basic distinction between labor and other factors is institutional rather than theoretical-economic. In a society where all labor was performed by slaves, it would obviously be pointless.

Moreover, neither labor nor capital, as a class of things, is properly a "factor of production." This term suggests internal homogeneity, with effective distinction from other, similar "factors," and fluidity, calling for a high degree of divisibility. The description is somewhat applicable to unskilled laborers as a separate group, and in less degree to other particular groups. Specialized, or skilled, workers are likely to be more or less attached to a locality and conditioned to a particular enterprise. Mobility of laborers over long periods of time is a matter of social stratification—the "non-competing groups" of Cairnes, though in more recent times and newer regions the groups or strata tend to fuse into a continuum. The degree to which this stratification rests on biological differences, in comparison with social institutions and conventions, is a matter on which learned as well as popular opinion has gone through several cycles since Smith so confidently asserted the eighteenth-century view that it is almost entirely a result of nurture. In a causal sense, all human capacity is socially and artificially created; in so far as its creation is under control and is controlled by economic motives, labor and its mobility form a subhead under the capital problem. A quantity of labor has meaning only in terms of value, which is the imputed share of product value.

On the capital or property side of the division, the outstanding fact is the contrast between short-run and long-run conditions. For capital goods, as they stand at any moment, homogeneity and distinctiveness of classes and other qualities are questions of brute fact, and the predominant fact is specialization, complementarity, and immobility, in almost infinite variety. In the long run, the question is one of the fluidity of capital between different forms of investment. On the side of exodus from any employment, fluidity

23. See pp. 52–53 of this article.

beyond that of the concrete agency depends (inversely) upon durability, while on the side of entry into an employment, it depends (inversely) on the period of construction. But mobility in the abstract is far less a problem than foreknowledge of conditions calling for movement, making it possible to plan for it a sufficient time in advance. In addition, mobility is not a matter of an individual agency or item, which, indeed, has little meaning, but of an interrelated complex in space and time. Specialized goods are complementary to other specialized goods and to specialized laborers and are produced by other specialized goods and laborers. Again, mobility is a composite of elements—time, or speed of transfer, and cost, which in turn includes direct outlays of many sorts and loss of efficiency. The mobility of the capital invested in any item is dependent on facts in infinite detail. None of the factors in it can be measured at all definitely, for there is no economic magnitude available as a standard which is not changed by any shift in the productive organization. Yet analysis has to recognize such differences, and the production manager must estimate them as accurately as he can.

Capital is the ideal "factor of production" and is theoretically (meaning in a society completely economic) all inclusive. Groups of concrete things approximate more or less to its empirical characteristics, while they exist as such. Obviously, capital is something very different from a class name for a group of things. The entire treatment of the subject of productive agencies has been vitiated by a confusion between the classification of things and the analysis of types or sources of productive capacity. This is particularly evident in the distinction between "natural" and "artificial." The productive capacity of any concrete agent may be more or less realistically analyzed into qualities resulting from previous human activity and those given by nature, and the previous human activity will have been more or less "economic" in intention and result. But to the extent that human activity in general is economic, all the exchange value represented by any agency will be accounted for in terms of that source, the "natural" attributes contributing nothing. Human beings might be similarly analyzed, or they might be classified, quite as realistically as non-human things, according to the predominance of the one or the other source of their productive capacity.[24]

24. As regards natural resources, the political interest is a further source of confusion. There is no contradiction between complete equality between value and economic cost of all such resources within any country, and the greatest difference between countries is the effectiveness with which existing productive capacity can be employed in producing these types of capital goods.

To explain the origin of the three-factor theory, we should go back to the historical conditions in which our economic conceptions were formed. General usage has long, and properly, recognized the three forms of income—wages, land rent, and return on capital (originally thought of as including profit[25] as well as interest). In postfeudal Europe, when our economic terminology was taking shape, the recipients of these three forms of income were fairly distinct social classes—laborers, landlords, and the middle class. The idea of distribution as a division of the total product among such classes is undoubtedly the point on which the classical economists went wrong.[26] But discussion of this topic belongs to the treatment of productive organizations (see Part III). The three social classes have no comparable reality today, particularly in the "newer" parts of the world; and in any case, if distribution is a phenomenon of competitive valuation, classes have nothing to do with it.

Another vital factor in the genesis and persistence of the three-factor view is undoubtedly the influence of the doctrine of pain cost as an explanation of the prices of products. The division might be systemized in these terms. Land would be defined by the absence of the effect of pain, presumably in both use and origin. The fallacy as regards use has been indicated when it was pointed out that the meaning of the pain of labor is the competition of non-pecuniary employments, and this obviously applies to land as well. The same reasoning fits the "production" of land also, as soon as it is seen to be produced, and the general relation of pain to production is understood.

Labor, of course, was virtually defined as pain, undergone for the sake of production, which was taken as the universal basis of value. This view has been criticized above.

As regards capital, one of the great inventions of the classical school was Senior's doctrine of abstinence. This functioned as a pain cost, corresponding to the interest element in the value of a product in a manner analogous to the pain of labor in relation to the wage

25. The classical treatment of the entrepreneur function and the corresponding type of income (or lack of such treatment) will call for notice in Part III.

26. See Ricardo, Preface, first paragraph; Senior, p. 88, heading. Mill's reference to classes is more casual and uncertain in meaning (cf. pp. 353, 417). Smith speaks of the different "ranks" of the people, in his heading to Book I, and of "ranks and conditions of men" in the brief "Introduction and Plan" (pp. 2, 4). None of the writers had any notion of a class as scientifically defined by sociologists.

element.[27] But there is much confusion here, which has also persisted to the present. Senior is emphatic that "abstinence" is the sacrifice incurred in *creating* capital. After capital "has become, whether by gift or by inheritance, the property of a person to whose abstinence and exertions it did not owe its creation," the profit ceases to be distinguishable from rent (p. 129). For Mill, however, "As the wages of the labourer are the remuneration of labor . . . the profits of the capitalist are . . . the remuneration of abstinence . . . what he gains by *forbearing to consume* his capital for his own uses . . ." (p. 405, our italics). Neither of them clearly saw the relation between the cost of capital in this sense and the direct, contemporary subjective cost of its use involved in giving up the use of existing capital for non-pecuniary enjoyments. The latter is the meaning of the "pain" involved in labor and is the only subjective sacrifice which can be held to be remunerated or motivated by the current money payment of interest.

This is most easily shown in relation to the non-consumption of existing capital. Assuming an interest rate of 5 per cent, one could enjoy double his net return by consuming the capital over about fifteen years. But to regard the $5 (per year on each $100) as pay for giving up $10 is palpably absurd. The only pecuniary incentive for not eating up the investment is the anticipation of having the net income beyond the fifteen years (or other period). But when this time arrives, as "now," the interest will, at the margin, exactly balance the day-to-day subjective cost of renouncing the use of the capital (viewed as permanent) for direct (non-pecuniary) satisfactions. That is, the capitalist never gets any pecuniary remuneration for non-consumption, and similar reasoning will show, *a fortiori*, that a saver never gets any for the original sacrifice of current consumption during the period of accumulation.[28]

27. See Senior, pp. 59, 89. Note the inconsistency in the definitions of abstinence, one calling it an agent, the other a kind of conduct. The germ of the abstinence idea is visible in Ricardo's repeated references to the time required to bring products to market and to the effects of the durability of capital on product value. In *Economica* for February, 1933, Mr. Victor Edelberg ingeniously argues that Ricardo expounded a "sound" theory of capital, *à la* Böhm-Bawerk. The present writer is unable to find in Ricardo's discussion very much either of Böhm-Bawerk's analysis or of a sound one, which to him mean very different things (cf. n. 29).

28. The paradox is identical with that raised, but not analyzed, by Marshall, in meeting Nicholson's objection to consumers' surplus (*Principles*, p. 127, n.). The choice involved in saving is analogous to that of moving from Africa to England in Marshall's illustration. If one lives in Africa on an income of £1,000

Saving involves abstinence, not "waiting," as later writers have erroneously preferred to call it, following Marshall, who took the term from Macvane. Mill himself glimpsed the fact (p. 405) that, even apart from the considerations brought out above, the capitalist could "often" increase his consumption during his own lifetime by consuming the capital. In fact, he could always do so, on the average more than doubling it, and in a majority of cases the saver decreases his absolute total consumption by saving.

Senior makes no attempt to connect the quantity of capital with the quantity of abstinence or to define quantity of capital in any way. It was left for Böhm-Bawerk and his successors to develop in this direction Senior's clear references to the interval, or period, which elapses between the employment of the labor, or the laborer and natural agent (p. 111 *vs.* p. 93), and the sale or completion of the product.[29]

In addition to the pain relation, it might be argued on purely general grounds that labor and capital depend for their continued existence upon their receiving a remuneration, while this is not true of land; and traces of this view may be found in the classical writers. The precise relation between the quantity of remuneration and the

per year, spending it rationally, one's total utility and its subjective cost is £1,000 per year, and in England it is the same. Yet there may obviously be a gain in moving, at a cost, because of the difference in the composition of the utility stream purchasable with the same money. Similarly, there may be a sufficient incentive to save in the privilege of securing in the future an enlarged utility stream at an equally increased cost (though that is not in any important degree the real motive of saving).

The notion of maximizing "total utility" (defined as whatever men do maximize in behaving rationally) will serve to explain the expenditure of a given income among given alternatives of choice. But any attempt to use it to explain movement from one economic situation to another seems to run inevitably into a double-counting paradox. For a present act must be explained by a present motive; and psychologically it seems that the books actually do balance from moment to moment—and not merely "at the margin," either. If we give up using quantity of utility to explain changes taking place over time, we are released from assuming that consumers' surplus is "real," and our reasoning harmonizes with the fact that no one in a routine situation experiences the free satisfaction pictured by the theory.

29. The main argument of this part should suffice to make it clear that there is no relation between the quantity of capital used in a society and the length of any "production period" or interval between production and consumption. Real production is simultaneous with consumption, while the time taken to build up the capital of society is its entire period of historical growth. The production period and service life of concrete things have no definite relation to the quantity of capital. Cf. also articles by the author in *Economic Essays in Honour of Gustav Cassel,* in *Economica* for August, 1934, and in *Economic Journal* for March, 1935; and also Part III of the present essay.

requirement for the existence of the factor is, of course, not discussed, but the same is true in the pain theory, and quantitative relations could not be discussed intelligently without bringing in the marginal principle.

In relation to land, we find clear evidence of another distinction, in the assumption that land is available for only one use, i.e., produes only one product, while labor and capital are subject to competition from a plurality of uses. There is, in fact, a fundamental difference between specialized and unspecialized agencies, but there is no correspondence between this distinction and that between natural resources and capital goods or labor. (And agriculture represents more a stage in production than even a distinct group of products.) Only an arbitrary classification of productive agencies can be made on the basis of specialization, which is purely a matter of degree. To discuss the fallacies in these views would require taking up in detail the separate questions of supply curves for productive agencies, for the services in pecuniary production of existing agencies, and for agencies or their services in particular pecuniary uses.

III. PRODUCTIVE ORGANIZATIONS AND DISTRIBUTION

INTRODUCTORY: IMPLICATIONS OF NATURAL PRICE DOCTRINE

The "correct" approach to the theory of distribution in economics is by way of a theory of productive organization; in fact, a sound distribution theory is hardly more than a corollary or footnote to an exposition of the mechanism by which resources are apportioned among different uses, and organized in each use, under the forces of price competition.[30] The "sense" in economics as a

30. Some apology seems in order for the absence of references to previous writers. A critique of previous critiques would be another labor equal to the survey itself, and I should not care to undertake it. Acknowledgments are also beyond my ability to state. I have learned from the better known historians of economic thought but am not conscious of indebtedness to any one in particular for any of the main interpretive ideas (such as they are) presented here. Except for running through a few chapters of Cannan's history of production and distribution theories, I have made no direct use of published work in preparing the essay, which presents the results of an effort through years of teaching to get at "what it is about" and makes no pretense to scholarship. I should be more interested in making acknowledgments to students who have written suggestive papers, but that also is out of the question. For a general check on the argument and aid in connection with references, I relied upon an able graduate assistant, Miss Rose Director (now Mrs. Milton Friedman), who was then working over the material intensively in connection with a more specialized study in the history of the theory of capital.

subject for study is derived from the idea of increasing the efficiency of action (i.e., of economy of resources) through mutual rendering of services by individuals. Historically, the development of the science may be imputed to the realization that purchase and sale represent and mediate such an exchange of services;[31] with a few individual exceptions, men seem never to have had this realization before the eighteenth century but to have regarded it as axiomatic that what anyone gains in a pecuniary transaction someone else must lose. Under analysis, a socially general effort to profit by exchange relations takes the form of a tendency toward a maximum (viewed as a state of equilibrium for the society as a whole), through the attraction of every increment of service capacity into its "best" use for the mutual advantage of both parties, i.e., the owner of the increment of capacity and the consumer of its service (who gets the service in exchange for that of some increment of capacity owned by him). If it is seen that this urge on the part of individuals as owners of service capacity is the organizing force in all price relations, and in the economic life which prices mediate and reflect, it becomes truistical to remark that the distribution of the product of all service capacity, considered as acting jointly, is on the basis of increments of yield.[32]

31. Services may be rendered personally or by granting to another the use of some external thing which one owns. There is no important analytical difference between the two sorts, either in economic theory, in social psychology, or in ethics.

32. All such statements should be accompanied by others emphasizing the considerations which tend to make nonsense (instead of sense) out of the study if they are not carefully taken into account: (1) The individual, including productive capacity in personal and property form, on the one hand, and knowledge, taste, and judgment as consumer, on the other, is taken as an absolute datum. (The severe limitations of this procedure cannot be developed here.) (2) The individual as a datum includes also his comparisons of present and future, and (3) either includes his attitude toward uncertainty (security *vs.* adventure), which cannot conceivably be formulated accurately, or else we are forced to make the impossible assumption of universal omniscience of the future. (4) It is assumed that individuals behave in a purely individualistic way, without collusion and without antagonism. This assumption, too, is highly unrealistic; in particular, it is theoretically impossible for two individuals in a system simultaneously to act intelligently in a way which at once takes the system as a set of given conditions of action and modifies it in any way, unless the action is fully preconcerted, which, of course, means collusion. It should be noted, too, that practically any aggregate of individuals within an economic system can profit by collusion; the only question is whether the gain will be greater than the cost of organization, which is a conception so subtle that analysis in general terms cannot be carried very far. (5) Finally, and perhaps worst of all, it is not true that the things really and finally wanted by human beings are typically, or in a major degree, physically measurable or that value-experience is a mathematical

Distribution really presents no special problem, unless the fact of indirect instead of direct demand may be regarded as such. The special theory of distribution usually given in our textbooks is simply a theory of joint demand, but, in fact, the demand for final products is overwhelmingly of that nature. The notion of indirect demand itself is purely a matter of degree; the designation of a really final product must be more or less arbitrary, and the results must be treated as final for the purposes of discussion, which are technically removed in various degrees from the theoretically final result of "psychic income" or whatever it is called. Moreover, distribution theory has little meaning apart from a theory of general equilibrium. For, obviously, the effective demand for any resource service depends on the distribution of income itself; and it is, of course, a reflection of the price of products, while the price of the service is a more or less price-determining element in the cost of the products. All the relations in question are relations of mutual determination in a framework of given conditions.

We should keep in mind, too, that a sound distribution theory must rest upon clear notions (*a*) of the meaning in quantitative terms of the resource-services priced, and (*b*) of the mathematical-logical principles of a functional connection between variables of small increments and variable proportions. On all such matters the classical writers were either unsuspecting or utterly confused.

The problem of interpreting the classical works in their treatment of distribution is more obscure than it would be if all theory of organization were absent. What we find, however, is that the discussions of value theory give, in connection with natural price, a fair indication of the general nature of the organization mechanism and process under price competition, but that the chapters on distribution ignore this reasoning and approach the subject from an entirely different point of view. In other words, the discussion of cost of production in relation to price is in general realistic, even if seriously incomplete, but the writers had little or no comprehension of the fact that the costs of production are identical with the distributive payments—that the two are simply the prices of productive services under different names. In the chapters dealing with distribution, i.e., with the various "shares," there is no approach to the subject in

---

function of physically measurable causes or sources. Economic values are really instrumental to values inherent in process rather than result and in a social context rather than the physical world.

terms of competitive pricing or of supply and demand; also, there is little explicit theory of organization, while such organization theory as is stated or most clearly implied is of another sort than the analysis of allocation and co-ordination of resources through price competition.

It is in Smith that we find much the clearest view of the organization process developed in connection with the theory of natural price.[33] Smith explicitly places the three types of productive agencies—"land, labor, and capital"—in the same position and role in the process of economic readjustment and treats them all as productive capacity, not as "pain."[34] Smith makes it fairly clear that the process of adjustment is one of transferring resources of any of the three kinds (individually) from less to more remunerative uses until the remuneration in all competing fields is equalized. In Ricardo and his followers, the essential phenomenon is the equalization of the return on capital, which is supposed automatically to equalize at the same time the return to labor.[35] All the Ricardian writers put land

33. See *Wealth of Nations,* Book I, chap. vii, "Of the Natural and Market Price of Commodities."

34. The question of the nature of cost of production, especially its relation to pain or sacrifice, was, of course, one of the main sources of controversy and of confusion in the whole body of classical literature. Two questions were really involved: (1) what it is that the money outlays of the producers really pay for, and (2) the meaning of sacrifice. On both points, the classical writers were in general wrong. What any outlay pays for is a service to the person making the payment and not a pain; and to the person rendering the service a sacrifice which is voluntary, or connected with a choice, is, in any rational view, simply the giving-up of one alternative to get another, which must be equal or greater, or the choice would not be made.

Regarding pain as the basis of production and of value, it is interesting to note that even Ricardo clearly recognized (chap. i, sec. 2) that the wage payments themselves do not correspond at all to the pain of the laborer, and Mill emphasized (p. 388) the tendency to an inverse correspondence where the wages go to different laborers in different wage groups. In the face of the unescapable facts, the related dogmas that labor is a homogeneous factor, rather than an indefinite plurality of kinds, and that prices must correspond with a meaningless pain cost, forced the writers into absurdity. The culmination in connection with labor was Cairnes's theory of value in terms of the "non-competing groups." As already noted, Senior's great contribution was the interpretation of capital as pain in the form of abstinence; the dimensional confusions in this notion were also pointed out above (see Part II, pp. 58 ff.).

35. Chap. iv in Ricardo gives the argument corresponding to Book I, chap. vii in Smith, under practically the same title, "Natural and Market Price." In Senior we have no separate section on the subject, but see his emphatic statements, especially on pp. 97, 101 ff. (He uses here the expression "labor and capital," but the argument as a whole will show that the meaning is not different from that of Ricardo; the heart of the matter is that a fixed amount of capital always "supports" a fixed amount of labor.) In Mill the equalization process receives relatively little attention in connection with the discussion of value but is discussed

in a special role in relation to cost (as does Smith, in part, in his chapter on rent, in contrast with the chapter on natural price). The details of the theory will be taken up presently.

Apart from his notion of three homogeneous factors, Smith falls short in two respects of giving a real theory of distribution. In the first place, and of chief importance, there is no clear recognition of the fact that his "ordinary or average rates" of wages, profits, and rent are themselves variables determined by the adjustment, being merely the rates at which the remuneration of each factor respectively is equalized among all competing uses when the available (or forthcoming) supply is fully employed in the best way. He seems to think of the transfer of any productive service into or out of any industry as affecting the price of that product (through quantity, a demand curve being implied but not clearly recognized) and of that service in that use, bringing both into harmony with the general average price paid for the productive service, taken as given. In the second place, there is no recognition of what is now generally treated as the central problem of distribution, namely the derivation of demand prices of factors separately through the imputation of the joint product, or its value, among the various agencies which co-operate in producing it (in connection with variable proportions in any productive unit).[36]

at length in connection with labor and capital (wages and profits) separately (see below).

Mill's discussion in the first section of his chapter on cost of production (pp. 451–52) is thoroughly muddled as to the meaning of cost. He says (p. 452.6): "As a general rule, then, things tend to exchange for one another at such values as will enable each producer to be repaid the cost of production with the ordinary profit; in other words, such as will give to all producers the same rate of profit on their outlay. But in order that the profit may be equal where the outlay, that is, the cost of production, is equal, things must on the average exchange for one another in the ratio of their cost of production: things of which the cost of production is the same, must be of the same value." This seems to be a reworking of Ricardo's statement (p. 50) to the effect that if a manufacturer should continue in a trade, "it would be only on condition that he should derive from it the usual and general rate of profits on stock; and that could only happen when his commodity sold for a price proportional to the quantity of labour bestowed on its production."

Ricardo seems at least to make his meaning intelligible, however untenable his doctrine, which can hardly be said of Mill. Ricardo's position, as we must repeatedly emphasize, is that a fixed amount of capital always employs a fixed amount of labor; capital cost and wages paid are identical and measure "labor cost."

36. This omission may be connected with Smith's earlier acceptance of the dogma that labor produces all wealth (related to the doctrine of pain cost) with which the chapter as a whole is in outright contradiction. The inferiority of the treatment in the later writers may also be due to their being still more influenced by this dogma.

Smith, of course, gives, following his chapters on wages and profits and preceding the chapter on rent, a separate discussion of differences in wages and profits in different employments. The same general pattern is followed by Mill, while Senior concludes his book with such a discussion. Ricardo gives only brief notice to the fact of differences, incidental to the argument of chapter iv (on natural price). All the treatments suffer from the theoretical defects just noticed; they fail to recognize that the process of equalization determines the general level or to explain the mechanism by which the factors separately are allocated among uses and among producers (and combined in each use and each productive unit). Indeed, the notion that labor and capital are separately movable contradicts the doctrine, so often stated or clearly implied, that the proportions of the two are fixed. And, of course, all the authors are wrong in not applying the same principles of equalization to land—which would force recognition, actually lacking, of the fact that uniformity of return in any connection has meaning only to the degree that the base is homogeneous.

GENERAL VIEW OF THE SYSTEM

When the classical writers, in their chapters treating of the distributive shares, turned away from the near approach to a realistic view of production and distribution presented in their discussion of value theory (natural price) and expressly took up our subject, they did not give up the notion of a "system" of distribution or even one of productive organization. Their theory is of little value as an explanation, because it ignores the essential phenomena of price competition and of economic organization through price competition, but this does not mean that it is false to the facts, still less that it is uninteresting. Beginning almost unconsciously with the idea of three shares, corresponding to the three social classes[37] and presumably to three social functions and three distinct sources of income, they attempted to picture a social process of division. The matter of most direct concern in the exposition seems to be the order in which the shares are assigned to the respective classes. In the very nature of their approach the actual mechanism has to be inferred, and any exposition of the system must involve debatable interpretations of diverse statements which can hardly be reconciled into consistency. It must be based chiefly on Ricardo and later writers, for Smith's

37. See Part III, pp. 58 ff.

strength was not in system but in realism of detail; but Smith provided practically all the materials used later.[38]

In form, the resulting Ricardian system of distribution is a double dichotomy. The social product as a whole is first divided between the land on the one hand and the labor-and-capital on the other, and then the labor-and-capital share is divided between its two claimants. The primary fact, in Ricardo's view, is the peculiar character of rent as not entering into the price of the produce.[39] The view of rent as a surplus taken by the landlord as a first claimant superficially simplifies the problem to a dichotomy; only

38. Except the idea of an increment of product associated with an increment of resource, of which there seems to be no clear trace in his thought.

39. If this doctrine meant what it said, that rent does not "enter into" or "form a part of" (Hume) price, it would imply that the aggregate value of the produce would be equal only to the sum of wages and profit, and the source from which rent would come is a mystery. What was meant was, of course, that the money payment for rent, and land use itself, are not causal in relation to price.

The general problem of interpreting Ricardo is too large and difficult to be attacked here, but one or two observations may be worth noting. Ricardo's primary interest in value theory was to make the theory of value monistic, and we might say absolute, in contrast with what seemed to him the pluralism and circularity (relativity) of Smith's reasoning. The task he set himself was twofold: to get rid of all use of prices to explain price, and to find some one thing, not itself a price, to which the price of a product must be equal. For fairly simple reasons, he picked quantity of labor. To explain price in this way, he had to explain away the price-determining roles of capital and land (or their remunerations) and to overcome the further difficulty that for common sense the price of labor as paid by the entrepreneur does not correspond to its quantity. Only one aspect of his procedure calls for notice here. He emphatically asserts (chap. i, sec. 2) that he is not concerned to explain the "absolute" value of commodities, but only the "variations in the relative value," which he says are not affected by the differences in remuneration of different grades of labor. The misuse of words is characteristic; he means that he is concerned with changes in relative value, not with actual relative value at any given time. In other words, his contention is that he is concerned with historical changes and not with equilibrium relations or tendencies, a position characteristic of many modern writers. The difficulty (as with his later emulators) is that a large part of what he says makes sense only in connection with a theory of equilibrium.

If we could view Ricardo's system in a purely historical light, as an explanation of contemporary events, it would, in a general way, fit the facts as to the outstanding changes in England during the half-century prior to the date of his book. The main fact was an increase of several fold in the prices of agricultural relative to manufactured products. And it would be correct to explain this, in the main, and speaking superficially, by the increase in the efficiency of labor in manufactures through inventions, and its decrease in agriculture, in consequence of the pushing outward of the margin of cultivation. (See especially Ricardo's "Essay on the Influence of a Low Price of Corn on the Profits of Stock.") The latter change was a consequence of the increase of population and the disruption of foreign trade by the wars. The first was a phase of the Industrial Revolution, which also underlay the growth of population.

one share need be really explained, the other is fixed by subtraction. The one more or less independently explained is wages, leaving profit as a residuum. Thus the treatment of distribution falls, or should fall, into two parts, the theory of rent and the theory of wages—in that order of sequence; and the organization mechanism must fit the same scheme.

The general conception of productive organization in relation to distribution is worked out by the classical writers only in connection with agriculture and with that only in a primitive form or aspect. Regarding every other phase of economic life, only extremely long-range and dubious inference is possible. In the situation the lines of which we can draw with some confidence, capital is thought of as in the literal sense "supporting" labor, and the two are "applied to" land. Production is carried on and directed by the "capitalist," who in the first instance owns all the product.[40] Production must be thought of as carried on in an annual cycle. At the end of the year, when the harvest is in, the capitalist-employer first pays his rent—if he uses any land superior to that at the margin of cultivation. He then divides the remaining product into two parts, one for his own use in consumption, and the other for the support of labor the next year. This second part replaces, continues, and constitutes his "capital," which is each year "advanced" to laborers. The rent or landlord's share (like that of the capitalist himself) is not thought of as advanced or paid out of capital. This can be rationalized only by assuming that the laborer is paid for his services (or the pay set aside and earmarked) at the beginning of the year, before they are rendered, while the landlord is paid at the end of the year. (In the writers' own exposition, none of the shares is treated as payment for

40. See especially Senior, pp. 93, 94; Mill, pp. 417–18; in Ricardo and Smith the assumption is clear beyond doubt. We find abundant recognition of lending at interest, but no separation of entrepreneur and capitalist functions. Karl Marx, who in so many respects is more classical than the classicals themselves, had abundant historical justification for calling—i.e., miscalling—the modern economic order "capitalism." Ricardo and his followers certainly thought of the system as centering around the employment and control of labor by the capitalist. In theory, this is of course diametrically wrong. The entrepreneur employs and directs both labor and capital (the latter including land), and laborer and capitalist play the same passive role, over against the active one of the entrepreneur. It is true that entrepreneurship is not completely separable from the function of the capitalist, but neither is it completely separable from that of labor. The superficial observer is typically confused by the ambiguity of the concept of ownership. The owner of an enterprise may not own any of the property employed in it; and further reflection will show that the same item of property may in different senses be owned entirely, or in widely overlapping degrees, by a considerable number of proprietors.

services, not even wages, though they all, even rent, are occasionally referred to as such, especially by Smith and Senior; but it is now impossible to think of distribution in any other way.) We now take up the classical analysis in detail, beginning with the share which was first segregated, i.e., rent.

RENT AND LAND UTILIZATION

Ricardo's treatment of rent is brief, and, in spite of the declaration in his Preface, it is oriented primarily toward the problem of rent in its relation to value and price rather than that of a distributive share. From the standpoint of this primary interest, it serves the purpose of eliminating an obstacle in the way of a labor theory of value. But, in spite of these facts, it is in connection with rent that we find the nearest approach in the classical writings to a real theory of distribution, meaning a process of imputation on the basis of final increments. In the theory, rent has two aspects; from the standpoint of production it is a surplus, an excess of the yield of capital, meaning capital-and-labor, over the yield in a situation where no rent is paid, while from the standpoint of distribution, it is a residuum after capital-and-labor get their joint share, determined by marginal productivity (pp. 48–49).[41] All through the chapters on wages and profits, as well as that on rent, Ricardo consistently develops his rent theory in these terms; capital-and-labor, viewed as a single, homogeneous factor, are applied to land in successive doses ("portions"), and their remuneration is determined by the product of the last increment, the land receiving the remainder of the product, if any. It is made fairly clear, too, that the order of application is such as to keep the product of equal final increments uniform in all locations. This reasoning obviously involves variable proportions of labor-and-capital with land, in two senses of the word.

Though it may seem hypercritical, careful reflection on the text as a whole forces us to raise the question as to how clearly Ricardo really grasped the meaning of the incremental principle. In spite of his consistency in making fairly correct statements (in terms of his assumptions), we find on analysis a staggering number of essential things that he certainly did not understand.

1. He did not see that all this is, or would be, under his assumptions, the condition for maximizing the product as a whole.

41. The use of the terms "surplus" and "residuum" in this technical sense appears later, though all our writers refer to rent as the surplus product of land. See, e.g., Smith, pp. 146, 147; Ricardo, p. 52; Senior, pp. 90, 91; Mill, pp. 427, 472.

2. The absurdity of treating capital-and-labor as a homogeneous factor has been mentioned, and the underlying theory will receive attention in the next section, dealing with wages and profits.[42]

3. It is equally absurd to treat land as homogeneous except for differences in grade. If Ricardo had attempted to give a definition of land "quality" (in the sense of grade) he would surely have been forced to see that its only test or measure is precisely the rent per acre—see below), and cannot be used to explain rent—unless one gives a thoroughgoing productivity theory.

4. Ricardo has no real notion of proportions between capital-and-labor and land, for he has none of quantity of land. He never connects rent with any particular quantity of land, or in general with land at all; it is the capital-and-labor (or capital) applied to the land which yields the rent (p. 49).[43] He generally refers to the total quantity of land of a given grade in a society; but on page 48.6 a clear reference of this sort is immediately followed by an illustration of a particular tenant and his land, without reference to the conditions under which the second £1,000 of capital would be applied to such a particular piece of land.

5. We may group here some other indications that Ricardo did not really understand the principle of variable proportions. (*a*) His "increments" are enormously large instead of negligibly small as a sound analysis requires. (*b*) The notion that it becomes "necessary" to take up new land or apply more capital to that already in use

42. Ricardo says expressly (p. 59.6) that using less capital is the same thing as using less labor. As far as the duality of the capital-and-labor factor is concerned we must recognize that if the proportions are assumed to be fixed (which generally seems to be the assumption in the discussion of rent), or if the use of more capital with a given quantity of labor through the payment of higher wages occurs but does not increase the total product (which is the assumption at some other points), then the grouping of two factors as one would not be illicit. (See next section.) The fallacy of treating labor as a factor would remain, and the treatment of capital in the same way would have to be justified by a clear explanation of capital quantity, which is certainly not found in the classical writers (and can be justified only with complex and fairly serious limitations).

43. His doctrine as a whole undoubtedly requires that only labor be considered productive, though, in the Preface and in the second paragraph of the chapter on rent, he refers to "the produce of the earth." Other classical writers make occasional statements more explicitly to the effect that rent is the value of the land-use or its product, which, of course, is a lapse into common sense inconsistent with the general position. (See Smith, p. 344.) Senior (p. 136) in one of his characteristic flashes of insight really commits himself to a productivity theory (cf. also p. 181), though he gives no hint of an imputation process. But on p. 140 he says that the amount is subject to no general rule and has neither a maximum nor a minimum.

(p. 47), and equivalent expressions, are not to his credit. (This usage is even more typical of other writers and of modern textbooks.) Even when Ricardo does refer to an "increase in demand" for agricultural products his case is not improved, for it is hardly possible to read into his text any economically defensible interpretation of the phrase. (His general usage of the term "demand" is hopelessly confused and inconsistent; see especially chap. xxx.) (*c*) It is difficult to interpret the famous discussion of two kinds of improvements in agriculture (pp. 57–59) in such a way that it does not deny the possibility of varying the proportions between capital and land.

6. Another point of major importance is that Ricardo (and his school) did not so much as glimpse the reversibility of the entire apparatus of dosing, diminishing returns, and residuals, with the consequence that the reasoning is circular, and is a vicious circle unless and until it is developed as a theory of mutual determination and of equilibrium in a system under stated given conditions. Of course, our criticism of the writers in this regard might be tempered by the fact that such notions only began to come into economic science the better part of a century after Ricardo's death and have been slowly making headway since that time.[44] A modern analysis would recognize that the entire theory can be turned upside down and viewed as a productivity theory of rent, with the capital-and-labor share as residual; and indeed this is closer to the underlying logic of the treatment, since the rent share is taken out first.

To see this, we need only fix our attention upon the form of the Ricardian statement (p. 47) which is followed by Mill (p. 425), viewing rent as the difference between the product of the same capital-and-labor when applied to a rent-yielding piece of land and

44. The notion of "dosing" an entire supply of one factor or group of factors onto the given total supply of other factors is as unnecessary as it is unrealistic. Even the postulate of continuity in the proportions of combination is superfluous. The correct notion is one of the increment of total effect secured by adding any concrete agency, or bargaining unit of a factor, to an organization as a whole. (The consequences of the actual finite size of the increment of productive capacity is a question to be examined on its merits in view of the facts in any case.) As for the residual theory in general, it practically reduces to saying that the effect of any change in a causal complex is the difference between what it is and zero, and that this fact is a causal explanation.

It may be worth noting that the analysis of distribution in the form of a double dichotomy with both rent and profit as residual does not involve the fallacy of two residuals in the same system, which is found in some later expositions, egregiously in that of F. A. Walker. (My own teaching was wrong on this point for years.) But, as we shall see, the fallacy of plural residuals does occur in the classical theory of profits and wages, which reduces to the absurdity that each claimant gets what is left after the other is paid.

when applied under no-rent conditions at the extensive or intensive margin, but with no statement as to proportions. (It must be the best amount of capital-and-labor for the particular piece of superior land, and the comparison must lie between the product in that use and the product when applied to the best amount of submarginal land, or in the best way at the intensive margin—"best" being defined in accord with the economic law that maximum total effect is secured through equalizing final increments.) It will be evident that the residuum left to the given piece of superior land after paying the capital-and-labor what it could produce at the margin is identical with the marginal or incremental product of the land itself, considered as a final small "dose" of its given kind and grade. For, under competitive conditions, if any (small) piece of land were held out of use, the labor and the capital properly belonging to it would be applied at the margin of cultivation. But at the margin of cultivation, each small increment of labor and of capital adds the same amount to the total product as the last unit on the superior land.[45]

7. A more technical, but quite fundamental, criticism is that Ricardo and the other writers had no clear or accurate understanding of the principle of diminishing returns, even in the limited and one-sided connection of the application of other factors to land, and overlooking the undefined and undefinable character of the variables they assumed. (This also is a recent achievement of the leaders of the science, which is still slowly making headway in the treatise literature.) It is true that Ricardo consistently speaks of the product (clearly meaning the increment of product) due to an increment of capital and labor in a combination. But in view especially of his controversial relations with other writers in his own day, it seems more than suspicious that the form of statement common in the literature at that time and since is a confused reference to different "proportional" changes in factor and in product. A correct formulation must, of course, distinguish two entirely different principles with no direct or necessary interconnection. One is the *proportional* law, stating that a given ratio of increase in a variable factor will give rise to a smaller ratio of increase in the total product. This principle is axiomatically true if the factors are combined intelligently but has no great importance for analysis since it affords no standard for selecting and using any particular proportions of the factors. For this we must have recourse to a different principle, the *incremental* law,

45. Cf. Allyn A. Young, in Ely's *Outlines of Economics* (4th ed.), p. 410, end of fine-print section.

stating that equal successive increments of a variable factor yield decreasing increments of product.[46] It is also necessary for valid analysis to distinguish between, and interrelate the effects upon, physical product and value product, and, in this connection, to distinguish carefully between a competitive industry and one in which there is but a single enterprise, i.e., a monopoly.[47]

8. Although the fact has been mentioned, it should be listed as a separate item that Ricardo's ablest followers clearly do not at all understand the significance of increments, even in the narrow and special setting in which Ricardo himself employs the concept. Senior, indeed, gives at one point a formally correct exposition of the Ricardian theory, though in connection with the express treatment of rent as a phenomenon of monopoly (see p. 115, table and explanatory text at bottom of page). But later (p. 126) he uses the absurd assumption that equal areas of land of different grades yield different amounts of produce at the same "expense"; and his discussion in connection with distribution (pp. 135 ff.) gives no definite theory and ends with the statement already quoted (p. 140) that the amount of rent is not subject to any general rule. (He makes the same assertion regarding monopoly price in general [pp. 97, 104, 111].)

In Mill's treatment of rent, there is no definite recognition of the incremental principle at all. He merely repeats (p. 425) the Ricardian formula that rent is the difference in the productivity of a given amount of capital on the rent-yielding land in comparison with that which yields no rent; but there is no clear reference to dosing or increments,[48] and no explanation whatever of the process

46. In a graph showing total product from a given amount of some fixed factor or factors as a function of the amount of a variable factor, the proportional law finds expression in the fact that the curve at a given point has a positive slope less than that of a line connecting the point with the origin of co-ordinates, i.e., a tangent at the point cuts the vertical or product axis. The incremental law is expressed by the fact that the curve of total product bends toward the base line (the variable factor axis).

47. Monopoly is, of course, almost always a matter of degree, a fact which has lately attracted a somewhat strange amount of attention. The views of the classical writers, including Ricardo, on monopoly value or price were absurdly confused (and they have no discussion of monopoly in connection with distribution); and, of the authors under consideration here, only Ricardo failed explicitly to treat land as a monopoly.

48. He does refer in the chapter on rent (p. 429) to a "portion" of capital applied to agriculture yielding "only the ordinary profits"; and in his chapter on "Distribution as Affected by Exchange" his language is "the least productive instalment of the capital employed on the better lands." Just what should be read

by which the quantity of capital to be applied on any particular amount of land of any quality is determined, which is the essential point for the theory of organization and so for a sound theory of distribution. He does emphasize the equalization of the return on capital through competition but gives no evidence that he understands the meaning of this as equalization of increments of return from equal increments of capital. The natural inference would be that he thinks of it as equalization of total return per unit, which is a fatal error. Mill's numerous references to diminishing returns are always to the proportionality form of the law.[49]

Smith's treatment of rent properly lies outside the scope of this essay, as he does not give anything like the Ricardian theory. But a few points in his treatment seem to be worth setting down. The first is the glaring inconsistency between his chapter on rent, especially the introductory section, and the treatment of rent as a cost in the chapter on natural price.[50] In the second place, Smith has no statement or clear implication of the principle of diminishing returns in any form.[51] Third, and most important of all, Smith shows at vari-

into this is a typical problem of interpretation. It may be argued that the process of dosing and equalization is taken for granted. But should it, or would it, be in such an exposition? The difficulty, as already pointed out, is that practically all the fundamentals of economic analysis are too obvious to be really overlooked by any observer who thinks about the problems at all.

49. There is an obviously accidental exception on p. 181. The first sentence on the page says that "the produce of land increases, *caeteris paribus*, in a diminishing ratio to the increase in the labour employed. . . ." This is really the incremental principle. But before finishing the next sentence the author quotes H. C. Cary as holding that "the produce increase[s] in a greater ratio than the labour." Senior also makes a similar accidentally correct statement of the incremental principle (pp. 105–6).

Both Senior and Mill treat capital-and-labor as a single homogeneous factor, referring to it indifferently as capital, or labor, or joining the two words in either order. (I have not noticed a statement by either paralleling that of Ricardo [p. 59.6] saying expressly that the two always vary together.)

50. See final paragraph of introduction to Book I, chap. xi; also the change made in the second edition in chap. vi (p. 51, n. 7). Ashley suggests that this was done at the suggestion of Hume (see his abridged edition, p. 46, n.). In the chapter on rent, Smith relapses by implication into an absolute labor theory of value, like that which Ricardo assumes in his book subsequent to chap. i, where the explicit argument is subject to a much more reasonable interpretation. Smith nowhere really argues for such a labor theory as cause or determinant of value, not even in chap. v. Moreover, his chapter on rent itself runs largely in other terms, and is much more realistic than those of the other writers.

51. Perhaps an exception should be made for two or three sentences relating to economic progress in colonies in the chapter on profits (Book I, chap. ix, p. 94.7).

ous points some recognition of the role of competition in different uses for land, and in particular emphasizes the special significance of unique or highly specialized land, in contrast with that which is subject to competition from various ordinary uses.[52]

LABOR AND CAPITAL: WAGES AND PROFITS

The classical theory of wages and profits contrasts with that of rent in that it continued to be controversial, while the rent doctrine was, from the beginning, accepted as definitive.[53] This, at least, is a good sign, for the theory sheds no light whatever on the economic principles of distribution and is an amazing tissue of inconsistency and irrelevance. These reasonings are interesting and important, not merely because they illustrate the workings of the best minds in one of the most important fields of thought and have, needless to say, some relation to facts and to real problems, but especially because they serve to warn against types of fallacy which seem to be perennially natural to minds not trained to be on guard against them. Modern discussion has recognized that the theory of profit does not get beyond the arithmetical truism of the residual idea; our examination will show, what is not so generally recognized, that the theory of wages is in no better state. The only sense in which the entire treatment gets beyond the narrow and vicious circle of each claimant getting what the other does not get, lies in the idea

52. The references are chiefly to vineyard land, on the one hand, and to competition between tillage and grazing, on the other. Similar passages occur in the discussion of natural and market price (Book I, chap. vii, pp. 62–63) and in the chapter on rent (Book I, chap. xi, p. 156, on vineyard land; pp. 149–50, 150, 153, 157–59 on competing uses). The passage dealing with payment of rent above a "natural rate" (p. 63) is especially significant. The argument as to which particular use determines the value in all other uses is, of course, confused.

It might be noted, too, that in at least one place (in Book II, see p. 344) Smith takes a productivity view of rent, saying that it "may be considered as the produce of those powers of nature, the use of which the landlord lends to the farmer."

53. Cairnes's brief parenthetical reference to rent (*Leading Principles*, pp. 58–59) might well be placed alongside Mill's oft-quoted reference to value theory as a topic on which nothing remained to be said. But as a matter of fact, the controversy in question raged around the composition of the wages fund. which is by no means the central conception in the doctrine of wages and capital; and, on the other hand, as shown above, the different writers did not really state the same theory of rent, though they were unconscious of the fact.

It will be recalled that it was really after the downfall of the older classical school (under the impact of the theory of subjective value) that Cairnes wrote his main treatise; also, that he wrote it for the purpose of rehabilitating the wages-fund theory (after the recantation by Mill), along with the other leading fallacy in the classical position, the labor theory of value.

that labor gets what it "has to have." This is not only meaninglessly indefinite but is in no defensible sense true, and, moreover, the same principle is advanced for the profit share also.

Viewed from the standpoint of a real analysis, the fundamental difficulty is, as already emphasized, the failure to treat the shares in distribution as competitively determined prices. But they have to be prices of something, which must be a measurable commodity. The absurdity of treating land-use as a homogeneous magnitude has been commented upon above; regarding labor, the fallacy has been pointed out often enough—quite typically by writers who go ahead to discuss "wages in general," as if the concept had meaning. Ricardo, whose main interest was the promotion of a quantity-of-labor theory of value, was not altogether blind to the latter difficulty, and his mode of evading it has been indicated above (p. 67, n. 39). For present purposes, we may follow the classical assumption that labor is a homogeneous and fluid fund, of which common agricultural labor may be taken as a type. But as regards capital, the entire discussion runs in terms of a rate of return, and it is necessary to have some conception of the meaning of a quantity of capital, homogeneous both in itself and with its return, if we are to talk sense about the problem at all.[54]

The problem of capital is crucial for distribution theory because of the fact that so much income is received in the form of interest, reckoned as a rate of return on a principal sum. It is strange, however, that anyone ever failed to see that the capital is always the value of some concrete thing endowed with earning power and is a distinct source of income, or class of sources, only in the sense that

54. On the treatment of capital, it might perhaps be observed first of all that the writers have nothing to say about the yield or income of concrete capital goods. This would, of course, tie up with rent theory; it conforms to the sense in which the term "rent" is used in everyday life, and recognition of the realities here would have gone far toward straightening out the entire system of concepts. (If "rent" is to be used in economics in a more specialized sense, to represent a theoretically peculiar sort of income, it should be the price-determined payment for the services of completely specialized productive agencies—which would naturally include a large fraction of wages.) But while the classical writers have much to say in various connections about various capital instruments—machines, buildings, etc.—they neither have anything to say about the earnings of such concrete things nor give any explanation of how they are quantified as abstract capital. The same statement holds for human beings and also for land; everything is abstract quantity, yet, of course, there is no indication of definitions in quantitative terms. Even the conception of rent as a surplus falling or accruing to the "original and indestructible powers of the soil" treats these powers as a homogeneous fund, though an attribute possessed in different degrees by different examples of "land."

it is restricted to things which are allowed to be owned and bought and sold, i.e., to property, excluding free human beings. Capital is the productive capacity of such things, except that it is measured by salable value at a moment of time, while the product of capital is a perpetual flow or stream of value. As already explained (in Part II), its quantity must be found by capitalizing a stream of value return, using a formula in which the chief unknown is a rate of interest, determined by the cost of creating additional income sources under the existing technical and economic conditions. (The cost of a capital item about to be created is also derived from an income-stream of some volume for some period, by a formula involving the rate of interest, but inverse to capitalization, namely accumulation; the yield must be viewed as a perpetual income-stream, since no yield can be counted until after complete maintenance is provided for.)

Nothing of this is to be found in the classical analysis of distribution. The notion of capital there assumed is simply a quantity of ordinary consumable product, accumulated as a stock. In this way the writers sidetracked any special problem of capital quantity, apart from the exchange value of a product for consumption use.[55] The distinguishing mark of capital is for them a special use of produce, its consumption in the special connection and for the special purpose of production, i.e., its own reproduction with an additional product, which is profit. But, since in the classical system only laborers produce, capital is limited in the first place to product consumed by laborers. However, not all laborers were considered productive, but only those actually engaged in reproducing capital, which they necessarily consumed, and so providing for the perpetual continuation of the production process. Thus capital is also limited to products suited for the consumption of laborers. But there are two further restrictions. First, laborers were supposed to live exclusively on material products, specifically excluding all services; and, secondly, in strict theory, only that consumption of products which actually enabled the laborer to work was held to be productive consumption, and only that part of actual consumption could count as capital.[56]

55. That is, they seemed to themselves to do so; to be accurate, they would still have required a rate of interest to define a quantity of capital. This is true under any conditions in which capital exists at all and is to be kept in mind as a special reservation whenever we speak of the incremental productivity of capital.

56. Of course, this notion of what is "necessary" to enable the laborer to produce is indefinite at best. As remarked at the outset, the classical writers did not understand the notion of functionally related variation and cannot be expected

But in classical theory there are still two additional circumstances necessary to give rise to capital, as distinct from other produce. Produce is employed productively (*a*) because the process of production requires time, and the producer (laborer) has to be supported during the period by produce previously accumulated and (*b*) because society is so organized that the laborer himself does not make this prior accumulation, but has it done for him by another person, who thereby becomes a capitalist. Now, since the capitalist is the entrepreneur and manager, and since, moreover, the activity of saving received so much emphasis, it is hard to give any reason for the view that the share of the produce consumed by the capitalist is not productively consumed and is not capital in the same sense as that which is advanced to laborers. Nonetheless, it is plainly an essential part of the system expounded by Smith and the Ricardians.[57]

---

to recognize a detail like difference in degree. Logically, the line would be drawn at consumption which increased production by more than the product consumed, and so yielded a profit. Such principles would have significance for a slave economy under perfectly rational exploitation, but it is hard to see their relevance to any free society. Needless to say, the writers, being human beings and endowed with common sense, did not stick to their definitions. Even apart from extensive animadversions on machines and other forms of capital which are not products in the sense here in question, and are not fitted into the theory of a rate of return, they always treated as capital whatever is actually paid ("advanced") to laborers as wages.

In discussing the notion of unproductive consumption, Senior makes an observation (p. 56) which contains much realistic economic insight and deserves especially to be brought to the attention of social reformers devoted to the equalitarian ideal: "We do not, of course, mean it to be inferred that all personal expenditure beyond mere necessaries is necessarily unproductive. The duties of those who fill the higher ranks in society can seldom be well performed unless they conciliate the respect of the vulgar by a certain display of opulence." Senior illustrates the point by the magistrate and ambassador, but the extreme paradoxical example is the minister of such a religion as Christianity.

57. Malthus held a diametrically opposite view, which was refuted by Senior (p. 64). Cf. also Smith, p. 58.

Exclusion from capital of the share of produce consumed by the landlord (when rent is paid) would be easier to justify, since the landlord was supposed to play a strictly passive role. (In fact, our authors discuss the division between labor and capital only at the land margin.) From the standpoint of a correct analysis, the landlord, of course, furnishes productive services to industry in a sense theoretically indistinguishable from similar activities on the part of the laborer, and is subject to a sacrifice, in the same sense, of giving up one valuable alternative to get another. The capitalist, as shown above (Part II), is in a somewhat different position, in so far as he not merely furnishes the use of capital, but abstains from consuming the capital itself, and perhaps saves it in the first place. But, of course, where land is private property in the complete sense, the individual landowner is in identically the same position as the owner of any other salable productive agency (ignoring the

The classical writers' general theory of productive organization and of distribution may now be restated with explicit reference to the division between wages and capital, and to profit as a rate of return. All production takes place in an annual *cycle,* starting anew from zero at the beginning of each year. During the year, all classes live on the produce of the previous year. The current year's produce comes at the end of the year into the hands of the capitalist. This functionary first pays his rent (if any) as already explained; then from the produce less rent, he sets aside a part—what is "necessary" —as capital, replacing his advances of the previous year and those to be advanced to labor as wages during the next year. The final residue is his own share or profit, which is reckoned as a fraction or percentage of the annual advance, the capital. Thus the capital of society is a wages fund, and the rate of wages is found by dividing the amount of the fund by the number of the working population.

Such a general view of organization and distribution must be sought in the chapters or sections dealing with profit; the fundamental conceptions met with in the explicit discussion of wages are utterly different, as we shall see. The theory as sketched was first given a fairly clear formulation in Smith's chapter (Book II, chap. iii) bearing the significant title, "Of the Accumulation of Capital, *or* Of Productive and Unproductive Labour" (our italics). Interestingly enough, Ricardo gave no explicit treatment of the topic of productive and unproductive labor. It is, however, referred to in terms which make it clear that he accepted it as established. It comes up several times in the first few pages of the chapter on taxes (chap. viii), where the wording is "productive and unproductive consumption" (pp. 131, 132, 133); but on page 135 we have "unproductive labourers." The latter is also the usage in chapter xx on value and riches (p. 263; on p. 264 it is the "reproductive" use of revenue); in chapter xxvi on gross and net revenue (p. 336) we find "unproduc-

---

deeper similarities between land and other agencies). But, from the standpoint of a really correct analysis, all of the contributors to production receive their remuneration instantly out of current production and not out of "advances" or "capital."

Some writers, but not in general those here being considered, identified the rate of return with the fraction of the produce accruing to the capitalist. The rent share is, of course, ignored or eliminated by thinking of production at a land margin, but the statement is still inaccurate, unless the capitalist's own share is considered as capital. But the statement is approximately true since the profit share may be assumed to be small in comparison with that of wages.

tive labour." It does not appear that Ricardo attached any meaning to the difference in terminology.[58]

Accepting the general approach, and framework of assumptions, of the system, two main problems leap out at once from the classical writers' pages treating of capital, wages, and profits. The first is, what actually determines the division of the produce-less-rent between capitalists and the laborers, or, stating the question in the form set by the treatment itself, what determines the amount which the capitalist must pay as wages, before he gets his own share, fixed by subtraction. The other problem is the more complex one of fitting into the theory of capital and profit the other forms of capital, so often and fully discussed, represented by things which cannot be viewed as reproduced in an annual cycle starting anew from zero each year.

On the first point, we get a fairly positive answer, if we consider only the treatment of wages which forms the body of the treatment of profits, leaving the latter as a residual. It is a very unsatisfactory answer, but it is at least verbally definite. Wages are determined by what is required for the support of the laborer (see Ricardo, p. 105.3; Senior, p. 191.2; Mill, p. 416.8). That is, we have a subsistence theory of wages. But the definiteness is purely verbal; the substance raises a number of crucial questions and really answers no questions at all. Since the theory purports to explain, and must explain, the division of the joint labor-capital share which actually takes place, it must be a short-run or momentary theory and not one which merely states or explains a long-run tendency; the laborer must obviously get what he has to have, "now." (The very different question of long-run tendencies will be taken up presently.) In the absence of any impersonal mechanism of market competition fixing wages,[59] the logic of the situation would be that the employer

58. The expositions of Senior (pp. 51–57) and of Mill (Book I, chap. iii, secs. 5–6) are somewhat easier to follow. Smith has a different arrangement of the material, but except for the refinement, his wages and profit doctrine is that of the later writers. His main discussion of the phenomena of capital is segregated from that of price and distribution theory in a short second book (Book II, "Of the Nature, Accumulation and Employment of Stock"), in chap. iii of which the doctrine in question is developed. His chapter on profits in Book I is brief and says little about general theory. (Its main theoretical point will be noticed later.)

59. Fixing them, of course, as the economic value of the service to the entrepreneur, which is their value to the consumer, under the given conditions. But no ethical implication attaches to the notion of the economic value of a

should pay what it pays him to pay; any individual laborer should receive the wage which yields the employer the maximum product. That is, wages would be fixed on the same principles as the feed and care of a beast of burden.[60] Thus the subsistence theory of wages rests on the deeper assumption that the employer-capitalist makes the division arbitrarily, and this is the clear import of the text. The minimum subsistence requirement sets the limit in that direction in which it pays him to go, and in the absence of forces setting any other limit, his self-interest makes the minimum the maximum and the actual wage. For those interested in raising wages, the suggestion of policy is obvious: it is only necessary to provide some form of compulsion in order to secure to the laborer "the whole product of his labour," which, again in accord with the principles of the classical economics, is taken to be the whole product of industry. But the notion that wages might be raised by bringing pressure to bear on those who pay them is, as we shall presently emphasize, antithetical to the dearest conclusion on policy of the classical writers themselves.

The deeper aspect of this theory, that capitalists make the division between themselves and their laborers by arbitrary fiat, is strongly confirmed by the tone of the discussion in Smith (Book II, chap. iii) and Mill (Book I, chap. v, sec. 9), which is one of downright fear lest they may not choose to "destine" to the support of productive labor enough of the product to maintain the social capital. Smith is obviously preaching (if not scolding), as well as analyzing mo-

---

service as a remuneration for the service, without a special examination of the whole problem from an ethical standpoint. All competitive values depend, as a matter of course, on the distribution of ownership of productive capacity (human and non-human) and on the knowledge and tastes of its owners as they affect the supply of services for various uses and the demand for various products. Persons who do not own some productive capacity in some form are outside the economic system altogether. See also above, p. 62, n. 32.

60. With the interesting exception that, since the workers are not actually slaves by inheritance, there is no reason why the individual employer should provide the worker with maintenance for a family. But this might be explained by assuming that the employer cannot prevent the worker from having a family and sharing his wages with them, and so must support the family to get the services of the worker. From a social-ethical standpoint, it is an interesting feature of the system that provision for all contingencies in the lives of the workers and their families becomes a responsibility of the workers individually, and one which they cannot adequately meet. But all individualistic societies alleviate some of the worst consequences of this inadequacy through various organizations for relief.

tives, in his emphasis on the "uniform, constant, and uninterrupted effort of every man to better his condition" (p. 325).[61]

The other phase of the theory, that wages depend on subsistence requirements, is supported by the fact that it has been taught ever since by the radical schools of economics, especially the Marxists, as the "iron law of wages" and is fervently believed today, with unessential modifications, by labor leaders and a very large section of the general public. Even when it is held in the form of a standard of living theory, the "necessary" standard is viewed as effective at the moment, and not over some long run of generations.[62] If Marx and the radicals are clear and emphatic about anything, it is the repudiation of Malthusianism and all its works. The theory then takes a bargaining power form; but there is no change in economic principles, the essential point being that there are no general impersonal forces determining wages and that, short of the whole product, the individual employer pays what he is somehow compelled to pay.[63]

Yet, viewed in the light of the whole text, even of the chapters on profit, Smith and Ricardo and their followers clearly do not really think either that wages ordinarily correspond to, or approximate, a literal minimum subsistence requirement or that they are fixed by an arbitrary fiat of the employer—in spite of the fact that they often seem to be trying to state these principles as unequivocally as possible. They believed strongly in the fixing of wages by impersonal forces, even by competitive forces, as the chapters on wages (to be

61. Senior and Mill make similar appeals, but Ricardo's preaching generally relates to public policy such as taxation, protective duties, and the poor law, rather than to private behavior. We should not leave the topic without noting that Ricardo and Mill also expressly state that profit must be at a level which will enable the capitalist to live! (Ricardo, p. 100.9; Mill, p. 450.5). Smith also calls profit the capitalist's fund of subsistence (pp. 57–58).

62. See below, on the classical long-run subsistence theory based on Malthusian population doctrine. This Malthusian doctrine is quite adequately stated by Smith (chap. viii, esp. pp. 81–83), along with characteristically sensible observations on the direction of the causal relation between scale of living and wages at a given time (pp. 77–78).

63. The practical conclusion which motivates the wish-thinking back of this theory—namely, that to raise wages it is only necessary to find some way to build a fire under the individual who pays them—illustrates a basic human trait. We seem to crave some enemy whom we can blame for anything that seems to be wrong and can attack as a method of correcting the evil. It is often implied, if not explicitly stated, that it would only be necessary to eliminate (liquidate) the employer and place the workers themselves (meaning the propagandists as their representatives) in charge of production in order to pay wages equal to the income which (successful) employers receive under competition.

considered presently) clearly show. Yet they failed to give any analysis of competitive process, hence of any real distribution theory. The reason is simply that they were discussing a problem which, self-evident as its main principles are, they only half saw and did not at all understand.[64]

The classical writers' explicit discussions of wages, to which we now turn (preceding their treatment of profit), develop two main explanations of wages, one for the short run and one for the long run; both are utterly different from the theory developed in the content of the discussion of profit, in arriving at that share as a residual. The short-run theory, or theory of actual wages, runs in terms of supply and demand. The supply of labor is the laboring population (not separated from the population as a whole). The demand for labor is the "funds destined for the payment of wages" or wages fund. As in the discussion of profit, so generally in that of wages, this fund is identical with the capital of society (sometimes only proportional); and, assuming an annual turnover of capital (without which it has no meaning), the wage rate is given by the simple formula, "capital divided by population." But capital itself is merely the portion of the produce-less-rent which is actually employed in the payment of wages; and, in the absence of a momentary subsistence theory of wages, we simply have no principle of division. Yet the argument clearly assumes both that wages are definitely above the minimum of subsistence and that the wages fund has some sort of objective reality, though subject to changes. The conclusion which the writers are evidently concerned to establish is that wages can be increased only by increasing the wages fund relative to the number of laborers. But two burning issues are raised:

64. As already noted, they make it clear that competition compels all employers to pay the same wages and equalizes the rate of profit among them all. (Generally in a separate discussion, not dealing with the general levels of wages and profits, but cf. Senior, pp. 191.6 ff. Ricardo, in chap. iv, talks constantly about the competition of different uses for capital, but only once uses the word, at p. 68.9.) This, of course, clashes directly with the notion of an arbitrary division between the employer and labor, but in no wise prevents their asserting the latter fact.

Smith repeatedly speaks of increased competition lowering the rate of profit. See pp. 89, 129–30, 335.3, 335.6. At the point of the last reference, he also has the competition raise the wages of labor (cf. also Mill, p. 343). The paragraph in Smith containing the last two references occurs in the chapter on interest in Book II. It is especially interesting as giving what is perhaps the fullest discussion to be found in his work of a demand function for a productive service, and as completely failing to give any indication of the real mechanism of competition, based on variable proportions and the significance of increments.

First, why should the wages fund increase?[65] Second, if it does increase, will the effect be to raise wages or to increase the number of laborers? On the first issue, we are left almost completely in the dark. (It is the first main unanswered question already referred to.) On the second issue we get both alternatives as answers and also (most clearly in Smith) a third more defensible view that it depends for the time being on the relative rates of increase in capital and population; but it is made clear that the rate of increase of capital cannot permanently be the greater, so that the final result is an increase in the supply of labor.[66]

65. One of the puzzling features of the classical exposition is the absence of any clear suggestion that an increased amount of capital, even in the primitive use of raising wages, should within some limits increase the output of given laborers. Smith's remarks (at p. 88.4) do not invalidate this observation, as it is the increased division of labor which increases the product, and the increase in wages referred to simply raises the question, "why," discussed in the text. At p. 259.5 f. there is a parallel statement with no reference to an increase in wages. On p. 84, Smith raises the question whether higher real wages lower efficiency, as the mercantilist writers generally held. Senior's discussion in particular (pp. 188 ff.) is put in a form to give him every opportunity and suggestion for mentioning such an effect, but it is conspicuously absent. In order to rationalize a raise in wages from the employers' standpoint, it would seem necessary to assume either that the labor supply responds instantly (see below) or that they deliberately maintain the higher rate for at least a generation in order to make possible an increase in the supply of laborers (which is supposed always to be tending to happen). But such conduct is out of the question under an individualistic system.

In the view of the classical conception of capital, an increase in wages is the same thing as an increase in the proportion of capital to labor. Only Senior of the writers under consideration seems to refer expressly to changes in the proportions of capital and labor as a condition affecting the division between them (pp. 140, 188, 189, 190); but even he makes no mention in this connection of a principle of diminishing returns or the significance of increments. Smith, in his discussion of colonial conditions, in his chapter on profits, mentions the proportion of stock to territory and of people to stock (p. 94). (The classical discussions of changes in the proportions of fixed and circulating capital have possible implications for this topic and for the theory of capital in general; but the problem is too intricate to take up here. But see below.)

66. The writers generally did not know whether they were talking about quantities or rates of change. When Smith says, at the beginning of the second paragraph of the chapter on profits, that "the increase of stock . . . raises wages," he means a "sufficient" *rate* of increase. The third answer above may sometimes be used to interpret the other two, but often the context makes this very difficult, definitely implying that more labor will always be on hand to consume more capital.

For the purpose of this essay, we must cut short the discussion of the wages fund with a note on its relation to the facts. The writers' objective, as already observed, was to show that wages cannot be raised by arbitrary action, or by any method which does not increase the amount of capital in proportion to the laboring population, or by inventions, which they treated in a strangely parenthetical tone. Of course, the application of inventions is generally connected

We have repeatedly referred to the long-run theory developed in the classical writers' treatment of wages, a theory based on the Malthusian doctrine of population. It cannot be subjected to critical examination here and is mentioned primarily to emphasize again its complete divergence from the short-run subsistence theory already discussed. Careful analysis must distinguish at least three different versions of the subsistence theory of wages in the classical writings. The first of the three (already discussed) is the notion that actual wages are determined by the subsistence requirements of the workers. The second is the doctrine just referred to, that, in the long run, wages are controlled by a "standard of living," through the tendency of population to increase or decrease whenever they are above or below the workers' psychological requirements which regulate reproduction. A standard of living, to operate in this way, must obviously itself remain stationary, or at least change slowly in comparison with the population changes which bring the supply of labor into equilibrium with reference to it. But, third, Smith and the Ricardians clearly recognize historical changes in the standard of living, which is normally under continuous pressure through the tend-

---

with an increased use of capital, and, with this qualification, the conclusion of the older economists was sound, though their reasoning was fallacious. Their major premise was that the employer's share of the product is either negligible or fixed. In recent years, statistical investigation has more and more impressed us with the narrow limits of the possibility of raising wages at the expense of interest and profit. With rent (in accord with any probable estimate) excluded. and allowance made for taxes, gifts for charitable and benevolent purposes, and necessary savings, the total share now falling to capital and entrepreneurship would not raise total wages by any large percentage, and it would have been much smaller a century or two ago. Of course, deductions from the capital share would make more difference if used to raise only the lowest wages. The amount of saving which ought to be provided for is indeed a large political question. As to rent, the modern disposition (with the exception of some Roman Catholic writers) would be to throw the landlord to the wolves first of all. But in Europe, under the feudal tradition, the rent of land was the chief means of payment for public services and for the maintenance of all cultural activities.

Even the distinction between types of product consumed by laborers and by capitalists, suggested by Senior, has vastly more significance for the problem of transfer of income than he recognized; a large part of the difference between large and small incomes would disappear under equalization in relative changes in the prices of "choice cuts" and those less choice, where the proportions in production are relatively inflexible.

From the standpoint of economic theory, the conception of capital as a fund for the support of labor over an interval between production and consumption is still profoundly important. It was reworked by Böhm-Bawerk, who combined elements from Ricardo and Senior to make the amount of capital a matter of the length of the production process, and in his form is still generally accepted and taught. For the fundamental fallacies involved, see Part II and references in this article.

ency of population to outrun the supply of provisions. It is natural to think of the movement as tending toward an ultimate equilibrium, set perhaps by the actual physical requirements of life (if the conception of the physiological minimum can be made to mean anything for human beings). The three equilibrium levels of wages implied in the three theories are all highly indefinite. Furthermore, the notion of currently "necessary" wages is ambiguous and might be subdivided into various shorter and longer-run conceptions.

On the second major unanswered question in classical wages and profit theory, we must be very brief. This has to do, as will be recalled, with the treatment of capital in other forms than the annual wage advances to labor, especially with the question of the quantity of capital in various capital goods, relatively permanent in comparison with food, and other things which may be thought of as used up and replaced in an annual cycle. The question is especially insistent and perplexing, not merely because of the prominence given to these other forms (more or less corresponding to the division between "fixed" and "circulating" in the general discussions and classifications of capital), but even more because in the illustrations used in explaining distribution theory the more durable forms are so largely involved.

The general position taken more or less explicitly by the writers is that the rate of return in other fields is determined by the rate on capital used to pay wages in agriculture at the land margin.[67] But in the first place, any view of the determination of a price in one section of a market by the price in another section is indefensible, as the causal relation in such a case is necessarily mutual.[68] But second, and more important, such reasoning is worthless without an explanation of the meaning of a quantity of capital "in" an instrument which is not a consumable product but has indirect utility. For

67. See Ricardo, "Essay on the Influence of a Low Price of Corn on the Profits of Stock," etc., in *Works*, p. 372 and second footnote; Senior, p. 188.7; Mill treats agriculture and manufactures together, failing to see that his theory approximately fits only the former (Book II, chap. xv).

68. It could at most be approximately correct if the demand for capital in the particular part of the market supposed to control were overwhelmingly large in comparison with all other demand. (It seems legitimate to say that the level of the water in the ocean determines the level in some particular bay.) Moreover, Ricardo's argument that a change in the level of profit in agriculture will change the level in manufacturing industry without a movement of capital from one field to the other is rank fallacy (see "Essay," in *Works*, pp. 379–80).

the value is struck "now" while the product (*a*) is to be enjoyed in the future, and (*b*) must be isolated by imputation. This is the central problem, almost the whole problem, of capital as a base for a rate of return; the classical economists never glimpsed the problem itself and, of course, have no light to shed upon it. All that it seems possible to say is that they had a fixed idea that all capital is the accumulated product of labor (or labor itself—the same thing in their minds), and that consequently the same principles which fit the advance of subsistence to laborers would fit all other cases (cf. esp. Mill, p. 418).

However, given a market rate of interest, the concept of capital quantity as cost, including interest, is so simple and obvious that no one who knew anything about business management and accounting could possibly be unfamiliar with its meaning. Consequently, it is easy, and no doubt justifiable, to read roughly correct general conceptions into the illustrations involving fixed capital which are used by Ricardo and other writers. They undoubtedly understood even the nature of capital maintenance as well as men need to do to administer capital intelligently in practice.

This suggests the fact that their crucial error lay in the theory of the primary. case, the interpretation of the nature and role of capital in the use of paying wages in agriculture and at the land margin. Even under the absurd assumption of a strictly annual and synchronous agricultural cycle in the production and using-up of physical materials, it is still true that, in correct accounting, the quantity of capital is theoretically constant; the writers simply forgot that the growing crop is capital! Perhaps conditions can be imagined under which their theory would be valid; but these issues cannot be further considered here.[69] The outstanding fact is the absurd unrealism of a periodic or episodic view of capitalistic production.[70] Capital is inher-

69. They have been broached above in Part II. The first requisite which comes to mind is that the physical cycles should not overlap, the capital-creation phase of one coinciding with the capital-consumption phase of the next. We may revert again to Böhm-Bawerk to note that his error was the same as that of the classical writers; that is, it lay not in assimilating the other forms of capital to the wages fund but in failing to give an accurate analysis fitting any case, under anything like real conditions.

70. In a deeper analysis, the error in the whole classical position (including, of course, Böhm-Bawerk) roots in the special character and role assigned to labor. More generally still, it consists in confusing conceptual analysis with ethical evaluation. From the former standpoint, labor and capital instruments, including land, are all alike, simply productive resources. It is in the contrast between

ently continuous, because production is continuous, as is all activity directed by thinking. It is the essential nature and task of rational accounting to make this continuity explicit.

capital as "supporting" and "aiding" labor, and labor as "using" and "reproducing" capital, that the immediate fallacy lies. The relation is symmetrically mutual. All the productive agencies use each other (or are used jointly by the enterprise), and all are jointly maintained and reproduced by all, in a continuing process.

III

Historical and Theoretical Issues in the Problem of Modern Capitalism[1]

DURING 1927 the third "volume" of the revised edition of Professor Werner Sombart's monumental treatise on modern capitalism was published under the title, rather impossible in English, of "High Capitalism."[2] Its claim to the designation "monumental" will be undisputed, even by those who most disagree with the author's views and conclusions. Recognizing himself (Vol. III, Part I, Preface) as the heir and continuator of Marx, who made capitalism a household word in all the languages of civilization, Sombart has, by this work and more specialized studies in the field,[3] displaced his predecessor as proprietor of the concept and its problems. For a long time to come the question of capitalism must be in large measure the question of Werner Sombart. In the pages which follow, no attempt will be made to review, or even to survey, the bulky literature which has grown up in a generation around the phases of the capitalism problem associated with Sombart's name. Rather the aim will be to present the reaction produced by some of this literature in the mind of a student of economics of the "armchair" variety, more or less equally interested in theory of the classical, deductive type and in the historical development and causality of economic institutions.

From this standpoint, the situation presents problems long dis-

1. Reprinted by permission from the *Journal of Economics and Business History*, Vol. I, No. 1 (November, 1928).

2. *Der moderne Kapitalismus: Historisch-systematische Darstellung des gesamteuropäischen Wirtschaftslebens von seinen Anfängen bis zur Gegenwart*, Vol. III: *Das Wirtschaftsleben im Zeitalter des Hochkapitalismus*. Like the preceding two volumes, this is in two "halves," the whole six running toward 3,300 pages, large octavo. The earlier volumes of the revision were published in 1916 and have run to a fifth printing. The first edition, in two volumes of over 1,200 pages, appeared in 1902.

3. *Die Juden und das Wirtschaftsleben* (1911) (Eng. trans., *The Jews and Modern Capitalism* [1913]); *Luxus und Kapitalismus* (1913); *Der Bourgeois* (1913) (Eng. trans., *The Quintessence of Capitalism* [1915]); *Krieg und Kapitalismus* (1913).

cussed but still both troublesome and challenging. During the greater part of the period covered by modern economic thought, historians and economists of different schools have been engaged in polemics over the question of what it means to explain economic phenomena. The result is, mildly stated, unsatisfactory. To a large degree we find one group of students in possession of the problems and another in possession of the data and the two living in separate universes of discourse. The attack on deductive analysis begun and continued by successive historical schools is kept up by the institutional economists, and now the statisticians are making it a three-cornered fight. To one who sees, or at least believes, not merely that all these methods and perhaps others are useful and necessary, but that friendly, intelligent co-operation among those who pursue them is equally so, it is disheartening to find them engaged so largely in reading each other out of the kingdom.

Human nature being a thing of limitations, it is natural for each scholar to think he is giving impartial consideration to the different points of view, when to the critical reader it is clearly otherwise. Sombart, for example, protests that he (and the newer historical school) must be classed as combining the theoretical and the historical (Vol. I, Part I, p. xiii). He insists that he is an economist rather than a historian, and even makes rather ill-mannered remarks about the "mere historian." Yet to the theorist the most striking feature of *Modern Capitalism* is the author's failure to understand the elementary mechanics of the competitive economic organization. Most of his "errors" are not at all peculiar to him; on the contrary, they are characteristic of historians generally and of other writers on economic subjects with the exception of specially trained theorists. In fact, they root in those primitive, popular misconceptions, the eradication of which is the despair of every teacher and writer in the field of economic fundamentals.

In the treatment of economic history, a confusion of money and wealth has become conspicuous in the handling of mercantilism; and here the viewpoints of historian and theorist notoriously clash most acutely. Sad as the fact is, it seems to be a safe prediction that an age of laborious education will be required before the two groups will cease to impress each other, in their treatment of this large and vital topic, as merely wagging their respective ears. And why? It ought to be recognized all around as legitimate and useful either to examine the historical background of an idea or policy or to consider it critically in the light of its wisdom as a means for achieving an end.[4]

It is not at all to the point to say, as Sombart and the Germans (cf. also E. Cannan) regularly do, that no one could be so stupid as not to know the difference between money and wealth, that the ancient fable of Midas is enough to dispel this illusion from any mind. Certainly the mercantilists did not identify the two explicitly (though they come near enough to that at many points), but it is just as unquestionable that only on the basis of such a premise can any sort of sense be made out of the great bulk of the mercantilistic utterances or policies. And why should it be otherwise? Conditions are no different today in most of the civilized capitalistic world. The man from Mars reading the typical pronouncements of our best financial writers or statesmen could hardly avoid the conclusion that a nation's prosperity depends upon getting rid of the greatest possible amount of goods and avoiding the receipt of anything tangible in payment for them.

An even more egregious, if practically less serious, example of the same confusion is found in Sombart's almost incredible position, argued and emphasized through a dozen pages (Vol. II, Part I, pp. 185 f.), that in the period following the new discoveries there was an increase in the aggregate demand for goods, constituted and measured by the amount of new money put into circulation. Undoubtedly he would admit, in the abstract, the basic axiom of an exchange economy (sometimes called "Say's Law") to the effect that the supply of one commodity is the demand for another and vice versa, and that consequently the aggregate demand and supply are necessarily equal, with money a mere intermediary. Yet there, in cold type, is the most explicit argument to the contrary. Fortunately, again, all this does not prove that Sombart overemphasizes the importance of the new gold and silver in transforming the

4. To the mere theorist it seems that even from the historical point of view the conventional treatment of mercantilism by the historians is open to criticism. To emphasize the *Staatenbildung* aspect is well and good, but to limit the description to that is surely narrow, if not misleading. Thus Sombart states (*Der moderne Kapitalismus*, rev. ed., Vol. I, Part I, p. 363, in italics) that "mercantilism is in the first place nothing other than the economic policy of the town extended to a larger territory." But on the third page following we read (also in italics) that "Aus der Güterversorgungspolitik der Städte wurde eine Geldversorgungspolitik der Staaten." This is surely the same thing with an important difference. If one goes on to list in parallel columns the main elements in the economic policy of the late medieval towns and of the mercantilists—military power, large population, colonial expansion, etc.—one surely finds the differences in the two lists more conspicuous than the similarities.

economy of Europe, which was undoubtedly great. It is typical of economists of all schools, the classical no less than the historical, to sense correct conclusions and support them with nonsensical reasoning. Our point is merely that more care in statement and more generous interpretation in reading are both requisite to the desideratum of more effective co-operation between scholars.

Another far-reaching case of failure to get clear of the level of folk-thought in economic analysis is found in the historians' common lack of grasp of the working of competition in bringing about an essentially impersonal, quasi-mechanical control of economic relationships. Few critics of capitalism see clearly enough that the entrepreneur in his "control" of production is relatively helpless as to what he shall produce, and where and when and by what instrumentalities and methods—and in particular as to what he shall pay for labor. Under perfect competition he would of course be completely helpless, a mere automatic registrar of the choices of consumers (and of laborers and property owners in so far as these have sentimental preferences among occupations or employers). Actual competition is undoubtedly very imperfect, but the degree of imperfection is quite as easily over- as underestimated. If one considers the range within which the manager can actually choose arbitrarily and remain in business, and averages out over a reasonable area and time period, it is evident that impersonal competition is after all overwhelmingly dominant.

Now the whole literature of capitalism is saturated with the view that its "spirit" is that of bargaining beween individuals. Nothing could be farther from the truth. There is relatively little bargaining in actual capitalism,[5] and under effective competition, again, none at all. And, on the other hand, when a seller or a producer is influenced by emulation or rivalry toward a competitor (and not ruled exclusively by an absolute calculation of his own maximum advantage), to that extent he is not following economic motives but is behaving irrationally, sentimentally.

In the popular mind, and of course especially in the Marxian and most other socialistic literature, it is viewed as an axiom that the owner of "capital," or "the means to labor," has the worker in his power. But the proposition is false or meaningless if employers are

5. The suggestive or hortatory element in advertising and selling is of course of the nature of primitive bargaining. But the relative importance of this element, in comparison with "education" of a proper and necessary type and the actual power of advertising in general, is as much overstated by superficial commentators on economic life as it is minimized by apologists.

in competition with each other and act in accordance with economic motives. The distribution of economic power in a competitive society is simply the relative market values of the property or labor services offered to production by different individuals. And if monopoly is assumed, each group will be equally in the power of the other.[6]

Associated with this misconception of the bargaining relation between property and persons, as a sort of counterpart, is another view held with amazing tenacity by thinkers of various schools as well as the folk-mind, namely, the belief that labor really "produces" the whole product. And permeating the whole complex is a bewildering jumble of unexamined and largely unconscious assumptions, dogmas, categories, concerning the relations between mechanical explanation and social criticism, between science and ethics. This is unescapably a philosophical problem, and the temper of our times is against philosophizing in social science. The tendency is sound, within limits; but carried too far it becomes philistinism and plain ignorance. Some of the insistence on facts which we hear today is in fact a refusal to face facts which are just as fundamental to the discussion as those recognized but are ruled out because they do not fit into a preconceived methodology. It is hard to begin a discussion in this field in less than a volume, but the issue as to the character of social facts and their relation to ethical judgments is so vital in any approach to the critique of capitalism that some notice must be taken of it. Again, Sombart has presented a beautiful bad example!

Scattered through the tomes on *Hochkapitalismus* are the bits of Sombart's theory of price (including distribution), or what passes with the author as a theory (see esp. Vol III, Part I, pp. 127–46). Marginal utility theory is an *Irrlicht* (p. 127), and all endeavor to "impute" a determinate share of the social product to the participating factors *grundsätzlich verfehlt*. These endeavors arise out of apologetic ends . . . (p. 140). The share of property (*Mehrwert*) is the expression of relative economic power and there is only an apparent difference between this conception and that of economic law (p. 141). The rest of his discussion is a mixture of considerations his-

6. Actually, the distribution of power is distorted in favor of property by the possibility of "capitalizing" it, living on the substance and thus securing ability to wait. If laborers were not guaranteed the "inalienable right" of freedom, that is, if they could make enforceable time contracts for work and thus capitalize their labor power they would in an economic sense be more secure—in the sense in which the slave has security.

torical and descriptive with "analysis" in a sense remote from mechanical principles or quantitative isolation of cause and effect. Indeed, the association of particular effects with particular causes seems to be repudiated universally as well as in economics by the later portion of the paragraph (p. 140) from which the first citation above is taken. Taking the author at his word, economic theorists are burdened with the enormous load of the sin of leading men to think in terms of cause and effect!

Comment must be so brief as to sound dogmatic. Again, the author has sound intuitions, while his statements are largely the perfect inverse of the truth. He is right in universalizing the imputation procedure. The method used in the productivity and utility theories is identical with that employed in science wherever any effect is associated with a particular cause, since all causality is joint causality. Through all discussion of induction and all classification of its canons stands out clearly the essential principle that nature is uniform as to the element of situations, that the diversity in event-sequences as wholes is explained by the presence of particular elements in varying amounts. Now the variation in degree is sometimes a simple matter of the presence or absence of an element in the antecedent, associated with the presence or absence of some element in the consequent, and the one is recognized as "the cause" of the other. More commonly, however, the elements in cause and effect are variable magnitudes and explanation involves showing the quantitative relation between them individually. And again this quantitative relationship is sometimes of the relatively simple character represented by a straight line (through the zero point of the scales), but usually it is a more complicated one. Typically, then, any effect element which we wish to explain is some curvilinear function of each of an indefinite number of cause elements. When this is true, the relation between cause and effect (in other words, factor and product or commodity and satisfaction) has to be stated as a function of the amounts of all the cause-elements acting and computed for infinitesimal quantities or variations in each. The marginal utility and marginal productivity theories are crude verbal approximations of the partial differential equation, which is the general form of a causal law. The principles have been commonplace in mechanics since the early nineteenth century at least, but economists only began to discover them around 1870 and only exceptionally have any clear idea of them yet.

However, it is in his reference to science and ethics that Sombart goes to the heart of the issue, but he has his main conclusion upside down—though here the great mass of economic theorists of the cloth are with him in the inversion. The theory of infinitesimal increments certainly states the logic of the economic cause-and-effect relationships since there are no other principles of causality met with in human experience or known to the human mind. And these principles apply equally, whatever type of causality is assumed, whether human behavior be viewed as choice determined by motives or as automatic response to stimulation, physical or psychical—just so it is in accordance with some form of law. But all such considerations have practically no ethical significance. The tendency under competition for any laborer and the owner of any piece of property to get as income his (its) causal contribution to production (or things equal to the same value) does not mean that they tend to get what they ought to have. The contrary would involve the postulate that effects "ought" to follow their causes, which is evidently nonsense. Moreover, neither the income distribution which we observe nor that which would result from the perfect competition of theory is to any great extent in conformity with any acceptable ethical standard.[7]

7. The fallacy of attributing ethical significance to distribution based on what the individual puts into the social total has several roots, of which only bare mention of a few is possible here. One is the feeling for expediency, that, in view of human selfishness, society must be so organized, or people will not work effectively. Of course any degree of positive correlation between reward and contribution would in theory accomplish this result. That identifying expediency with ethics is another way of denying the existence of ethics in the common-sense acceptation, many economists would admit and welcome the consequence. It is demonstrable, however, that the same logic which does this will annihilate the expediency concept in turn and reduce economic behavior to mechanical inevitability and will end in impossible absurdity; but this is not the place to present the argument.

In our opinion the essential confusion back of the assumption of an ethical significance in productivity is the fact that one factor in productivity is effort, which does have ethical significance for common sense. But the recognition of effort as a factor in a sequence takes the discussion out of the realm of science, as that term is properly used; for it is of the essence of the scientific conception of causality that nothing of the nature of effort is involved in it. Thus there is an ultimate contradiction between the scientific and the ethical premises of thought.

No task in the field of economic thought would be more interesting or more important than that of tracing through the literature the concept of production and separating its causal and ethical aspects and implications. Perhaps—if so much as a perhaps may be ventured here—one would discover a tendency to use the word "produce" in a causal sense, and unconsciously drag in an ethical implication when speaking of the property factor, and to make the ethical sense primary when referring to the role of persons. But in reality, again, there is not

From considerations largely of an economic-theoretical character we must now turn to the more historical aspects of the capitalism problem.

In the past generation there has been a pronounced movement away from emphasis on the machine-industry side of modern economic life, away from the inventions, the period of the industrial revolution, and from England, to a broader interpretation in terms of culture history. Sombart and Max Weber stand out as leaders in the emphasis on non-technological factors, political, psychological, intellectual, and religious, underlying economic change. In some ways, the revised *Der moderne Kapitalismus* represents a return toward more conventional views, as compared with the first edition. The earlier work dated the capitalistic age from 1204, the year both of the capture of Constantinople by the Crusaders under Venetian manipulation and of the publication of Leonardo Pisano's work on mathematics which introduced the Arabic notation into Christian Europe. The new edition divides modern from medieval history at the usual date and also separates the former into two periods at about 1760, the date of the introduction of the coke process in iron smelting. From about 1500 to 1760 is the period of "Early Capitalism," from the latter date to World War I that of "High Capitalism." The volumes on the Jews, on war, and on luxury presented extreme statements of special theses, as the author now admits, and the theories of these and of the first edition of the general work are much toned down and worked into better perspective in the new *Modern Capitalism.*[8]

Although in general Sombart shows little reverence for his critics, the decidedly negative comment which greeted many of his theories in their earlier statement must have had something to do with the marked improvement in the new work. Indeed, he virtually admits yielding ground under the influence of Strieder[9] on the question

---

much more ethical significance in the second source of income than in the first (a common illusion of radicals). Personal capacity is, nearly as much as wealth, the result of inheritance or luck rather than effort or any ethical source.

8. A French admirer (who classes the author among the five great names in modern economics—Smith, Marx, Walras, Pareto, Sombart) goes so far as to say that the revision has only the name in common with the first edition (G.-H. Bousquet in *Revue d'histoire économique et sociale*, Vol. XV, No. 2 [1927]). This seems to the present writer a great exaggeration of the change.

9. J. Strieder, *Zur Genesis des modernen Kapitalismus: Forschungen zur Entstehung der grossen Kapitalvermögen am Ausgange des Mittelalters und zu Beginn der Neuzeit, zunächst in Augsburg* (1904). See *Der moderne Kapitalismus*, rev. ed., Vol. I, Part II, pp. 637–38 and note.

of rent as the practically exclusive source of capital in the early modern development. His original contention was that commerce itself, trading profit, was unimportant as a source of accumulation, which he held came from the money plethora in the hands of aristocratic landlords. Strieder's interesting book on the Augsburg fortunes as evidenced in the tax records, together with Heynen's study of Venetian history[10] and articles by Häpke, Nuglisch, von Below and others,[11] seemed to leave little possibility of reconciling the "rent-theory" with the facts. However, it is often possible to find an interpretation which will go far toward reconciling theories where the parties in controversy see nothing but absolute contradiction. In this case, the view of Max Weber makes it appear that both Sombart and his opponents are substantially right. Weber[12] holds that money was made in trade by traders, but that the initial capital did come largely from the landowning nobility under the form of commenda-contracts or other credit arrangements.

Obviously related to this theory of rent versus trade as the source of the early modern capital is Sombart's second highly controverted position, on which he is much less disposed to yield any ground in his revision. This is the contention for a "handicraft" (*handwerksmässig*) characterization of medieval trade.[13] The issue here involves the "quintessence of Sombart," his theory of the essential contrast between earlier economic life and that under capitalism—specifically "high capitalism," with "early capitalism" as an intermediate, tran-

10. Reinhard Heynen, *Zur Entstehung des Kapitalismus in Venedig* (1905).

11. Rud. Häpke, "Die Entstehung der grossen Vermögen im Mittelalter," *Jahrbuch für Nationalökonomie*, Vol. XXI, Series 3; A. Nuglisch, "Zur Frage der Entstehung des modernen Kapitalismus," *Jahrbuch für Nationalökonomie*, Vol. XXVIII, Series 2; G. von Below, "Die Entstehung des modernen Kapitalismus," *Historische Zeitschrift*, Vol. XCI.
To these criticisms should be added the thorough overhauling given Sombart in Lujo Brentano's essays in the volume, *Die Anfänge des modernen Kapitalismus* (1916). The date is that of Sombart's own revised *Der moderne Kapitalismus* and though some of Brentano's essays had been published before, Sombart shows no knowledge of them. Heynen was a student of Brentano.

12. *General Economic History* (Eng. trans.), pp. 343 f. The question is closely related to that of the origin of the medieval towns. Henri Pirenne's book *Medieval Cities* seems to the writer to give a one-sided view of them as the exclusive creation of the merchants. He does not mention Sombart. For reference to Pirenne's views see *Der moderne Kapitalismus*, rev. ed., Vol. I, Part I, p. 175. Professor H. Sée, *Les origines du capitalisme moderne: esquisse historique*, esp. pp. 34, 190, refers to Sombart's argument with respect but dismisses it as unconvincing.

13. See his defiant restatement in chap. xviii of the revised edition (Vol. I, Part I, pp. 279 f.), with an Appendix answering his critics (pp. 309 f.).

sitional form. It is a question of the "spirit" of life in the different periods. In his formal definition of capitalism (Vol. I, Part I, p. 319) it is, to be sure, the form of organization which is put to the front, with the capitalistic spirit in the position of a codicil; but in his work as a whole it is clear that the spirit is the inner heart of the matter. In his view, the spirit of capitalism is that of exclusive direction of activity toward increasing the sum of money (in contrast with the handicraft endeavor to satisfy needs) combined with economic rationalism. The last, again, is analyzed (p. 320) into the three elements of (*a*) planning in advance (*Planmässigkeit*), (*b*) intelligent direction (*Zweckmässigkeit*), and (*c*) control by exact, quantitative evaluation of ends and means (*Rechnungsmässigkeit*). A little later (pp. 327, 329) the capitalistic spirit is described as a combination of the Faust spirit of the modern European soul—"enterprise," reaching out toward infinity—with the "bourgeois" spirit of order, industry, and frugality. It is the qualities of abstract quantitativeness and unboundedness which constitute the essential contrast with the craft spirit.[14]

Leaving entirely aside for the moment the question of historical causality, there is no doubt that the capitalistic spirit is the most important fact of modern economic history or even of modern history at large. And it is Sombart's work, along with the strikingly similar utterances of Max Weber, which has taught the reading world to appreciate the importance of *quantitative rationality* as a phase of the modern social mind. This must stand as one of the great intellectual achievements of the age. It seems to the present writer, furthermore, that Sombart is more right than wrong in his emphasis on the abstract goal and unbounded striving. To be sure, it is easy to understate both the amount of the getting-ahead spirit present in the Middle Ages and the role of making a living in the present day. That making money is after all making a living is one of those facts which the teacher of economics finds difficulty in getting the student and the public to appreciate. Yet the former, almost universal, centering of attention on the achievement of a fairly definite and limited standard of living (though varying widely with social status) seems to be the most important difference between medieval and modern economic life.[15]

14. See also, in accordance with the references given in this connection by the author, Sombart's essay in Vol. IV of the *Grundriss der Sozialökonomik*, and his book *Der Bourgeois* (Eng. trans., *The Quintessence of Capitalism*).

15. In this connection it is inevitable to recall the sharp difference between Sombart and Pirenne (none too generous on either side and rather nasty on that of Sombart—*Der moderne Kapitalismus*, Vol. I, Part I, p. 175) and to note

In the way of causal explanation of the revolution in world view which has given us the modern man, in contrast with a mere historical description of the change, there are not many offerings to be listed. That sort of thing has been out of fashion in historical writing for some time. The mere dogma of inevitable progress, through the cumulative growth of knowledge and improvement in technique, is plausible on its face but breaks down in view of the obtrusive fact of decadence. Emphasis on particular technical advances, themselves viewed as accidental or simply taken as data, which serve as keys to a large sequence, is often illuminating. Sombart's view of the importance of the Arabic system of notation seems hardly exaggerated—until we ask why it did not form the basis of a development among the people who invented it similar to that which it seems to have occasioned when introduced into Italy and Europe. The most famous hypothesis of a causal nature in connection with modern capitalism is no doubt the religion-theory of Max Weber.

Two years after the first appearance of *Der moderne Kapitalismus*, Weber published the first of his essays on Protestant ethics and the spirit of capitalism.[16] He essayed to prove specifically that Protestantism, particularly Calvinism, and most particularly English Puritanism, was the main *cause* of the capitalistic movement, and not a mere rationalization of its standards; his argument is based on the strength of Puritanism among the *petit bourgeois* classes who were

---

that, in spite of all, they complement (where they cannot compliment!) each other. Pirenne's observation, or theory, that the whole modern development was the work of successive "waves" of new men, each successive group retiring to live at ease as soon as they were in a position to do so, is strikingly in harmony with Sombart's view of the contrast between the medieval and the modern economic spirit.

There is no space here to comment on Sombart's significance as an economic historian in the general sense, apart from his special theories, nor is the present writer competent to do that. But we must record the impression of a staggering amount of work of a very high order having gone into the making of his books.

16. *Archiv für Sozialwissenschaft und Sozialpolitik* (1904 and 1905). There followed a considerable controversial exchange in this and other periodicals, and in 1912 E. Troeltsch's book, *Die Soziallehren der christlichen Kirchen und Gruppen*, which gave general support to Weber's position. See references in Brentano's *Der wirtschaftende Mensch in der Geschichte* (1923), p. 372 n. This volume incorporates the essays contained in the earlier *Die Anfänge des modernen Kapitalismus* and prefixed reprints of several other valuable papers dealing with the relations of religion and ethics to economics in the course of history. All references to Brentano in this paper are to the later book. Weber's original essays are republished in his *Gesammelte Aufsätze zur Religionssoziologie*, Vol. I. His views are summarized in Part IV of the *General Economic History*, now published in English translation. A convenient statement of them is given in two articles by the Rev. P. T. Forsyth in the *Contemporary Review* for 1910.

not in a position to practice acquisitive business on an appreciable scale. Sombart, in *Die Juden und das Wirtschaftsleben,* took over the main idea and attempted to extend it by arguing for a similar religious morale among the Jews and for their having played a decisive role in the development of capitalism. Both phases of the religion-theory are destructively criticized by Brentano (*op. cit.,* essays X and XI) with expressions of personal deference for Weber and of its absence for Sombart! It seems to be a fairly safe rule that the negative will have the better of a debate over any far-reaching principle of historical causality, if not any historical generalization whatever. More recently, R. H. Tawney has studied the role of the Protestant churches in a scholarly and beautifully written volume[17] in which Sombart and the Jew theory are not mentioned, and Henri Sée makes some judicious and impartial, if rather non-committal, remarks on the questions in his short but able historical sketch.[18]

The result in all cases is rather negative, so far as any satisfying view of causes is concerned. Tawney sees religion, as a social organizing force or power in private life, simply whipped out and driven from the field by the irresistibly rising power of greed, and looks with eloquent longing—mainly backward—toward a different state of affairs. We miss any adequate objective survey of either the actual policies (ends or means) of the medieval Church as a political power, or the ethics of workaday economic relations, in contrast with the fair-sounding preachments of religious and moralistic writers. Mr. Tawney seems to exaggerate both the identity between religion and the religious organization and the difference between the conduct of ecclesiastical and other bureaucracies in power, to say nothing of possible differences of opinion regarding the ethical aspects of either comparison.

From this standpoint, of the dominating spirit of activity, Brentano puts forward a very interesting theory of economic evolution. The central concept is the changing composition of the economic unit. He holds, in brief, that the spirit of an economic unit is universally and always that of hostility and unbounded acquisitiveness in its relations with outside units, combined with brotherhood or communism in relations between members of the unit itself. What

17. *Religion and the Rise of Capitalism* (London, New York, 1926). Cf. also three articles on "Religious Thought on Social and Economic Questions in the Sixteenth and Seventeenth Centuries," *Journal of Political Economy* (Chicago, 1923). Tawney's book has been widely discussed by reviewers.

18. *Les origines du capitalisme moderne: esquisse historique* (Paris, 1926). Cf. esp. pp. 26–27 and 108–10.

has happened historically, then, is the transformation and disintegration of the economic unit. As long as the primitive family group could expand on a basis of relative self-sufficiency and independence of other groups, the communal principle was maintained, but as the group became more interdependent with other groups, through trade, the external ethic seeped into intragroup relations. Hence unlimited gain-seeking has come to be the spirit of economic dealings between all individuals, with limited exceptions within the modern small family. His essay on the beginnings of capitalism explicitly traces its lineage from war, of which trade is at first the twin brother; this again recalls one of Sombart's main emphases.

Sée is inclined, as already intimated, to be prudent and avoid commitment to explanatory theories and large generalizations. He recognizes the Puritans and Jews as "among the most active agents" of modern capitalism (p. 47) but points out (p. 109) that the movement in Holland was in full swing before the coming of the Jews at the close of the sixteenth century. His main emphasis seems to be on the geographical factor, which is naturally right for the final result of the application of rational procedure but less satisfactory for its beginnings. His word for the spirit of the movement is "individualism" (pp. 47, 191–92). The most conspicuous weakness of this as an explanation is the virtual absence of reference to the state and the movement of political thought. Statism is surely as prominent a feature of the sixteenth century as individualism. Sée refers explicitly to the Reformation as a parallel manifestation of individualism; he fails to note that if Luther declared the individual's religious independence of pope and clergy it was but to relegate him to an equally abject subjection to the territorial prince and economically and politically to all established authority. Was there a real individualist in religion among all the founders of Protestantism, or in any other respect among all the great names of the century? And in any case, is individualism anything but another word, perhaps a somewhat better word than capitalism itself, for the change in outlook? Brentano is better, with his emphasis (*op. cit.*, pp. 53, 370, etc.) on the twofold roots of the whole movement, in the revival of paganism with its emphasis on the state, and in the religious revolt, which he also treats as essentially individualistic.

Whatever one may think of his Puritanism theory, there is surely one respect in which Max Weber towers above all the other writers noticed; he is the only one who really deals with the problem of causes or approaches the material from that angle which alone can yield an answer to such questions, that is, the angle of comparative history in the broad sense. It seems to the writer that the question of the origin of capitalism would gain by being stated in negative form: Why did capitalism *not* develop (in the sense in which it did not) in other times and places than modern western Europe? Especially, why was there no development comparable to that of modern times in the classical and ancient civilizations? Max Weber discusses these questions. His *General Economic History* is a mere sketch, available only in an editorial patchwork from students' lecture notes, but in this fundamental regard it stands in a class by itself.

Reflection upon the literature sampled in the foregoing pages suggests many questions which it would be interesting to follow out, but in conclusion we can note only a few points. The first is that, as indicated at the outset of the paper, the historical writers are handicapped by a lack of clear understanding of the capitalistic system. The essential thing, on the organization side, is not at all, as Sombart following Marx holds, the dominance of property over propertyless labor. The subjection of workers to owners is certainly less extreme now than it was in the precapitalistic age, due to the fact of impersonal competition. However imperfect and occasionally ineffective competition may be, it is categorically different from servitude embodied in the political constitution of a society. What is essential is the change in the content of the property concept, its differentiation into numerous forms, and the liberation of both men and things from the prescriptions of authority and tradition. In contrast with these, "contract," though very different from ideal freedom, is truly a great liberation. In theory, and largely in fact, the "owner" of a business today is in the same relation to the capitalist or ultimate owner of wealth and to the laborer, the last two sharing a common lot. Thus Sée is right—one suspects more right than he realizes—in placing the emphasis on the loan at interest as the essence of capitalism (*op. cit.*, pp. 26, 193).

Again, on the side of the "spirit" of capitalism, the talk of bargaining and conquest is even more definitely upside down. It was also remarked at the beginning that competition and bargaining are antithetical concepts. It is rather other times and peoples that have bargained and conquered, or especially—and this is more vital—have *thought* in terms of bargaining and conquering. They have all had their self-made generals, priests, thieves, artists, traders, men who got on in the world. It is true that the bulk of the people in China, India, the European Middle Ages, in Rome, and even in Greece did not personally look at life in those terms, but they knew and admired such lives. What is new in the modern world is not conquest but the conquest of nature. Now this is in contrast with the conquest of other men, though it may be fundamentally a method for the conquest of men. This is largely true in fact, as those who delight in pounding capitalism (e.g., the author of a book called *The Sickness of an Acquisitive Society*) must sometime recognize. We hold no brief for capitalism and have insisted that there is practically nothing ethical about it; but it has been also constructive, whereas such spirit of enterprise as existed in previous ages was almost purely acquisitive. And still more does capitalism think of itself as constructive. The modern businessman views everything he does as productive—in general naïvely and about one-half falsely, to be sure, but the spirit is fully as important to the historian as the deed.

The novelty is, in a phrase of the Beards, the invention of invention. Early technological progress was not based on invention in the true sense, but was, we must assume, essentially accidental, a slow Darwinian process of the preservation of spontaneous variations which happened to be favorable. Now all this is changed; the conquest of nature has become a field of deliberative action and a means of individual advancement. Max Weber has not overemphasized the importance of a spiritual religion in contrast with magic, or Sombart that of an arithmetical notation making it possible to teach the masses of mankind to work quantitative problems and get the right answers. Apparently technical progress had to proceed by gradual, trial-and-error methods up to a certain point before it could become deliberate and rational. And perhaps it had for long ages to make its painful way in a rigid social framework of authority and tradition, and then have the torch passed to a more primitive and lawless people. In this connection it is especially interesting to note that the five particularly important technical advances by means of which Europe seemed to lift itself from medieval to modern status were all Asiatic in origin—the compass, the Arabic system, gunpowder, paper, and printing. And centuries later Asia begins to learn of capitalism from Europe.

Finally, it is suggested that the process by which slavery and servitude were eliminated in parts of Europe, without anyone seeming to think much about it, is one of those crucial differences between the modern age and classical antiquity which is deserving of especial study on the part of those who would understand the coming of capitalism.

IV

The Common Sense of Political Economy
(Wicksteed Reprinted) [1]

ALL students of economics are placed deeply in debt to the London School of Economics, to Professor Robbins individually, and to the publishers by the bringing-out of this work. In it are included not only the "Common Sense" but, in addition, all of Wicksteed's economic writings of importance except the *Co-ordination of the Laws of Distribution*, which has also been reprinted, but under separate covers, in the London School series of reprints. These other papers fill nearly two hundred pages of the second volume. The two volumes are offered for sale separately, the first, with an admirable introduction by Professor Robbins, containing Book I of the "Common Sense," which makes Wicksteed's general statement of his system available in convenient bulk for use in elementary classes. The reviewer has some doubts as to whether there will be any great demand for the work for this purpose in the United States, where the elaborate illustrations in the barbarous system of pounds, shillings, and pence will form a considerable obstacle to the undergraduate mind. And there are deeper reasons which will be obvious from the following more critical comments on Wicksteed's work.

In writing any discussion of Wicksteed's work (and making excuses for the tardiness and unconventional character of this note), it is necessary for the present reviewer to make some statements of a somewhat "confessional" character. To begin with, my own published ideas on economics have frequently been compared, not to say bracketed, with those of Wicksteed, especially by the editor of these volumes. I therefore feel compelled to say not only that I never read the "Common Sense" until recently in this reprinted form, but that when I once "thumbed through" the book about

1. Philip H. Wicksteed, *The Common Sense of Political Economy and Selected Papers and Reviews on Economic Theory,* ed. Lionel Robbins (2 vols.; London: George Routledge & Sons, Ltd., 1933).

This article is reprinted by permission from the *Journal of Political Economy*, Vol. XLII, No. 5 (October, 1934).

1923 or 1924, I found it intolerably prolix; and, furthermore, that I get much the same feeling now. It seems to me to use endless pages in saying what could be more intelligibly and forcefully said in a fraction of the space. This might not deserve putting into print were it not for the second fact, which I hope is of more importance. It is considerably over a year since, at Professor Viner's suggestion, I took the copy of the reprint for the purpose of writing a brief and rather perfunctory notice in this journal. About the same time, the publication of Viner's article on cost theory in the *Weltwirt-schaftsliches Archiv* led to some discussion of that subject in the theory group at Chicago. It became necessary for me to "straighten out" my ideas on the subject of cost before I could write my notice of the book, and in that connection to study through Wicksteed's theoretical position. The result is a considerable reconstruction of my own system, so that it no longer agrees so closely with the position of Wicksteed, which is practically that of Wieser and the present-day Austrians; and I have to modify quite materially some doctrines previously expounded in print. The following pages present briefly this change in position and constitute, not, indeed, a "review" of Wicksteed's book or work, but a discussion of the pivotal doctrine in his position.

This master-theme is that economic theory is merely a clear working-out of the "common-sense" of the administration of resources, and particularly that the same principle governs the organization of production and consumption. Producers, like consumers, spend money in the way to make it buy the largest result. Productive services, like individual incomes, are said to be allocated on the principle of equalizing marginal increments of the result—value-product in one case, utility in the other. In an economic system so conceived, prices are equal to money cost, and can be said to be determined by cost, money-cost outlays representing payments to productive services, which payments in connection with any one product reflect the competing offers of producers of other products for productive capacity. Thus, equality between price and cost is but another view of the fact that resources are so allocated as to be equally productive in all uses, and the real cost of any product is a displaced quantity of competing product, which at equilibrium must be of equal value. Resources specialized to any particular use get a "rent" or a "price-determined" remuneration and do not affect the price at all.

A short article of mine, published in 1928, which expounded this general view, received some favorable comment.[2] But it contains one rather crucial and, to me now, painfully obvious error, which I think applies also to the general position of Wicksteed and the Austrian school on the subject of cost. That is to say, the general principle of alternative-product cost so carefully and elaborately expounded by Wicksteed is subject to a sweeping limitation. It has to do with the question of "irksomeness" or subjective cost, which was the central cost concept of the older classical economists but is virtually eliminated from consideration in the general equilibrium theory of Wicksteed and the Austrians. The relative "irksomeness" of different occupations (the same notion really applies to all factors as well as to labor) is supposed to have no effect. And it does not if money earnings are in fact equalized; but the error is that they need not be equalized even at equilibrium and under freedom of movement.

In my own paper above referred to, the example of the deer and beaver used by Adam Smith was made the basis of the argument; but my own statement, as a matter of fact, contains a clause which starkly calls attention to the fallacy, although I did not see it for years. (These personal details seem to me worth giving because they are so typical of what has happened all through the history of economic thought and should be helpful in emphasizing caution and preventing errors.) A passage of the paper (*loc. cit.*, p. 356) reads: "Suppose for example it be found that deer hunters 'voluntarily' work twice as many hours per week as beaver hunters for the same reward in deer or beaver at their market ratio, or 50 per cent more hours for two-thirds the reward." It should, as it now seems, hit any critical reader in the eye that under the first assumption the alternate-product principle is valid, but that under the second it is not. That is, it is palpable that if, say, the workers in two occupations of different degrees of "irksomeness" are indifferent between the two at the same total wage, if they compensate for the difference in irksomeness by working a different number of hours per day, or in any other of several possible ways except the money earnings, the alternate-product principle of cost is valid; the cost of a unit of deer is the quantity of beaver of equal value, and vice versa. But if the difference or any part of it is reflected in total earnings, then it is palpable that resources are not at equilibrium distributed between the two uses in such a way as to equalize the *pecuniary* return, and

2. "A Suggestion for the Simplification of the General Theory of Price," *Journal of Political Economy*, June, 1928, pp. 353–70.

the addition to the output of one product resulting from subtracting a dollar's worth from the other will not be exactly a dollar's worth but somewhat more or less.[3]

It now seems to me that the reference to the possibility of the reward being two-thirds in one use what it was in the other was a "slip" in writing, that what I really thought was that such a result was inconsistent with rational choice between occupations on the part of the laborer. The reality at the back of the irksomeness notion is a competing possibility of using productive capacity in other ways than to produce income—say for recreation, or, in the case of labor, leisure (see below). Certainly after the issue was clearly defined in my own mind (in which process discussion with T. O. Yntema was perhaps especially stimulating), I for some time felt it sound to argue that the same rationally choosing subject would not combine pecuniary and non-pecuniary utilities in different proportions in different occupations. This would be sound if all pecuniary utility were really of the same kind and all non-pecuniary utility likewise, or, in general, if all the alternatives were composed of common elements which could be combined at will in any proportions. But it is now clear that such is not the case; the composite non-pecuniary alternative given up in working is an extremely complicated and subtle concept and would never be identical in two occupations. That is, it would never be the same *function of time*, and time enters into such comparisons in a peculiar way, being the one independent variable which is a real physical dimension of both and all alternatives compared. And while the pecuniary alternatives will probably be less divergent, they will rarely be the same either. A man will typically spend his money for a different list of products, or at least for the same list in significantly different proportions, as a consequence of changing his occupation. And any con-

3. The alternative cost principle which goes with the notion of general equilibrium in terms of pecuniary return can be formulated in terms either of value of sacrificed alternative or of physical quantities. It tells us more about the situation, is a more complete analysis, to keep values and quantities separate. This means expressing the condition of equilibrium as an equality between a physical ratio and a value ratio rather than as an equality between two mixed magnitudes each a value of a physical quantity. In the simplest common-sense form, equilibrium means that the physical quantities of any two products which have identical costs in transferable resources will have identical incremental utilities to all consumers (who consume both—see below). The ratio form of statement is accurate only for mathematical derivatives in a rather complicated form. There is no definite ratio between either utilities or costs of finite magnitudes of product, as there is none between any two subjective magnitudes except at the point of equality or ratio of 1:1.

siderable change in the composition of a utility complex affects the utility of every element and makes it a new complex. Worse still, expenditures for enjoyment can never be accurately separated from those which are properly costs or deductions—such as transportation, special clothing, and location and mode of life which go with the job. Hence, it cannot at all be assumed that one will strike a balance at the same pecuniary income, if perfectly free to proportion "working" and "not working" at will. (In general, a worker has this freedom only in a limited degree, but it is in order to assume the greatest flexibility at all justifiable in relation to the facts.)

Following up this reasoning, we find that the conception which is the very cornerstone of Wicksteed's work, namely, the conformity of the economic choices in consumption and production to a common principle, is subject to a sweeping limitation which seems to have generally escaped economists, as it did the present writer; or, if it was sensed by the pain cost and real cost theorists, it has not been correctly and clearly stated. In consequence of the principle of division of labor in particular, and more generally the fact of diversity of ownership of resources, there is a fundamental nonparallelism between the theory of the allocation of income among competing uses by consumers and the allocation of resources among competing lines of production in society as a whole. An essential principle in the former case is that every consumer, in apportioning his income rationally, will establish the same "relative marginal utility" between any two products, with the result that this relative marginal utility of different products is, in a sense, "objective" for all exchangers, even though it is in essence a subjective magnitude.[4] The same formal principle holds for the entrepreneur's apportionment of his expenditures among different productive resources, and hence the relative marginal productivity of every resource is equalized over the whole system in the same way as relative marginal utilities—in the aspect of resources *as things bought* by the persons who do buy them, and in so far as different entrepreneurs can be said to buy and use the "same" resources.

But if differences in the psychological attitudes of different resource-owners (especially, but not exclusively, laborers) are taken

4. Failure to grasp this principle profoundly disturbed Wieser and the later Austrians and gave rise to the spurious "rich-man–poor-man" difficulty in the utility explanation of value. It was all clear to Jevons, who repeatedly and explicitly emphasized that there is no comparison of utilities between individuals except as to equality of ratios; it was possibly understood by Menger also, though he is not so explicit.

into account, then to the degree that such attitudes in fact differ the resources furnished by different owners to different occupations are not the same, and no statement can be made about the equalization of return to different owners, since there is no common base of reference.[5] This, as already suggested, is a plain consequence of the general principle of specialization elliptically referred to as the "division of labor." Because of this principle, the individual as "producer," i.e., owner of labor or other resources, does not allocate productive resources among different uses as the individual consumer allocates income. And in the absence of specialization—in a society consisting of self-sufficient individuals—there would of course be no problem of money costs.

What lies back of the notion of irksomeness, as already suggested, is in any rational view of conduct the competition of "other uses," apart from money-making, for the productive capacity owned by an individual, whether in the form of labor power or any other form. In the case of labor, we are likely to think of this competition as leisure or recreative use of time. But even a superficial analysis must recognize both (1) that non-monetary alternatives are open to other resources as well as to labor, though with differences in detail, and (2) that much more is involved than different uses of time. On the first point, the clearest illustration is perhaps "land," particularly agricultural land. The typical farm-owner will use a part of his land for producing things for sale and a part for such direct uses as buildings, lawns, etc.; and on a larger scale, land for agriculture and other commercial uses has to compete with such employments as parks, game preserves, golf links, etc.

But the difficulty does not end with a simple dichotomy between uses, or, in the case of labor, with the fact that the human individual is relatively indivisible between pecuniary occupations, while every individual distributes or allocates his potential labor capacity in some way between pecuniary and non-pecuniary production. The case of agriculture again suggests that the owning farmer also uses some of his land for such purposes as growing garden vege-

5. The principle of "equal wages for equal work" so glibly argued, even by economists like Pigou, and also fought for, can be given no definite meaning, unless (a) both the "work" and the "wages" are measured finally and absolutely by the estimation of each individual worker, and (b) the performance is measured by that of the purchaser; and in that case there can never be any possibility of inequality. It is peculiarly interesting that the argument always centers around the inequality of money wages. In the abstract there is no more presumption that the same dollars represent the same utilities in consumption to two workers than there is that the fact of equal payment proves equality of "sacrifice."

tables, a part of which may be sold on the market and a part used at home, and the part used at home displaces and is equivalent to things which are bought and to things which are sold in the market. Again, these things which more or less displace and equate commodities in the market shade off into other human interests which do not properly come under the economic principle of rational quantitative comparison between uses of resources and maximizing of total return at all. We have to recognize a "trichotomy" of interests and motives lying along a scale from values definitely, sharply, and completely measured in pecuniary terms by (in theory) perfectly competitive market dealings (or opportunities) at one extreme, to motives which must be designated for the purposes of economics by such negative terms as "imponderable" at the other.

It is impossible to draw a clear-cut boundary around the sphere or domain of human action to be included in economic science. The most nearly objective boundary would shut out all interests or activities the results of which do not actually go through the market. But practically it is absurd to make an absolute distinction between commodities or services actually bought and sold and those which are or come infinitely near to being absolutely the same thing, and which would come into the market or go out, more or less, with the least shift in price in either direction. This last category obviously includes a very considerable bulk both of productive services of the various kinds and of their products in the form of commodities and direct services. In so far as behavior is to be interpreted in terms of economic categories and principles, we have to assume that the individual divides the use of any kind of productive capacity between money-making and other employments on the basis of the same kind of comparison and marginal equalization which underlies the choice between different uses of income. But the apportionment between different money-making uses (an aspect of which is the theory of alternative costs) conforms to this principle only to a limited degree.

This negative statement holds especially for labor, in consequence of the indivisibility of the human individual and the principle of division of labor, i.e., of the general facts which lead to the division of labor and to social economic organization in general. With regard to other forms of property,[6] there are no such sharp physical and technical limits to the division of the productive capacity owned by

6. In a property system labor power is the "property" of the laborer; and, in fact, most of it is the product of investment.

a given individual among a multiplicity of employments; but there still are limits to such apportionment, and, in fact, some new considerations working against it come into play, but they need not be considered here. On the other side, there is no reason for the apportionment, comparable to that which leads to the apportionment of income among commodities—no diminishing relative psychic utility of one line of use in comparison with others, as the one in question is extended.[7] The main reason making for apportionment of his property by the individual owner is the reduction of his personal risk, a consideration which does not apply under perfectly economic conditions at all. Any risk which can be recognized as compatible with rational economic choice will be eliminated by insurance in some form, i.e., by organized relations with other individuals.[8]

On point (2) it is obvious that there are other ways of dividing the use of one's labor capacity between money-earning and other uses, and of changing the proportions in such division, in addition to shifting segments or increments of the time stream bodily from one field to the other. Here the problem relates especially to labor, which can obviously vary its productivity in a given occupation by working at varying degrees of intensity for a given fraction of the time as well as by changing the fractional distribution of the total time-stream of 24 hours per day and 365 days per year between the occupation and "leisure" employments. It is also obvious that these other modes of variation are, marginally at least, equivalent to changes in the distribution of time. For by working at a slower pace, or with less close attention, or in more satisfactory stretches, and the like, one can save "energy," literal and figurative (or physical and

---

7. This argument naturally leads to the observation that the "objectivity" of the utility theory itself, even in the sense in which it has objectivity, i.e., that the quantities of two commodities having the same incremental utility are the same for all individuals, is also subject to limitation. As regards any two commodities, it is true only for those individuals who do consume both, or at least are actually on a margin of indifference with respect to doing so.

8. "Risk-taking" is in reality a motive on its own account, but it is one which cannot possibly be brought under economic principles unless, again, the risk is measurable and hence insurable, and very doubtfully even then; at least, I do not see how the principles of rational choice through quantitative comparison of increments can be applied to the desire to gamble, even in such a mechanical case as the roulette wheel, where the essence of the interest is ignorance as to whether the result will be a gain or a loss. The converse notion of gambling as a disutility, paid for on the basis of marginal productivity, though argued for by Pigou, is even more unintelligible to me—not to mention that if a businessman knows how much "risk" he is taking he is not taking any at all or is merely playing roulette.

"spiritual"), from one's work for other purposes (which again will be more or less comparable quantitatively with the things actually measured by the money denominator). Many different ways in which energy may be saved could be distinguished, but such analysis would be difficult and vague at best—beyond the factor of physical speeding at least—and would rapidly run off into dubious subtleties. With regard to "property" (apart from labor capacity), there are also possibilities of varying the intensity of performance apart from redistribution of time, but the question is still more subtle and vague.

A rational theory of the apportionment of productive capacity between pecuniary and non-pecuniary employments must rest on the assumption that the human individual considered as a productive instrument, and every other productive agency, actually has a given fixed productive capacity, the use of which is fractionally apportioned. This given capacity could only be quantitatively defined as the maximum pecuniary income which the individual or instrument could produce in the most remunerative employment open. (Capacity not available for making money income is completely outside the ken of the economist.) The difference between this income and lesser actual earnings would have to be treated as representing the use of the corresponding fraction of the total capacity to create some "other," "non-pecuniary" utility. It is evident, however, that virtually any change in the general economic conditions, physical or psychical, in the economic system in question, would change the definitions of all these magnitudes. We must face the fact that the notion of given magnitudes in economic life is itself an assumption subject to severe limitations.

Finally, it should again be emphasized that even under given conditions in the strictest sense, the concept of economy and the economic is subject to severe limitations as a principle of behavior interpretation. Most of the individual's activity outside of the sphere actually organized through market dealings is not properly or fully amenable to such interpretation. A rationalizer from the outside may indeed argue that the choices involved in play, sociability, friendship and the love-life, and in aesthetic, cultural, and religious activity, do come under the principle of comparing increments of desirable result obtainable from the use in different ways of increments of "productive capacity." Wicksteed himself seems to take this position (Book II, chap. i), and Canon Rashdall has even more explicitly defended it in his book on *The Theory of Good and Evil* (especially

Vol. II, chap. ii).[9] But it is surely evident to common sense that if the behaving subject himself attempts to view his behavior in economic or mathematically maximizing terms, he changes its character and in most cases "spoils" the interest in and enjoyment of the activity. One of the most inspired products of the phrase-maker's art is perhaps the observation of Professor John M. Clark that an irrational passion for dispassionate rationality may take the joy out of life.

It may be interesting to glance at the history of the discussion of cost from the standpoint of the issues which have been raised above. The classical school of economics of course started from the "axiom" that cost is labor cost. This principle is expounded in *The Wealth of Nations* (Book I, chap. v). But in Smith the view is limited to his "philosophical" treatment of the value problem; when he comes, in chapter vi, to discuss price concretely, he starts out from the familiar deer and beaver illustration, in which the underlying meaning is obviously that of relative cost of two commodities in terms of perfectly mobile and indifferent labor. In reality, this makes the cost of a unit of either product a definite quantity of the other (constant cost), it being assumed also that the productive capacity is valued only for its exchangeable product. As long as the commodities compared are produced under such conditions—a single homogeneous resource of any sort, whose "owner" is indifferent between the occupations on the basis of equal time—it is possible to measure the cost in terms of resource time, if one prefers. (It possibly deserves explicit remark that the feelings attached to employment or unemployment have nothing to do with the case; the argument holds in every detail in the same way if we substitute acres for laborers.) When the costs are heterogeneous, this can no longer be done, and the *only* measure is displaced alternative product, or, in a developed economic situation, the complex of competing products reduced to

9. Interestingly enough, the outstanding critic of the position in English so far as the writer knows is John A. Hobson; see his *Work and Wealth*, especially the last chapter. For a brief criticism of Rashdall, cf. R. Kingsdown Pemberton, "The Commensurability of Values," *International Journal of Ethics*, October, 1922, pp. 23–33. The issue raised is undoubtedly the real crux of the problem of marginal utility about which so much that is not very profoundly relevant has been written on both sides. Cf. also R. B. Perry, *The General Theory of Value*, and his article, "Economic Value and Moral Value," *Quarterly Journal of Economics*, XXX (1915–16), 443–85, and critical discussion of his work, and, indeed, the entire literature on the relations between economics and the various types of value recognized by the philosophers. The work of German social-organism economists like Spann is also in question.

a common denominator in terms of money. In Smith's later argument, especially in chapter vii ("Of Natural and Market Price"), he makes it even clearer that the mechanism underlying the cost reasoning is simply that of equalizing the yield of resources by correct apportionment among competing uses, in which labor, land, and "stock" are put on the same basis. Many details are, of course, not worked out, and others are confused; but the essential position is that of modern "Austrian" economics.[10]

Both Ricardo (*Principles*, chap. iv), and Senior (octavo ed., p. 101) even more explicitly worked out the cost theory in terms of the flow of resources from one use to another and equalization of yield. Abstracting from incompleteness and error in detail, this is again the general equilibrium theory, in which the real cost is a displaced alternative product. Ricardo argued in chapter i for labor cost as an approximation, and in his work elsewhere assumed identity between labor cost and value as a kind of metaphysical dogma without any argument whatever. Senior, however, made his best-known contribution to economic doctrine in the form of a supplement to pain-cost theory in the form of the abstinence doctrine, and this position was even more definitely adopted by Cairnes.

If resources are considered mobile from one use to another, and indifferent between uses in the sense indicated at the outset above, namely that at equilibrium, under freedom of choice, they earn the same total income—compensating in any way other than money for differences in "time-irksomeness," the different relative appeal of income and alternative fruits of each time unit—then any doctrine of pain cost or resource cost involves a simple failure to see the obvious relativity of the price and cost idea. (Not to mention the impossibility of measurement; under specialization only final products are directly compared and reduced to equivalence.) If the real alternative to employment in producing (the final unit of) the commodity actually produced (the alternative which would be chosen) is at equilibrium with the production of an equal value of some other commodity, then it is this quantity of the other commodity which is the cost; and neither "pain" nor resource use as such, nor

10. It is impossible to make any sense out of a doctrine of labor cost in harmony with this position, whether labor cost is taken in a philosophical or other meaning; the philosophical doctrine is as "wrong" as a labor-cost theory of price empirically considered. It is not labor cost, but scarcity relative to need or desire, and the necessity of choosing, which is the ultimate basis or essence of value when the latter is taken as a magnitude in any sense. This principle was as well and clearly stated by Senior as it has ever been since.

any concomitant of the latter, has anything to do with the case. The only connection in which pain or consumption of resources becomes significant in relation to the price of products is, as already indicated, that at equilibrium a small transfer of resources from one use to another will for some reason actually involve a change in the total amount of pain undergone or resource capacity used in the making of money income; this change is indicated and measured, of course, by a change in the total amount of money income earned, and ties up with a shift inward or outward in the boundaries (contraction or expansion) of the economic system as a whole.

However, there is a positive side to the matter, along with failure to understand. Alongside this equilibrium view implying an alternative cost or displaced product-cost doctrine, there seems to be a more or less implicit admixture of a different conception of cost altogether, one in which cost as pain has somewhat more meaning. This view, separated out and stated explicitly, considers all production as due to labor, i.e., subjective sacrifice by individuals, but assumes that every laborer is completely *immobile* or specialized to the particular product on which he actually works. The "supply curve" of any product, then (to use modern jargon), is entirely a matter of variation in the amount of work done, whether arising out of variation in the distribution of time or in any or all of the factors making up "intensity." This, as already noted, makes the pain-cost doctrine somewhat more meaningful, although, if the conduct is rationalized at all, "pain" and "pleasure" in any literal sense have nothing to do with it, as choice is again simply a matter of apportioning between alternatives in the use of capacity, in this case the alternatives of working at the particular occupation and the composite of "not-working"; the individual choosing might be either maximizing pleasure or minimizing pain, according to the accidental zero point of this personal scale at a given moment—if the notion has any meaning at all.

Such a cost theory is so far from the facts of life that it is naturally difficult to attribute it conclusively to any writer. It seems, however, to be the theory generally in the mind, or implied in the words, of Jevons, particularly; and John Stuart Mill is open to the same accusation. Both of them emphasize labor cost, and neither expressly or clearly recognizes, as do Smith, Ricardo, and Senior, the shifting of resources as the essential process underlying price fixation. This applies to Mill's direct discussion of cost; in the treatment of international trade, he is explicit that the essential peculiarity in the situ-

ation is the *immobility* of capital and labor. (All the classical economists, including Marshall, assume, or argue as if, "land" has no mobility affecting the supply and price of products.)

It is clear that an inclusive theory of cost in relation to price must
take some account of both these viewpoints. For it is a fact and is
significant that each individual resource-owner is on the one hand
limited—and, in the case of labor, quite narrowly—in the proportional allocation of his resources among the various uses theoretically
open, while at the same time each owner must make, and has some
choice in making, an apportionment of his productive capacity between pecuniary and non-pecuniary uses. But in a general summing
up, the theory of cost and price will have to run primarily in the alternative cost terms of Wicksteed's "Common Sense." Most of what
can be done to make it more realistic and true to fact will take the
form of recognizing limitations and specifying in a general way the
kinds of divergence from reality which are to be expected and their
causes; relatively little seems possible in the way of formulating
supplementary theories with any degree of generality. It is, of course,
true that, in so far as an individual is free and chooses rationally, he
will equalize the utilities derived from the final increment of any
resource in all fields, pecuniary and non-pecuniary and both in indefinite multiplicity. But this freedom of apportionment is so limited as to make the theory highly unreal; and, as already emphasized,
the fact and the desirability of rational quantitative comparison in
choice are also limited. It seems impossible to formulate meaning-
fully the conditions under which equality of money earnings will
be a condition of indifference between the money-earning alternatives, and the bearing of all the relevant complexities upon the
determination of the relative prices of commodities simply does not
admit of any workable general formulation. The only general-cost
theory which can be maintained will, after all, be that of alternative
cost, best formulated as displaced product cost, but this must be
stated subject to the qualification that it is true only "in so far" as
at equilibrium the indicated conditions obtain.

The "other" theory already referred to, of supply curves based
on variability in the amount of productive service rendered by given
productive agencies, specialized to particular uses, cannot be given
much weight. In the first place, the dominant fact affecting the supply of a commodity is, in general, unquestionably the competition
of other pecuniary employment for the services and not variability
in the amount of specialized services offered. In the second place,

the direction of the variability which may exist is a serious question. One of the difficulties of the labor-cost theory, which gradually forced its way to recognition (by J. S. Mill, and especially by Cairnes) was the obtrusive fact that, in general, the higher remunerations are paid for smaller and not greater sacrifices. The reasons for this are complicated and need not be taken up here; they include many things in addition to the variation in the supply of services from given agencies as prices vary, other things being equal. The nature of this variation itself is an unanswered question, and one which probably admits of no general answer.[11]

It is, of course, necessary to avoid confusion as to the meaning of changes in the supply of productive services, i.e., as to what changes affect price-determining costs, and how they work. (Money costs will always equal prices if full and accurate accounts are kept, but such payments may be either price-determining or price-determined.) In the first place, it should go without saying that the general conditions of a stationary economy are assumed, meaning especially a given supply of productive instruments or agencies of every type. In view of the foregoing argument, fixity in the productive capacity of existing agencies must also be specified as coming within this category. A change in either respect is a "historical" or "progressive" change (of the sort generally miscalled "dynamic"). The supply changes in question are, then, changes in the supply of salable product-making services from specialized factors, at the expense or to the benefit of use of their capacity for other purposes. Of course specialization is a matter of degree and, it would be more accurate to say, "changes in the supply of services in so far as they are specialized." In so far as any service is perfectly mobile among all pecuniary uses, changes in its supply will affect the (relative) prices of products only through the different elasticities of demand of different products. But "perfect" mobility would have to include perfect flexibility in combining proportions, which would contradict the most fundamental principles of production.

Only with such qualifications and reservations can the central

11. Obviously, "leisure" and "products" are complementary goods. If it can be assumed that they are complementary in the special sense that the utility function for the two together is of the nature of a product $[U = L^a P^b]$, then simple mathematical manipulation will show that the proportional division of productive capacity between commodity production and leisure, or the amount of leisure exchanged for income, is independent of price, depending only on the ratio between the exponents in the formula. For other mathematical forms of complementarity, the problem has not, as far as I know, been studied.

doctrine of *The Common Sense of Political Economy* be maintained, plausible as it is and widely as it has been and is held. But the historically opposed doctrines of pain-cost and real-cost are not thereby vindicated and are indefinitely farther still from the truth.[12]

12. A fuller exposition of the theory of cost as now understood by the writer has been published as two articles in the *Zeitschrift für Nationalökonomie* (Vienna, 1935).

III

V

Social Science[1]

WHEN we speak of social science we are reminded that originally and etymologically the word "science" is more or less a synonym for knowledge. Our inquiry has to do with what we know, and can know, and how we can acquire knowledge about society. The question inevitably runs into that of the meaning of knowledge itself and, as a part of its meaning, its function, or why we want it, and hence raises at the outset the ultimate problems of philosophy. In this field, as elsewhere, knowledge is wanted both for its own sake and for use. It is a serious reflection that the unsatisfactory state of affairs in social science has largely resulted from the very progress of science, the revolutionary development of techniques for acquiring and applying knowledge, which is an outstanding feature and achievement of civilization in our own and recent time.

The primary function of a discussion such as this—at least such is the main point contended for in this paper—is to correct a fallacy which is particularly current in social science circles. The fallacy is that social science is a science in the same sense as the natural sciences, in which the revolution has occurred, that its problems are to be solved by carrying over into the study of society the methods and techniques which have produced the celebrated triumphal march of science in the study of nature, and that this procedure will lead to a parallel triumph in our field, both in the yielding of knowledge and insight and in the transformation of life.

In this connection in particular—more or less characteristically for social problems in so far as they can be solved—it would seem that a clear statement of the issue ought to be sufficient to resolve it definitively. It ought to be obvious that the relation of knowledge to action cannot be the same or closely similar, nor can knowledge itself, apart from the question of action, be at all the same where the knower and the known are identical as where they are external to each other. In a genetic-historical view the fundamental

1. A paper presented at a joint session of the American Philosophical Association and Section K of the American Association for the Advancement of Science, Philadelphia, December 28, 1940. Reprinted by permission from *Ethics*, Vol. LI, No. 2 (January, 1941).

revolution in outlook which represents the real beginning of modern natural science was the discovery that the inert objects of nature are not like men, i.e., subject to persuasion, exhortation, coercion, deception, etc., but are "inexorable." The position which we have to combat seems to rest upon an inference, characteristically drawn by the "best minds" of our race, that since natural objects are not like men, men must be like natural objects. The history of British-American social thought in modern times is particularly interesting in this connection. In general, it has represented a combination of positivism and pragmatism—two philosophical positions with respect to the nature of man and his place in the cosmos and specifically with respect to social action, which are at once contradictory between themselves and equally indefensible as a basis of social action. For man, conceived in positivistic terms, could not act at all; and conceived in pragmatic terms, he could not act upon himself.

So much for the negative view of the problem, which brings us to the point at which the discussion ought to begin. From an affirmative or constructive standpoint the case is far less simple. For, on the one hand, there certainly can be and are, within some limits, "positive" sciences of man and society—not one but many—and these are in widely varying degrees of a like kind with the sciences of nature. And, unquestionably, these "natural" sciences of man not only yield genuine knowledge but are of genuine and profound relevance to action. In view of what has been said the possibility of such sciences as well as their necessary limitations becomes a mystery to be explained.

As these statements imply, any truly rational attack upon the problems of knowledge and of action, in connection with human and social data, must at least provisionally rest upon a pluralistic conception of the object matter. It is an indisputable fact that man is a physical object and that man, as an object, and the phenomena into which he enters are in part to be explained by physical science. And man is also a biological organism and as such is in part to be explained, with the phenomena in which he plays a role, by biological science.[2]

Next, it is as indisputably a matter of fact, in the inclusive sense, that man and human phenomena present characteristics which any

2. Of course this raises the issue whether biological phenomena might ultimately be explained as physical phenomena merely. The question cannot be argued here, beyond noting that biological science does use teleological categories, like struggle and adaptation, and that it is sheer dogmatism to assert that they could be reduced to purely physical or positive content.

discussion must and does recognize as sharply different from those of non-human biology. Man is a being who thinks, and acts on the basis of thinking, in a way which sharply differentiates him from any other organic species and which, we have to assume, is not characteristic of inanimate nature at all. Other distinctions will be developed in the detail allowable as we proceed. It should be clear that man is at the same time many different kinds of being or entity which are not reducible to any one kind. The urge to treat man scientifically in the sense of the natural, and specifically the physical, sciences can itself be readily explained. Man as an intellectual inquirer is characterized by a craving for intellectual simplification and unification, for monism as against pluralism. And since "he" cannot deny that "man" is a physical being, this craving leads him to deny that he is anything else. And, of course, the triumph of physical science and technology, in yielding intellectually satisfactory knowledge along with power to transform his environment and his own life, contributes largely to the strengthening of the prejudice. But why these considerations should actually lead man as inquirer to deny to man the characteristics of an inquirer (even the faculty of denying) must be allowed to remain in the status of mystery so far as the present essay or the present writer is concerned.

We enter upon the domain of social science with the naming of the next familiar distinguishing characteristic of man—that he is a "social animal." The statement does not of course have for us its original significance of a member of a *polis*. But it has a profusion of other meanings, at least three of which must be distinguished. In the first place, the sociality of man is in fact utterly different from that of any other species, and it is for the most part the differences which enter into the subject matter of social science. It is not as an animal that man is social, and the designation of a social animal is misleading and essentially untrue. In the subhuman animal kingdom there is no clear line between aggregates which consist of associated individuals and others which are to be viewed as individual organisms composed of units or cells. Human society is again pluralistic in that it presents both characteristics to a striking degree, but it presents both in a highly distinctive sense.

The important fact about human society, whether from the standpoint of knowledge and understanding for their own sake or for use in action, is that it is made up of units of the general character insisted upon in the next to the last paragraph, i.e., of rationally purposive individuals. Man is an individual in a special and unique sense—a sense which goes infinitely beyond the meaning of the term in any other connection. Yet this particular kind of individual is also social, in a sense just as distinctive and unique. The kind of society which human society is, presupposes such uniquely individualistic individuals, and at the same time the existence of such individuals presupposes the existence of such a society. This relationship is embarrassing to the analytical student in making it difficult to discuss either man as an individual or human society prior to discussion of the other.

Man and society necessarily developed from animal life in a historical process of creative interaction of individuals upon each other and of interaction between individual and group, extending over a long geological epoch. The history of this development, which would no doubt help a great deal toward understanding and exposition, is almost completely and irrevocably lost. The biological strain which led to man must have branched off from the evolutionary tree at a point where life was not social in either of the main possible senses of the word. The most developed form of animal society is a termite colony. Its structural organization, its functioning, and all the phenomena which belong in it are (presumably) based upon instinct. But human society involves a widely different animal type, belonging to a branch the other orders and families of which are not truly social. It is not based on instinct, and it is more than doubtful whether this type of social life could have evolved out of instinctive social life. It would seem as if there had to be, as an intermediate link, society in a third meaning, based upon tradition or "institutions." Institutional life is a quasi-mechanical concept, involving habit in the individual and the transmission of the pattern of associative life by unconscious imitation, i.e., by social or cultural, in contrast with biological, inheritance. Traditional or institutional associative life was important in human evolution because it allowed for adaptive modification independent of biological and biologically inherited change, whether by natural selection of random variations or by mutation.[3]

Because human society is an association of consciously purposive

3. Cf. preceding note as to instinct and mechanism. It may be doubted whether purely institutional social order is conceivable, apart from a degree of individualism on the part of the units; and it is still more doubtful whether such a picture of human development is in harmony with the facts, such as are available as a basis for inference, in existing primitive societies and in the evident incipient rationality of the higher animals, and even more in their emotional makeup.

individuals rather than an organism to be viewed as a unit and analyzed into individual components (or, while it is both, the former viewpoint is more fundamental), the individual is logically prior to society. A more decisive reason is that the study of society is, and cannot be kept from being, relative to social problems—problems of social action; and in a society which has the essential character of human society such problems arise out of the individual nature of the individual human being rather than out of his social nature. In a society based upon instinct or even in one based exclusively upon tradition and institutions there are no problems, either individual or social, for, or to, either the society itself or the individuals which compose it. Human social problems arise out of conflicts of interest between individual members. From this point of view a termite colony is in principle of the same kind as an animal organism, the individual members being in the position of cells. And the same would be true of a society which was purely a phenomenon of socially inherited patterns of associative life.

The argument so far shows that man must be described in terms of at least five fundamental kinds of entity or being. He is (*a*) a physical mechanism; (*b*) a biological organism, with characteristics extending from those of the lowest plant to the highest animal in the biological scale; (*c*) a social animal in the traditional-institutional sense; (*d*) a consciously, deliberatively purposive individual; and, concomitantly, (*e*) a social being in the unique sense of an association of such individuals. (He may also be to some extent a social animal in the proper instinctive sense; but, if so, it is to such a limited degree that for present purposes it may be left out of account.)

It is evident that at least the first three of these types of existence can each be the subject matter of a distinct positive science or group of such sciences. And these sciences have already been more or less extensively developed. We do have more or less distinctively human physics and chemistry, human biology, and institutional science—sociology or culture anthropology. And of the last, in particular, there are many branches, including institutional economics. Each of these sciences deals descriptively with an aspect of human phenomena which is isolated and treated in the positive terms of "uniformities of coexistence and sequence," which is the general pattern of a natural science. At least one further distinction must be made—a fourth type of scientifically describable form of existence recognized. Consciousness is not necessarily or always active, deliberative, or problem-solving. And to the extent that it is not of this character but is phenomenal (or epiphenomenal), it is possible, in theory, and more or less so actually, to describe consciousness in positive categories. Such description is the task and subject matter of another highly developed science—that of psychology—in the meaning indicated by the statement, which is its original and proper meaning, in distinction from various special physical and biological sciences such as neurology, physiology, and "behaviorology."

It is also evident that all these sciences must in a sense take account of the social nature of man. Yet they are not social sciences, with the exception of culture anthropology. This is in a sense *the* science of society, if the word is restricted, so far as the subject matter allows, to the category of a natural or positive science. But it should hardly be necessary to emphasize that the content of culture anthropology as a positive science—namely, institutions—is not learned like natural science data through sense observation merely but primarily through intercommunication. And the science can have no direct significance for social action in the society of the scientist himself; for if it results in such action, its conclusions are no longer true. It does, however, need to be emphasized that culture anthropology may have for its subject matter a very large range of the phenomena characteristic of societies which do face and solve problems, which "act," on the basis of deliberation by the society as a unit. The phenomena of our own society are very largely of the traditional institutional character, and this must be true of any society which is even intellectually conceivable, just as any real or possible society must involve human beings in all their "lower" aspects. The study of these phenomena may bring them above the threshold of social awareness and make them problems of social action.

The study of actual or possible society must involve a large congeries of special positive sciences, more or less effectively interrelated, co-ordinated, and unified, according to the actual possibilities of such an achievement, which are to be discovered only by trying. But such study must also involve other sciences not of the positive sort, or only partly so, but still sciences, bodies of knowledge. It must involve social science in a distinctive sense, the nature of which must be considered in the light of the nature of the human individual as the real unit.

The main distinctive characteristic of the human being has already been mentioned; he is individualistically and rationally purposive. But this concept calls for further analysis. One aspect of rationality appears in the use of means to achieve ends. And it goes without saying that any means used by an individual are used to realize ends which are individual (though they may also be social) and are at the same time individual means. The human individual, then, inherently involves two aspects—individual ends and individual possession or control over means or power. These two aspects, factors, or elements constitute the economic man—a concept methodologically analogous to the frictionless machine of theoretical mechanics and essential to analysis in the same way.

The notion of power in turn includes two factors: (*a*) possession or control of means in the narrow sense of actual things or instruments used in purposive activity and (*b*) knowledge of the use of means (with skill in an ambiguous position). The confusion between means in the concrete sense and procedures for using means, the content of knowledge in its economic aspects, under the inclusive term "means," is one of the serious confusions in our everyday terminology. A much more important confusion prevails with reference to the meaning of the end in economic behavior (the behavior of the economic man). The concept of economy clearly implies a *given* end and one which is measurable, or quantitatively comparable with other ends, in terms of the means to be employed. Economic behavior implies or is, in the degree in which it is economic, the use of means in such a way as to realize the maximum quantity of some general end or objective, embodied in specific wants and conditioned by the limited means available to an individual subject. The general end, now usually called "want satisfaction," is to be realized by correct apportionment of the given means among various modes of use, bound up in a "preference function" with intermediate specific ends or wants. Further analysis or discussion cannot be undertaken here. The essential point at the moment is that in economic behavior as a concept ends are given, defined by actual preferences on the part of the subject as an economic man as he stands at the moment of making any choice involving the disposal of means. A preference is a datum, whether it represents merely individual taste, or good taste, or the solution of a value problem reached in preceding "calm, cool hours" of deliberation.

Thus the notion of economic behavior defines a particular form of rational-deliberative or problem-solving activity or conduct, involving what may be referred to as economic rationality. Such behavior is the subject matter of several descriptive social sciences and of theoretical economics. Economic activity is to be sharply distinguished from other, and higher, forms of rationality or problem-solving, to be noticed presently. But economic rationality requires further discussion because it exemplifies problem-solving at the level of greatest simplicity, and the general features of problem-solving activity are crucial for our discussion as a whole. It is of the essence of such activity, and hence of distinctively human behavior (conduct), that, by virtue of being problematic, the course of events involved is not accurately predictable in advance in terms of any possible knowledge. That is, it is conceptually distinct from a mechanical cause-and-effect sequence and so cannot be made the subject matter of any positive science. A problem is not a problem unless the solution involves effort and is subject to error, features or notions which are absolutely excluded from mechanical process or positive cause and effect.

But human behavior, in an essential part, element, or aspect, is problem-solving, and first in the limited sense of economic problem-solving. The human being does confront the problem of using given means to realize given ends and does solve this problem more or less correctly. To think of its always being solved correctly would be to deny that it is a problem and to deny an undeniable fact. Thus perfect economic rationality, while applied as a "limiting case" in the notion of varying degrees of it, is as a real concept self-contradictory. (It is exactly like the concept of universal causality in this respect.)

Another significant aspect of the notion of economy, which should not be overlooked in any discussion of methodology, is that as a quality of motivation it is a purely intuitive idea. Even the propositions of mathematics can be derived and verified inductively, to a degree of generality and accuracy to which there is hardly any limit except that of cost in time and effort; but no mere sense observation can give any indication as to whether any conduct is economic or in what degree. Even the subject himself cannot know at all accurately, even afterward.

But economic rationality as a description of deliberative conduct is limited in two further respects, fully as important in principle as the fact that actual results of action diverge in all degrees from the intention of maximizing a given end. First, the end is rarely or never actually given in any strict sense of the word; rather, it is in some degree redefined in the course of the activity directed toward realizing it, and the interest in action centers in this definition and discovery of ends, as well as in their achievement. That is, the end is always itself more or less problematic, as well as the procedure (use of means) for realizing it. One of the most absurd items in the common folklore about human beings is the idea that they know what they want or that "there is no disputing about tastes." It may be seriously doubted whether there is any thinking at all about conduct which does not center on determining the end to be aimed at, or what end is "right" in various senses, as well as the type of activity which will realize some end. An actual problem may be to any extent that of the end or that of procedure—except the limiting case at either extreme. Deliberation about ends in turn takes many forms, but detailed exploration of these must be omitted here. The form most important in connection with social science in relation to action—which is necessarily one vital aspect of any science, though never the whole problem—is the selection of good or right ends. This is the problem of value—moral, aesthetic, or intellectual—to which we must return presently.

The second limitation to which the notion of given ends is subject—ultimately rather an aspect of the same fact that they are not given but problematic—is that to the extent to which an end is given, it is not really the end in the sense of finality. Given, concrete ends are means, or intermediate steps, in the achievement of *purposes*, which even more clearly are not and cannot be *data* in any definite sense. This would come out most sharply in a discussion of "non-serious" conduct. In play, it is obvious that the objective—what a player is trying to do—is a means, first to victory, and, beyond that, to a good game. Again, casual conversation is one of the most characteristic human activities, and it can hardly be said to have any end. This is one of the most seriously neglected aspects of conduct in general. Play, diversion, recreation—the "moral holiday"—is just as essential to human life as even nutritional activity.

A clear and adequate recognition of the nature of individual economic activity is essential as a prerequisite to social science, first, because all conduct whatever has this character in some degree, along with other aspects. The aesthetic, intellectual, moral, and even the religious life involve the use and the economy of means, as well as what are usually thought of as sustenance activities. In fact, provision for these values makes up the greater part of the sustenance problem itself, as measured by cost, at any level of life which can be called civilized or properly human. In the second place, the ends of individual motivation, and even more the purposes to which they are essentially relative and instrumental, are also social, and in two senses. They are partly created by the unconscious cultural process- es of society and partly decided upon or chosen through intellec- tual activity, which is always fundamentally social in character. Fi- nally, individual desires and purposes are largely realized through economic activity which is socially organized, and conflicts between individual ends and purposes, centering in the use of means or pow- er, form the main source of the important social problems in our culture. It is primarily in connection with such problems of con- flict between individuals wielding power that it is at once necessary to have and difficult to secure the agreement which is required to maintain the degree of peace and order requisite to rationally pur- posive life, individual and social.

These statements, especially in their excessive brevity, tend to overemphasize the importance of economics in the picture of social science and its conceptual and methodological problems. They must not be taken in this sense any more than economic interests and problems are to be dismissed as trivial or sordid. Man is not only a rational animal; his emotional nature is as real and important as his thinking (in a sense even more fundamental), and rationality also includes much more than economic rationality. It is difficult to strike a correct balance here. On the one hand, economic problems are relative to problems of ends and in that sense are subordinate. But, on the other hand, the correct use of means is not only a uni- versal aspect of all problems of action but is an indispensable condi- tion of their solution and of all achievement of purpose or creation of value. The fundamental category of economic activity is *power*. It is equally (because in both cases completely) essential to any good activity to have power and to direct its use "rightly"—and in particular not to treat the acquisition of power as an end or purpose on its own account.

The two main currents of social-ethical thinking in modern Western civilization—namely, Christianity and liberalism—respec- tively embody the two evils suggested by this last statement. The one is a naïve, romantic-mystical voluntarism, the other a naïve, in- strumentalistic intellectualism. The central tenet of the Christian ethic is the repudiation of power, the denial of real value to goods dependent on the use of means. Virtue, defined as "love" of God and man, is left without content other than a feeling attitude and a vague neighborly helpfulness to persons in distress through some calamity. In particular the teachings of the Gospels enjoin indifference to political power and obedience to any established authority, which clearly seems to exclude the good Christian from any participation in political activity as well as from wealth-getting or wealth-using.

On the other hand, modern utilitarian liberalism, including pragmatism as its most recent phase, has tended to see the whole problem of life in terms of the acquisition of power and efficiency in its use. It virtually ignores the problem of values to which concrete ends are usually, if not always in some degree, instrumental. And the social ethic of liberalism has emphasized individual liberty and, specifically, the economic freedom of the individual. Its conception of social policy is, or was, the maintenance of such freedom. This logically and necessarily means that the individual is to be left free to use power in his possession in practically any way he pleases—including its use to acquire more power, indefinitely—subject to the important restriction that he does not act in such a way as to infringe the equal freedom of others.

It will be seen that while the ideals of Christianity and liberalism for the individual life are antithetic, their conceptions of social ethics are not so far apart. Christianity repudiates any concern with politics, while (the older) liberalism was chiefly concerned to restrict the functions of law and the state to the negative field of preventing interference by individuals with one another's freedom of action (though sweeping exceptions were made by Adam Smith and other advocates of laissez faire). Christian non-resistance is closely akin to liberalist non-interventionalism. In both systems the main substance of social life is left to unconscious processes—to an "invisible hand"—whether this is interpreted in theological terms or those of historical-cultural mechanics. And neither system has any place for social science with any relevance for social action.

Social science must, on the one hand, strive to tell the whole truth, to recognize all the facts, in the large sense of the word, about society and about man as a member of human society. It must not stultify itself by oversimplification, by stressing a particular set of facts or a particular aspect of the facts, in response to an intellectualistic prejudice on the part of the scientist. This is just what it has largely tended to do in the past. And the absurdity is especially egregious because it involves ignoring in, or denying to, man in general the very characteristics of individual and social interests and activity which are distinctive of the scientist himself as a human being. For science itself is problem-solving, both in the economic sense and in the higher sense of exploration and creation in the realm of values. Scientific activity is the pursuit of truth. And truth is essentially a value, not merely a want; and still less is it merely an effect in a causal sequence.

The contrast between (*a*) fact (interpreted in positive terms of cause and effect), (*b*) end (as given, the object of desire or wish), and (*c*) value (or purpose) is of the essence of the meaning of all three. And all three are inseparably involved in any true description of man and/or of society. Man as an individual acts to achieve ends, and these, in turn, are instrumental to purposes and to rational purposes or values. And no description of him and his behavior makes sense if it ignores this fact. Among the kinds of value pursued is truth, which is a value as well as being instrumental to the achievement of ends in the narrower sense. In a sense, truth includes all other values, however classified. It is typical of all value in that men want it without knowing concretely what it is, but as the solution of a problem, and especially in being desired *because* it is a value. The thing that men most characteristically want is to be right. Truth is at once a social and an ethical category. All truth, even as fact, or as instrumental, or as a value, is arrived at by co-operation among individuals acting freely and in a spirit of ethical, even religious, integrity. Such co-operation in its ideal form is equalitarian or democratic in the ideal sense of that concept; it excludes any exercise of power or wish to exercise power over other participants in the quest, on the part of any individual. The pursuit of truth or of value in any form is the ideal type of ethical association, which is to say of all true society; it represents the type of life-activity properly described as social in social science itself.

Furthermore, any genuine science must, even as science, be relevant to action. But natural science itself, in its relevance to action, must certainly recognize that the action to which it is relevant is not merely action upon natural objects, which are inert and passive, but is also action by a subject who does act and who consequently has a fundamental nature categorically opposed to that of the object matter of action. Social science must also be relevant to action and to the kind of action to which it is relevant. But this is not action upon an inert, passive object matter. To some extent men do indeed act upon other men. Indeed, they also must do so in the actual world, or in any possible world, as in enforcing law and in education. But, on the one hand, it is clearly of the essence of that ideal human social life which men as men strive to realize that no individual ought to use any other as a means. Action of man upon man is necessary or defensible only to the extent that the man acted upon is not a moral person in the ideal or complete sense. And it must be one of the basic ideals of social policy to reduce to a minimum both the fact and the need of such action, to treat all men as free and equal persons, so far as obviously greater evils are not involved. When any individual does act upon another, the relationship is not truly social. And, incidentally, the technique and concepts involved in such action are sharply different from what is involved in the action of men upon inert objects. Action upon men takes such forms as coercion and deception, which have no meaning in the relations of man to physical nature—in addition to being universally recognized as intrinsically immoral.[4]

Social action, in the essential and proper sense, is group self-determination. The content or process is rational discussion, of which science itself—the pursuit and establishment of truth—is the primary type, for truth is a value, established by criticism, and a social category. Discussion is social problem-solving, and all problem-solving includes (social) discussion. As directive of social action, discussion has for its objective the solution of (i.e., the truth about) *ethical* problems, the establishment of agreement upon ethical ideals or values, for the reconciliation of conflicting interests. Ethical ideals have for their content right or ideal relations between given individuals and also, and more fundamentally, ideal individuals, to be created by ideal social institutions, which form the immediate objective of social action.

In their social, superindividual, normative character, values are objective. No discussion can be carried on in propositions beginning with the words "I want." Everyone—when not momentarily defending a theory to the contrary—recognizes a difference between individual preference and what ought to be, between personal taste and good taste, between personal opinion or wish and truth. Thus values belong to a value-cosmos which has the same kind of validity, or reality, for our thinking as the external physical world.[5]

4. Competitive social play calls for discussion in this connection and also the vital problem of leadership.

5. The only significant difference is in the possibility of measurement, in various senses, in physical phenomena, whereas values, like preferences, are quantitatively compared by estimation only. The prior claim to validity made for data of sense-observation is untenable, for the reason that objectivity in this field is established only by verification by other observers, which depends on intercommunication and also on the competence and integrity of the observers.

Social action consists, concretely and for the most part, in making, which is to say changing, the law, including public and constitutional law, which is the main repository of social institutions as subject to socially voluntary and deliberate change. In practice, social policy is discussed chiefly in connection with the selection of individuals who are to act as agents of society in carrying into effect the policies decided upon, or who in varying degrees are intrusted with the concrete formulation of the policies themselves. The social problem in the strict sense, however, is purely intellectual-moral. All physical activity involved in social-legal process is carried out by individuals who act as the agents of society, in so far as they are true to the trust confided to them. Social action, which is social decision, uses as data both facts and cause-and-effect relations, pertaining both to nature and to man. But the social problem is not one of fact—except as values are also facts—nor is it one of means and end. It is a problem of values. And the content of social science must correspond with the problem of action in character and scope.

VI

Social Causation[1]

R. M. MacIver's book is more a philosophical discussion of the meaning of causation with reference to social phenomena than an essay on scientific method, or even "methodology," in social science. What can be done in reviewing such a work, in a compass about one-twentieth that of the book itself, must be limited to indicating its general character and briefly discussing the author's position on a few major issues. To be useful, one must necessarily be somewhat negative; and to be brief, one must be somewhat dogmatic. The difficulties are rather especially great in the present case because of the unusual extent to which the reviewer finds himself in general agreement with the author's position and yet dissatisfied with its development and exposition, while recognizing the high intellectual and literary quality of the book. It is likely that the major differences of viewpoint between the reviewer and the author are connected with the reviewer's approaching the general problem more from the standpoint of a social science other than sociology—namely, economic theory, which in its methodology resembles natural science of the theoretical and quantitative type represented by mechanics. The problem set by the title is, of course, to bring out what social causation has in common with causation in other fields of inquiry, and the important differences. Thus, the author's task calls for a survey of the whole field of knowledge and for an effort to distinguish its main divisions, from the standpoint of the types of explanatory thinking involved.

In the reviewer's thinking, the philosophical issue in the interpretation of causality centers in the ambiguous and varying relation between knower and known, or, in philosophical jargon, between "subject" and "object." That is, the difficulty in the analysis of knowledge lies in the varying kinds and degrees of opposition or assimilation between these two entities. At one extreme we have the direct self-knowledge of the individual subject. Here the pri-

1. R. M. MacIver, *Social Causation* (Boston: Ginn & Co., 1942). Reprinted by permission from *The American Journal of Sociology*, Vol. XLIX, No. 1 (July, 1943).

mary fact is assimilation or identity; and, while separation and inter-relationship are evidently involved in the knowing relation, they present a peculiar difficulty for discursive thought and linguistic expression. At the other extreme we have the matter-of-fact knowledge, through sense perception, of the external physical world of inert objects. Here the primary fact of common sense—especially in the modern, scientifically sophisticated variety—is opposition between knower and known. Yet philosophical analysis is forced to recognize that man is also a part of nature; and the superficial opposition also breaks down from the other side, for physical objects have an ultimate kinship with mind.

Between and around these two poles of thinking lie many complications and perplexities. Of these, the most important center in the intermediate and ambiguous position (for the individual knower) of other knowers, who have to be recognized as both objects and subjects, in a relationship which is fully as puzzling for the individual, though in a different way, as the relation between himself as knower and as known in his own self-consciousness. The crux of the difficulty here is that the individual must immediately recognize, as soon as he begins to think seriously about it, that all knowledge is itself "social"; it is based on intercommunication between individuals, each of whom is both subject and object, both to himself and to all others in the thinking community in which knowledge has its being. Apart from society, we can perhaps conceive of mental life, but only in the sense of unordered, chaotic "fantasy" or the equally unorganized perception of the "buzzing, booming confusion" which William James attributed to the newborn infant. Certainly, neither would be "knowledge," to say nothing of understanding.

It seems to the reviewer that the first, and perhaps the major, hiatus in Professor MacIver's treatment is his complete failure to confront this fact of the social character of knowledge. From this point of view, human society is fundamentally intellectual activity. But modern thought cannot envisage man in any aspect without being driven back to a genetic and evolutionary view; and, from this standpoint, overt action is unquestionably prior to thinking, both in social life and in that of the individual. Our author fails completely (at least in this book) to give any explicit consideration to conduct, either individual or social, in its relation to thinking and knowledge. He does not mention the fact that in the animal kingdom, particularly in the "social" insects, we have empirical knowledge of society without thinking, so far as we know and must assume, while human association also is conscious only in part. In short, he ignores the functional significance of knowledge and thinking. Moreover, he has written a philosophical treatise without any explicit reference to the great historical schools of thought in the field of his subject—pragmatism, positivism, and idealism, to mention only the major divisions and contrasting positions. The result is, to this reader, confusing and difficult to interpret.

To come to grips with causation as the principle of order in the object-matter of knowledge, we begin by confronting the relations between subjectivity and objectivity, in the form of activity and passivity. This opposition enters into all interpretation of persistence and change. The final impression of the book upon the reviewer is that of a kind of vain twisting and turning, almost a squirming, through four hundred pages, in an effort to "have it both ways," in the conception of reality. There is equal insistence that causality is an *active* principle, and, on the other hand, upon concrete methods of problem-solving which are "scientific" in the sense of natural science as purely empirical, phenomenalistic, and positivistic. The main criticism of the book is that the author sees both horns of this intellectual dilemma but fails to recognize it and to see that it has no real solution. The issue arises in connection with every type of subject matter, from physical science through psychology and sociology to the study of "values" in logic or epistemology, aesthetics, and morals. The author wrestles with it over a large part of the field, but he never makes clear either the issue itself or his own position toward it. Rather, he seems to take first one side and then the other, in bewildering confusion. In the mind of the reviewer the only tenable position is to recognize that causality always has both aspects; it is at once an empirical and a dynamic concept. Yet the two principles are logically opposed, even antithetical, in meaning. The nearest we can come to a solution is through a kind of pragmatism. For "practical" purposes—and this includes the purposes of knowing as well as of acting—we must adopt the empirical, descriptive view; causality is a matter of discoverable and describable order in phenomena. But it is also true that this empirical or positive knowledge is never satisfying and that, further, we never really stop with generalized phenomenal description; in the discussion of any subject matter we always use interpretive principles of a non-empirical, metaphysical, more or less dynamic, character.

This is conspicuously true in physical science, where the metaphysical principles in question take the form of "forces." (In modern physics these are replaced by "field theory," running in terms of some conception of "hyperspace," which is even further from empirical knowledge than is the concept of force.) "Force" has bothered students and thinkers from the beginning of modern science, and they have struggled to get rid of it (on the principle of "Occam's Razor") and to use only equations of motion. But this simply cannot be done. Prerelativity physicists, notably Poincaré, made it clear that a purely empirical mechanics is impossible. The conception of some kind of "real interaction" between physical bodies is indispensable to thought. The simplest mechanical phenomenon—that of impact—cannot otherwise be pictured or thought of as real. MacIver himself really argues for this position throughout chapter ii and effectively criticizes such phenomenalists as Pearson, Russell, Cohen, Ogden, and Richards, and the sociologist Lundberg, as well as Hume, who "reduce" causation to uniformity or regularity of sequence (p. 63). But he himself remains ambiguous as well as halfhearted. He really comes out with the positive position that causality is simply "the ways of things" (an expression quoted from Montague), though the last section of the chapter insists upon the reality of the principle of causation as something more than empirical sequence (or accompaniment).

MacIver's position is weak in his refusal frankly to recognize that the positivists are right in insisting that causality in this "real" sense is "anthropomorphic" or "animistic," epithets which to the scientific mind are even more damning than "metaphysical." Men cannot think about anything in wholly unanthropomorphic terms. This is hardly a mystery. Long before the advent of Ward and Whitehead, Huxley pointed out in connection with Hume's example of the billiard balls that we cannot finally picture physical objects as real—as persistently and actively real—without reading into them some rudiment of mind, some kinship with ourselves. Pure existence cannot be thought of entirely without activity, and the only intelligible meaning of activity is that of will. If one is determined to have a "monistic" theory of reality (which to this reviewer is absurd as well as dogmatic), it must certainly be formulated in idealistic terms. The difficulty with this position is that if it is carried to its logical conclusion it results in solipsism, or perhaps in the sheer dogma of an "absolute" cosmic mind into which the reality neither of individual minds nor of "objects," as known to experience, can be fitted intelligibly.

The ambiguity and untenability of MacIver's position—or his lack of a position—come out in his repudiation of indeterminacy with reference to the Heisenberg principle (p. 32), and most clearly in a long chapter on "Cause as Responsible Agent," where he comes nearest to confronting the fact of will (Part III, chap. viii). Here, while formally insisting on the nature of human beings as "dynamic participants" (p. 236) in the causal order and on the reality of the act of choice (p. 240), the substance of the argument reduces to the conventional positivistic "explanation" of freedom of choice as an illusion. The contradiction, or equivocation, is apparent throughout Parts III and IV, which present, respectively, the author's "Analytic Approach" and his "Interpretation." He argues nobly, effectively, and correctly for the reality of motives and for the necessity of taking them into account for the understanding of human behavior and social phenomena. But the nearest he ever comes to interrelating the two factors, empirical uniformity and "real" cause, is in the presentation of a sharp antithesis between the physical and the social realms. "The chain of physical causation does not need mind except for its discovery. The chain of social causation needs mind for its existence" (p. 263).

The antithesis is false in both parts. Physical causation also ultimately needs mind, of a sort, to be "real"; and social causation does not need it and cannot use it for the purposes of "science," properly interpreted. The author presently adds:

There is no point in seeking to apply to social systems the causal formula of classical mechanics, to the effect that if you know the state of a system at any instant you can calcuate mathematically, in terms of a system of co-ordinates, the state of that system at another time. We simply cannot use such a formula. It fits into another frame of reference.

But social "science," in so far as it goes beyond mere taxonomy and attempts to explain events and at the same time sticks to scientific concepts and methods, does use precisely this formula and no other. If it also recognizes conscious states or attitudes as a factor in its subject matter, these are treated as "epiphenomena," as simply "parallel" to the empirical order, without adding anything to the latter, and as superfluous for scientific discussion. Motives in human behavior play the same role in discussion as forces in mechanics; they are essential for ultimate intelligible interpretation, and in this case we know them as directly and as certainly as we know physical objects; but they are supernumerary, for science itself is descriptive and analytical. As far as science is concerned, free will, which is the only real dynamism, is either an illusion or simply a methodological limitation. Social science should recognize this limitation and admit that it has nothing to say about it beyond recognizing its existence as a limitation upon regularity and its place in our interpretive thinking. In so far as the activities of will are to be made intelligible, it is the task of philosophy and, perhaps, of literature and art.

However, the limitation due to freedom is relatively unimportant in a quantitative sense and with reference to any phase of social phenomena which anyone would think of discussing in scientific terms and in sober, non-figurative language. Free choice, based on genuine mental activity and not finally explicable in terms of antecedent conditions, is of very limited scope even in the individual life, even though infinitely important. Its significance as a limitation of scientific treatment is greater the narrower the area within which one may be interested in "predicting," i.e., describing, in terms of reliable and stable patterns of uniformity of coexistence and sequence. But, even in the narrowest range, factors which we must call "caprice" and "accident" are indubitably more important than will or free choice in setting limits to scientific generalization, though the two categories cannot be clearly distinguished. The great bulk of individual conduct, bodily and mental, must be conformable to established patterns as a condition of the individual's own effective functioning, specifically as a "free" individual; and this is more pronouncedly true of that part of his conduct which is properly called "social." For the most part, social phenomena come under the "laws" of physics and chemistry; of biology and psychology, including logic; and of anthropology, as the general science of culture.

If we examine social phenomena and our knowledge about them, with a view to discovering the differences between social and natural science, as science, the major difference will undoubtedly be found in the enormously greater role played by "history" in contrast with non-historical science. That is, the "independent variables" and the forms of their interrelations are to a vastly greater degree "functions of time"—of chronological as well as clock time —in comparison with the constant or recurrent features. MacIver refers to history several times, particularly in Section II of chapter ix (from which we have quoted just above), which is entitled "The Special Case of the Social Sciences." He mentions "the unreturning stream of history" (p. 256) and here and elsewhere stresses the "uniqueness of historical configurations." But what he is interested in is the limitations of experimental method, and he nowhere discusses the relation between history and science, in the narrower meaning in which it contrasts with history, or the relation between social science (in this narrower meaning) and human history.

There are, of course, historical sciences dealing with nature, inanimate as well as animate; such are historical astronomy or cosmology, geology (in contrast with physical geography), and evolutionary biology. But, when we speak of "science" without qualification or explanation, we naturally think of laboratory science or of statistical induction. The propositions of such sciences are hypothetical for the most part; they describe associative relations among phenomena or events, not phenomena or events as actual, at a particular point in space-time. They run in the form of "if this, then that"—or, correctly speaking—if "this" is present in a certain magnitude or degree, "that" is to be expected to accompany or follow in some corresponding magnitude or degree. MacIver's weakness with respect to the quantitative aspect of science will call for notice presently, in another connection. Our point at the moment is simply that the historical character of social data presents a difference from natural science only in degree, and no difference in the ultimate meaning of scientific method. The propositions of history, natural or human, are also essentially "timeless," in the metaphysical sense, in so far as history itself is scientific. This quality of science, even when it describes irreversible changes and non-recurrent sequences, is surely familiar to anyone who has made any serious study of the philosophy of science. It is often expressed by saying that, for science, time is essentially a spatial dimension. The philosophy of Bergson in particular centered around the contrast between such time—mere duration—and "real time." The latter, as Bergson also emphasized, is intelligible only in terms of will—really active or creative change.

We have mentioned, as an important limitation of MacIver's treatment, that he has so little to say about quantity and quantitative relations. This comes out particularly in his discussion of the notion of equilibrium and most specifically in his references to economics, which he uses as the main illustration of "error" in the use of the equilibrium concept (see especially chap. vi, Sec. I, "Equilibrium and Precipitant"). The entire chapter, entitled "Cause as Precipitant," shows a predilection for the "romantic" view of causality, as centering in catastrophic events or discontinuities, and a repugnance for the conception of it as orderly process, and particularly for stable quantitative relations. The meaning of the very concept of an "event" is interpreted in this way, which, of course, is in harmony with everyday usage, reflecting the interests of the man on the street. Numerous examples are cited, such as the spark which starts a forest fire, the assassination which precipitates a world war, etc.

It is true that there are such phenomena and that they present a certain difficulty for the quantitative conception of causality favored by scientific thinkers. That the difficulty is not insuperable for scientific method in general is proved by the simple fact that men are able to predict the consequences of such events, and even the events themselves and their magnitude, accurately enough to make such knowledge useful for action. The root of the apparent anomaly—the failure of quantitative correspondence between cause and effect—is well brought out by the case of a spark and the resulting conflagration or explosion. The phenomenon centers in the release of stored "potential energy"; this is admittedly a non-empirical, metaphysical conception and is somewhat repugnant to the scientific mind, but it has to be recognized and used in scientific thought. All the higher phenomena of life, everything beyond photosynthesis (which is the opposite phenomenon), consist essentially of the release of potential energy. All animal life is a species of combustion, including all that goes on in our own bodies. And practically all our control over natural phenomena, all our ability to use nature for human purposes, centers in the mysterious capacity of thought and will to direct the mode of release of potential energy in living and non-living nature, beginning with our own nerves and muscles. To a limited extent we are also able to direct its accumulation, especially in agriculture. But the growing plant is finally no exception to the downhill flow of energy. Like a hydraulic dam, the fixation of a certain amount of carbon merely catches and temporarily imprisons a minute quantity of energy radiated from the sun.

Physical science recognizes unstable as well as stable equilibrium, but it is no exaggeration to say that in fact the latter is infinitely more important. And it is also vastly more important in biological phenomena, and even in those of psychology, where apparent discontinuity and the absence of discoverable quantitative equivalence are most striking. Modern electronic physics is, indeed, based on the notions of ultimately unstable equilibrium and ultimate discontinuity. Here quantitative theory runs in terms of statistical probability.

But for all "gross" phenomena, for all change subject to any kind of direct observation (with possible reservations for thought itself), an event, in the everyday meaning, is simply a case of exceptionally rapid change, and quantitative relations still hold between what happens and its "conditions."

What MacIver says about economics tends to confirm the reviewer's impression that it is futile for an economic theorist to discuss the problems of this discipline with a sociologist. One or the other seems to lack those primary perceptions of fact and principle in this field which make relevant communication possible—and the question of which one it is can hardly be fruitfully discussed by the parties themselves. To begin with, the writer does not know of any expression by economists which has the implications criticized in the section referred to—e.g., that "change advance[s] by a series of jumps and halts as disturbances successively interrupt states of equilibrium" (p. 164), or that "change itself [is] the incidental and temporary interruption of a persistent order" (p. 169). We do not believe there is any implication in the writings of any recognized economist that the concept of equilibrium implies either stationariness or that change is "slow," whatever that may mean. And the word "normal," as used in the writings of reputable economists, has (so far as known) no other meaning than the reference to equilibrium under conditions defined with respect to the problem under discussion—and entirely different according to the problem. Consequently, such theory does not "minimize change in favor of the *status quo*" (p. 169) except as all scientific explanation of change runs in terms of the unchanging. If one were to look for the "cause" of the sociologist's attitude toward economics (which is virtually that of the man in the street), it is not far to seek; it roots in the abhorrence of the romanticist for anything that can be interpreted as defending anything that exists and the natural suspicion that this is what others are doing. However, it is true and important, if unfortunate, that scientific explanation of what is demonstrates that it is inevitable under the given conditions, which is easily interpreted as a defense.

The meaning of equilibrium in economic theory is best shown by a mechanical analogy. The explanation of a price (or, in fact, any other economic variable) is closely parallel to the explanation of the level of water in a tank or reservoir where water flows in by one pipe and out by another. Given the head of the inflow and the relevant characteristics of the outflow (and the density of the fluid), it is fairly easy to calculate the head in the tank itself which will equalize the two. But it goes without saying that this head will actually prevail only "at equilibrium," when the two rates of flow are in fact equal and the head is stationary *in relation to the given conditions*. There is, to repeat, absolutely no implication that these conditions will be constant over time. The intellectual confusion in denying the relevance of these equilibrium concepts centers in ignoring the practical significance of the role of time. If a change is introduced in any of the conditions taken as given, the actual level of the water in the tank at any moment could be predicted from all the given conditions; but it would be a complicated function of time, in relation to the "conditions" themselves as functions of time. The equilibrium method is practically indispensable in the interpretation of reality because the given conditions are changing, *not* because they are stationary. It is necessary because changes in the value magnitude to be predicted lag behind changes in the given conditions which ultimately determine it.

It is not usually possible to predict the actual magnitude of a dependent variable at any moment, as a function of time, because the necessary data are not available. The use of the method is chiefly to predict the direction of change and to give some idea of the magnitude and speed of the change to be expected; this is possible to the extent that the changes of the independent variable themselves are predictable. These changes, in turn, can often and to a useful extent be predicted through the use of the same method, by bringing them into relation, as dependent variables, with others which are treated as independent, or causal, in relation to them. Thus, the method of economic theory on the whole proceeds by steps or stages from the variables of primary interest back to others which those who apply the theory—businessmen or statesmen—must know, as constants or as functions of time, deriving their information from factual data of the situation in which they act. Of course, it is a part of economic science as a whole to give instruction as to these data or the sources from which they may be obtained; but it is *not* a part of the task of general theory.

A vitally important fact which is almost systematically ignored by the critics of economic theory—including most specialists in other social sciences and many who are called economists, as well as the man in the street—is that the subject as expounded in modern times has been developed with definite reference to the practical needs of free society. This means that "society," represented by the statesman, is not interested in the concrete content of the economic conduct of individuals. The practical relevance of economic theory is chiefly to the problems of social action. But in free society the objective of social control is not usually to make individuals behave in one particular way rather than in another; it is simply to create the conditions under which individuals will be able to realize their individual objectives to the maximum degree, i.e., to act harmoniously, with a minimum of conflict and mutual frustration.

Economic theory is the science which deals with general principles, first, of individual conduct, from the point of view of quantitative means and ends. This is the meaning of "economic behavior," which is one meaning of rational behavior. It takes individual ends as given and is concerned with the rational use of means in realizing ends, i.e., in realizing them to the maximum extent possible with the available means, including knowledge of the ways of using means (technology) as well as concrete resources, material and human. There seems to be some innate repugnance in human nature against this whole point of view, against rationally facing the problem of choice as a comparison of possible alternatives. Human nature seems to be fundamentally romantic in this regard; men in general hate any reference to "costs," which means simply the deliberate comparison of alternatives.

This attitude (prejudice?) is reflected in such statements as those made by MacIver to the effect that the works of an artist or a prophet are primary values because some people get direct satisfaction from them, while "a similar statement does not hold for the trader or the manufacturer or the banker or the engineer or the armament maker" because "the utilities they provide remain also means for those who provide them" (p. 278). To this writer such a statement is a sheer absurdity, a distinction without a difference. Books and pictures, and manufactured products, mercantile services, and anything that is salable are patently alike in being sources of direct satisfaction to their "consumers," who pay money for them and so give up other satisfactions because they prefer these. What MacIver presumably means is that "the direct satisfactions" in the one case are in some sense "higher," on a scale of absolute values, than they are in the other. We need not enter into a discussion of the question raised, beyond suggesting that the author might have said what he meant and observing that it does not fall in the field either of economics or of any other social science, unless this field is made to include all philosophy as the theory of ultimate values. And the answer to the question would not in any way affect the validity or significance of economics as a special science.

Only in a provisional and preliminary sense, however, is economics a science of individual behavior. In its main content it is a social science. It deals with interindividual relations, with co-operation or organization between individuals for increasing efficiency in the use of means to realize their ends. Modern economics treats chiefly of a particular form or mode of co-operative organization—that which is worked out through the exchange of goods and services in markets (more accurately, their purchase and sale against money as an intermediary in exchange). When economists approve or condemn the system, they are speaking as social or moral philosophers, or as ordinary human beings, and not as scientists. Whether they "ought" to do this or not is another problem of values. (But we may note again that any scientific explanation presents a superficial appearance of justifying the results which it explains, since it treats them as necessary consequences of causes.)

It is worth noting also that all "free" co-operation takes the general form of exchange. Moreover, it is difficult to discuss social relations in purely hypothetical or factual terms, entirely free of value judgments, especially if motives are taken into account. In particular, it is difficult to discuss social relations in the context of our own culture without assuming or implying that individual freedom is a good as well as a fact; hence, that the individual has a right to be the judge as to his own wants. It might be better if even these normative judgments were kept more clearly separate from scientific analysis than is usually done in economics textbooks; or it might not; that, again, is a question of values. But sociologists would hardly claim to be in a position to throw stones at economists on this point—and the statement applies to the work under review. As a sociological datum we may throw in the observation that the traditions of literature and learning as well as religion manifest a romantic-aristocratic prejudice against "the market"; practically anything that has a connection with money is regarded as "sordid." But the market is simply a mechanism for organizing relations of mutual advantage, which is assumed to be a good; and, incidently, the free-market organization leaves any persons who do not like the terms of co-operation established in the market, by the meeting of minds of all interested parties, free to adopt any other terms on which they can agree as better.

These more detailed criticisms bring us back, by way of conclusion, to the larger issues raised by MacIver's treatment as a whole. This discussion must be reduced to the briefest compass and most summary form. The main issue centers in the relation between science and interpretation and the corresponding implications of the concept of causation. As already noted, Part IV, which comprises the last third of the work, bears the title, "Interpretation." It starts out in the same general way as the book as a whole. The first section (of chap. x, "The Realm of Conscious Being") deals with "The Dynamic Realms" and presents a classification more or less parallel with the "Modes of the Question Why," distinguished in chapter i, Section II. As in the rest of the book, the author constantly insists on "real" causation, here under the name of "The Dynamic Assessment" (meaning essentially the rational evaluation of objectives); but, at the same time, whenever he gets down to the brass tacks of concrete problems, he insists on sociology's being a "positive" science of descriptive analysis and generalization. This dualistic view is, in the mind of the reviewer, philosophically correct. The procedure is open to criticism, first, in the detail (but surely a very important detail) that the treatment of scientific method seems to strive to ignore the quantitative aspects of cause and effect and the logical method of "concomitant variations," which has become nearly the whole procedure of modern inductive science. The author's theory of method ignores the conception of "function and variable"; and, even when he is explicitly discussing statistical procedure, he seems to strive to avoid quantitative correspondence so far as possible. In fact, of course, the "all-or-none" relationship is extremely rare in nature, if it occurs at all; and it is logically a special case of the broader principle. But our author prefers to think in terms of the methods of agreement and difference, with the main emphasis on difference (see especially p. 65 n.).

The more general criticism has to do with the failure to distinguish between science and interpretation and to bring out the relation between the two. In the abstract, or logically speaking, the method of science is the same, regardless of the nature of the subject matter. It consists in the discovery of uniformities of coexistence and sequence, regularities or stable patterns in the time and space relations of observed data, which are not apparent in the data themselves. The main differences in the meaning of causation in natural and social science center in two facts. The first is the meaning of observation. Strangely enough, our author does not mention this difference in either of his discussions of the major divisions of the field of knowledge. If the fact that social data are derived through intercommunication rather than through direct sense observation may be regarded as not belonging to the nature of causation, this certainly cannot be said of communication as an essential feature of the social process—unless one adopts the position of physical behaviorism, which the author is throughout particularly concerned to combat (and it is one of the most useful features of his book). Moreover, if intercommunicative activity is relegated to the realm of interpretation rather than to that of observation and induction—a kind of quasi-behaviorism—it nonetheless calls for explicit discussion in a book of this sort. But communication seems to be mentioned but once, and rather cursorily (in the concluding paragraph of the last chapter of Part III, p. 264), as incidental to the notion of "imaginative reconstruction."

With respect to the division of the field of knowledge, from the standpoint of principles of interpretation, the schemes given in chapters i and x are difficult to reconcile, and both seem vulnerable at many points. Attempts of this sort are, of course, familiar, especially from the hands of sociologists, back to the famous hierarchy of Auguste Comte. The results differ widely from one author to another, and the problem raised, however important, cannot be discussed here. But the writer would offer two or three criticisms of MacIver's second scheme (pp. 272–73), with only brief reference to the more elaborate (and more confused?) layout given in chapter i.

The first step is a division of all "Being" into three realms: the physical, the organic, and the conscious. These must be interrelated in some way with the scheme of four "nexi" (p. 271): the physico-chemical, the biological, the psychological, and the social; presumably they correspond to the first three. The third is said to have three varieties or aspects, "exhibiting, respectively, objective, motivation, and design"—all modes of "teleological activity." The author continues:

In this form of activity we introduce for the first time the relation of means and ends, the emergence into the realm of consciousness of the relation of organs and functions. As this form of activity becomes socially articulate, two interdependent systems or orders gradually become distinct, the system of apparatus or means, and the system of values or ends. These we designate respectively the technological order and the cultural order. The social order itself is the scheme of relationships between social beings.... In the social order the ... social nexus for the first time appears [p. 271].

Then we are told explicitly that the three orders—cultural, technological, and social—lie "within . . . the realm of conscious Being" (p. 272).

After close study the reviewer finds much of this scheme unintelligible. We can understand the ideas of physical being, with and without life, and of life with and without consciousness. But the relation between conscious being and society is quite obscure. For symmetry, the meaning would be that conscious being may be either social or non-social; but in that case "social being" should be introduced as a fourth level. The intent of the discussion, in this chapter and in the book as a whole, seems to be rather to identify the social and the conscious. But the facts surely call for recognition both of conscious being, which is not social, and of social being, which is not conscious. Specifically with reference to human society and to its scientific discussion in sociology and anthropology, conscious activity plays a highly various, problematic, and, on the whole, rather limited role. The distinctive interpretive conception would rather be habit, formed in the individual and transmitted in the group by unconscious imitation. And a place must certainly be made for social forms and changes which result unintentionally and unconsciously from acts which are individually conscious, in the sense of purpose or (conscious) teleology. If teleology is not restricted to conscious purpose, then the biological nexus of function all comes under this head. It would seem that the bulk of social process and change consists of activities which fall within the realm of behavior which lies somewhere in this region of the "functional" (in a broad, loose interpretation) but unintentional, whether conscious or unconscious.

The author's scheme not only leaves the order of categories confused and obscure but finds no place for conduct which is at once consciously social and consciously purposive, i.e., for all deliberate group activity. That is, it excludes the phenomena of democratic political action and the similar activities of the infinite variety of voluntary private associations—unless, again, these are to be dealt with in physical-behavioristic terms, in accord with the canons of positive science in the strictest and narrowest interpretation. If they are to be dealt with "realistically," in the higher meaning of the term and in accord with the position our author so ably espouses in the central section of his book, it is clearly necessary to recognize the category of "social mind," of group feeling and knowledge, and of group deliberation and choice.

Finally, the identification of values with ends conceals or denies one of the most important distinctions which has to be made in any realistic discussion of conscious teleology. This is the distinction between thinking or deliberating about the procedure for realizing given ends (the appropriate use of means) and deliberation about what ends to pursue, in terms of more general purposes or ideals. (Confusion on this point has been noticed in connection with the author's misconception of the meaning of the economic as a behavior category.) Partly, no doubt, because popular usage and thinking eschew anything resembling careful analysis, there is no established terminology for clearly referring to this distinction; but the minimum departure from general usage would seem to call for the use of the words "end" and "value" for the purpose—though value has other meanings, including both economic value (relative magnitude of different given ends) and even pure mathematical magnitude as such.

VII

"What Is Truth" in Economics?[1]

It seems that a great many thoughtful people in the world are like Pontius Pilate in that they ask a question of our title, but "do not wait for an answer." But a considerable number differ from him in the interesting respect that instead of asking others the question, they volunteer to give the answer themselves, to others and to the world, without waiting to be asked. This leads to the writing of books of varying character and size, which one suspects are more interesting on the average to their authors than they are to any considerable number of readers. And to many of those who do read them this may be a comforting thought, since it means that books on methodology probably do not do much damage. The chief reservation would be that they are most likely to be read and taken seriously by the young.

Hutchison's methodology or philosophy of economics is of a sort which is particularly irritating to this reviewer, especially because it is so common, among people who "ought to know better." The author is a positivist, i.e., one of those who always think of "science" with a capital *S* (if they do not always write it that way) and use it in a context which conveys instructions pronounced in the awe-inspired tone chiefly familiar in public prayer. This emotional pronouncement of value judgments condemning emotion and value judgments seems to the reviewer a symptom of a defective sense of humor. The attempt to build a social science on these foundations suggests that the human race, and especially a large proportion of its "best minds," having at long last (a very long last) found out that the objects of nature are not like human beings—are not actuated by love and hate and caprice and contrariness, and subject to persuasion, cajolery, and threats—have logically inferred that human beings must be like natural objects, and so viewed by the seeker of knowledge about them.

1. Review of T. W. Hutchison's *The Significance and Basic Postulates of Economic Theory* (London: Macmillan & Co., Ltd., 1938). Reprinted by permission from the *Journal of Political Economy*, Vol. XLVIII, No. 1 (February, 1940).

We read only a few pages into Hutchison's book before coming to the development of the all-important distinction between science and philosophy, illustrated by an example which in fact admirably illustrates the superficiality and dogmatic oversimplification involved in the author's own position.

The reason why scientists, unlike philosophers, can build on and advance their predecessors' work rather than each being simply "influenced" by it and starting afresh right from the beginning at the same problems with some complete new system, is that "scientists" have definite, agreed, and relatively conclusive criteria for the testing of propositions, solutions, and theories which "philosophers" do not accept [p. 7].

The meaning, if it has one, is clearly, "go thou and do likewise." The illustration is that of two imaginary economists in an argument as to whether the check system did or did not exist in present-day Paraguay. If they were scientific, they might themselves go to Paraguay and investigate. In that case, the argument might be settled by their actually having a check before them. "Then, having settled the scientific dispute, they might begin a philosophical dispute . . ." as to whether they had got "the real check-an-sich" or only "the idea or appearance of a check" (p. 8). Now it is surely obvious, without any reference to transcendental reality, that it would be impossible to assert on the basis of any printed slip of paper or other object "before them" whether "the check system" existed or not. One would certainly have to know the history of the "object" and the laws and business usages connected with it. In fact, it is inadmissible to speak at all of "the" check system, if one is making any serious pretense to accuracy; and if one is talking about a check system at all, one is certainly concerned with purposes aimed at and results achieved as well as with the existence and paths of motion of printed pieces of paper or any physical events.

In short, such a contrast between glorified science and a caricature of philosophy is not helpful but rather the opposite. But Hutchison's conception of science has a specious plausibility and a strong intellectual appeal, and that is precisely what makes it dangerous and pernicious and in that sense important, especially (again) because of its appeal to the young. It is utterly remote from "reality," in the "real" sense, in contrast with the artificial and arbitrary use of the word by positivist philosophers, who at bottom are simply bad metaphysicians. The appeal of this method is oversimplification which amounts to serious falsification. Where there are or can be "definite, agreed, and relatively conclusive criteria for the testing of propositions, solutions, and theories," there are no very serious intellectual probems and no methodological problems whatever. The problem of truth in Hutchison's subject matter is not one of finding such tests; any tests which can be proposed would rather themselves have to be tested by the propositions of economic theory as already understood.

Hutchison continues: "The scientist proceeds by means of the two inextricably interconnected activities of empirical investigation and logical analysis, the one, briefly, being concerned with the behaviour of facts, and the other with the language in which this is to be discussed" (p. 9). This statement, like the generalization previously quoted, may pass as a definition of science, though obviously a restricted, if not an arbitrary, one. If science is so defined, the fraction of human knowledge which is "scientific" is almost disappearingly small and includes no knowledge of human or of social data, or specifically of economics, and most specifically of economic theory—if the key words (including "empirical," "logical," and "facts") are taken in the meaning of ordinary usage.

One who has read critically so far in the book will be moved to read on with the particular object of finding out what the author actually means by such terms as "empirical" and "logical." He will not have much success. But he will find that Mr. Hutchison does not stick at all to the principles so emphatically put forward in chapter i—which fact is on the whole rather to his credit, though it means that he really has no philosophical position at all. As to observation, he will be able to discern, on coming to chapter v (the last in the book except for a conclusion and an appendix) which in some measure comes to grips with some of the more common and familiar concepts of economics, that the author has quite dropped his rigorous and "hard-boiled" (dogmatic!) pose. Speaking of propositions about such mental attitudes as expectation and the derivation of utility from a commodity, he simply states that he *prefers* "the ordinary usage by which such propositions *are regarded* as definitely verifiable or falsifiable" (p. 146; my italics). He finds a "core of truth in the common-sense 'comparison of utilities' [between persons]" (p. 148), and approves of including "welfare economics" in "economic science." This is a "far cry" from looking for printed pieces of paper (where even the meaning of the printing is assumed to raise no questions).

In the few pages in which the meaning of testing is considered, our author first finds a " 'conventional' element" in the tests which "one lays down" (p. 145) and then apparently asserts that all tests are "purely conventional" (p. 152; also 147, 148, etc., on the "ordinary use of words," and *how words are in fact used*" [author's italics]). According to this theory, a logically or factually wrong statement is on the same level as a piece of faulty grammar which in no way affects the meaning of what is said. Certainly no one believes that to be true. But in the meantime (p. 147) we also learn that propositions and concepts fulfil the scientific criteria (of empirical testability) "if we *choose* to define them as doing so, and do *not* fulfill it if we do not choose" (author's italics). Here truth is merely a game in which the players are free to make any rules they please.

Thus when our author "gets down to cases," he seems to abandon entirely his stern insistence on factual testing and to fall back upon the naïve conceptions of common sense. His philosophical position, in the brave passages where he professes one, would seem to be that of "logical positivism"; that is—if one can hope to state a position which one does not believe to be tenable in a way that would be acceptable to someone who does believe it—knowledge is (or true propositions are) relative to objects of two sorts: (*a*) "things," such as printed pieces of paper, which can be identified by pointing and naming, and (*b*) verbal definitions, which are a pure matter of the use of language in accord with conventional or arbitrary rules: "Purely theoretical analysis consists in the manipulation of concepts in accordance with the rules laid down in their definitions" (p. 30). It is simply assumed that there is actually no disagreement—that no "test" is ever necessary or in question—either as to observed facts or as to the meaning and the truth of any stated inference. One must suppose that there is never any question even as to whether there is disagreement or not, or whether rules arbitrarily laid down are actually followed.

Now, in the present writer's opinion, all this is fundamentally misleading and wrong, if not actual nonsense. The fundamental propositions and definitions of economics are neither observed nor inferred from observation in anything like the sense of the generalizations of the positive natural sciences or of mathematics, and yet they are in no real sense arbitrary. They state "facts," truths about "reality"—analytical and hence partial truths about "mental" reality, of course—or else they are really "false."[2] Economics and other social

2. I must deny that any conclusion which can claim any sort of logical validity, or even any meaning, can be drawn from any proposition which is really arbi-

sciences deal with knowledge and truth of a different category from that of the natural sciences, truth which is related to sense observation—and ultimately even to logic—in a very different way from that arrived at by the methodology of natural science. But it is still knowledge about reality. Its character will be considered in more detail after a few general observations about the knowledge problem.

The starting point of any discussion in this field is recognition that all discussion ultimately rests upon statements of fact and principle which are assumed to be accepted as true and which cannot be defended by argument if they are denied or questioned. If one begins with confident and sweeping assertions about "tests," one is under a corresponding obligation to make it unambiguously clear what sort of propositions do and what sort do not need testing and what tests are accepted as valid and not themselves in need of testing. This follow-up is just what we do not find in Mr. Hutchison's essay.

Even the briefest survey of the problem must recognize at least three types or fields of knowledge, in contrast with Mr. Hutchison's two, and the third type, not considered by him, is by far the most important for the problems of economics with which he is supposed to be dealing. The three fields are: first, knowledge of "the external world," including both the plain man's knowledge of everyday reality and the physical scientist's knowledge of his primary data of observation; second, the truths of logic and mathematics (the problem here is whether knowledge of this sort is knowledge about the same objective reality as the first category or whether it is about thinking or mind—or what is the relation between the two); third, knowledge of human conduct. It is of course in this last field that economic problems lie, though, as will be emphasized, they consti-

---

trary, including mathematics and formal logic itself. This will be more fully explained below. Statements by mathematicians and mathematical logicians which are partly careless formulation and partly based on error of fact are in my opinion largely responsible for the prevalence of this untenable view.

As to economics, Hutchison approvingly quotes Professor Schumpeter's statement that Gossen's law "is not a law of economics . . . but an assumption," which is "in principle arbitrary," and "we could . . . make the opposite assumption, and it could not be called false" (p. 134). I must say categorically that we could not make the opposite assumption, or any divergent assumption, and tell the truth or talk sense about economic behavior. The principle referred to as Gossen's law is a descriptive fact about such behavior, which is a reality. As Whitehead has said of natural science, economics is not a fairy story.

tute but a small fraction of that field and only one of several categories which must be recognized within it, and a still smaller fraction of knowledge about human "behavior," if behavior and conduct are most correctly and usefully defined. The subject matter of relevant knowledge of conduct, in contrast with mechanical response, is primarily human interests—interests in action, in contrast with the interest in knowledge—and the relation between interests and action, in our knowledge of both and in action itself.

Regarding our knowledge of the external world, the first fact which calls for emphasis is that the data of immediate observation cannot be taken on their face, but must be "tested." The bare fact that an individual sees, or thinks that he sees, or reports seeing a physical object or event—in everyday life or in a laboratory—by no means establishes that event as real, or a proposition reporting it as true. In many familiar situations it does not do so even to the observer himself; he sees the "straight staff bent in the pool"; and when observing a sleight-of-hand performance everyone knows that what he "sees" is entirely different from the "reality." Validity has little relation to vividness in the impression or fervor in the report. The "snakes" seen and reported by the sufferer from delirium tremens are probably by no means inferior in such respects to the observations of the scientific zoölogist.

And a second fact, of even greater importance, if possible, is that testing observations is chiefly, and always ultimately, a social activity or phenomenon. This fact makes all knowledge of the world of sense observation, whether that of the plain man or that of the scientist (not to mention knowledge of social data), itself a social activity and a social phenomenon. In addition, it means that all such knowledge is inseparable from (*a*) self-knowledge of the knower and (*b*) knowledge of other knowers and of their knowledge, or of their "minds," and hence of the nature and conditions of knowing and thinking as such. The concrete nature of this testing process is the subject matter of treatises on scientific method, and it is neither possible nor necessary to discuss it in detail here. The essential point for our purposes is that knowledge of external reality presupposes "valid" intercommunication of mental content, in the sense of knowledge, opinion, or suggestion, among the members of a knowing group or intellectual community. A conscious, critical social consensus is of the essence of the idea of objectivity or truth.

Moreover, a consensus regarding truth is itself by no means a "mere" (undisputed) fact. It rests upon value judgments as to both the competence and the moral reliability of observers and reporters. (It is no matter of a majority vote!) Without a sense of honor (as well as special competence) among scientists—if, say, they were all charlatans—there could be no science. And if ordinary normal human beings habitually and systematically lied, or talked dream talk (or reported free association), there would be no possibility of any knowledge, or of the existence of minds or intelligence. There could be no "feeling" of truth or of reality; we could never form these notions, or have any communicable, and hence any intellectual, experience. "We" could not exist at all as minds or selves. There might, indeed, be animate beings, or animate objects, making biologically "correct" responses to their environment and to one another's physical behavior. But anything that can properly be called knowledge on the part of any subject is unthinkable apart from self-knowledge and valid intercommunication with similar (competent and trustworthy) knowing selves, living, thinking, and acting in and in relation to a common world of not-self, which is the general object of knowledge. This naturally suggests the question as to how we do know (imperfectly, of course) the content of one another's minds, or how we intercommunicate. This is the problem of the third field of knowledge. But we must first make a few observations about the second field.

With respect to the highly abstract propositions which form the axioms of logic and mathematics, the essential fact is that all such knowledge is at the same time knowledge of the external objective world and knowledge, in a special sense, of the way in which minds work. In the former aspect it differs from the more concrete knowledge which forms the content of the sciences only or primarily in the degree of generality or abstraction. The propositions of algebra, as well as those of arithmetic (in contrast with those of economic theory, as we shall see) are verifiable in the crude empirical sense of that term, to any degree of accuracy which is thought worth the cost, by counting beans. (The "beans" may be imaginary if the problem-solver's memory and imagination have sufficient power and reliability.) In fact, most of the content of arithmetic and algebra consists essentially of "short cuts" or procedures for saving time in computation, as compared with the prohibitively slow and costly method of getting results by counting. And the propositions of geometry are also empirically verifiable, to any worthwhile degree of accuracy, by drawing and measuring figures.

This will probably not be disputed for the "ordinary" algebra of real numbers and "ordinary" geometry, the geometry of Euclidean space. When we go beyond these realms the matter may seem to be otherwise, but a little critical reflection will show that it is a rather superficial seeming. Propositions which involve such concepts as imaginary numbers, or non-Euclidean space, merely represent a higher degree of abstraction; they are still descriptive of the real world.[3] The fact that we can hypothetically reverse some axiomatic propositions, such as that parallel lines never meet, or postulate the opposite, and use the result in valid reasoning, creates no serious difficulty. We can do this with any proposition with content, as long as there is no explicit contradiction. There is a difference only in degree, not an essential difference in kind, between such reasoning and inference from the simplest hypothesis contrary to fact, such as supposing that an object had been in a different position or had been moving in a different direction or at a different velocity than was actually the case, in discussing an automobile accident or a laboratory experiment.

The apparent universal necessity, or *a priori* validity of any proposition which seems to have it, is far less mysterious than is often represented. It may be true to say that universally necessary propositions are "forms of thought," or laws of intelligence or mind; but such a statement does not mean at all that they are not truths about the real objective world. Rather the *a priori* necessity of any proposition is simply and, in this writer's view, correctly explained by the fact that our minds lack any power of really creative imagination or original intuitive knowledge of superempirical reality, and not by the fact that we possess any such powers. Any statement which "must" be true under all conditions is simply a statement of a fact about the world which is so universal and fundamental for experience that we cannot "think it away" or imagine a situation in which it would not be true. (Hutchison frequently refers in a very matter-of-fact way to what is "conceivable"; e.g., pp. 104, 142.) The real mystery (insoluble to the present writer) is how any mind could imagine, or think it imagined, that there could be a real contrast between the most general features of reality as experienced and what a mind living in and formed by it is able to imagine, or between the fundamental laws of nature and those of thought. The

3. For a brief and particularly illuminating discussion of these problems see the essay "Intelligence and Mathematics," by Harold Chapman Brown, in *Creative Intelligence* (New York: Henry Holt & Co., 1917), pp. 118–75.

higher the degree of abstraction involved, the easier it is to regard a proposition as a form of thought rather than as a fact about the world.

All this must by no means be taken to imply denial or questioning of the reality of reasoning as an activity of mind. But extremely little light is thrown on the nature of reasoning by the traditional treatment of formal logic. The heart of intellectual activity consists in the discernment of similarities and differences, the conjunction and separation or "concomitant variation" of attributes, including behavior over time or associated changes in attributes, all of which is fairly well summed up and indicated in the word "analysis."[4]

With regard to the relation between deduction and observation, or intelligence and the senses, in our knowledge of nature, there is not much that should need to be said. Surely anyone who has made any progress at all in the study of philosophy, or even in private reflection about its problems, can be assumed to know that any simple antithesis between observation and inference is utterly untenable, if not downright foolish. The question as to the primary or immediate data of consciousness is perhaps the main perennial, unsolved and probably unsolvable problem of the theory of knowledge as a whole. What is observation and what is inference are questions on a par with what is truth, if they do not simply restate the same question. It has been a commonplace, at least since the time of Kant, that ordinary "sense perception" is very largely an intellectual operation. And since the dawn of modern science, it has been a matter of arbitrary choice of viewpoint whether what we *actually* "see" is things, qualities, or sensations, or even nerve currents. It is also essentially a commonplace that what we perceive, or are able to perceive, is largely a matter of the "apperceptive mass"—and this involves both expectations and interests.

It should now be clear that we cannot separate the discussion of reality from the discussion of the knowledge of reality, the nature and structure of thinking and the conditions of its validity, or the workings of "mind" (meaning minds). There are two senses in which a distinction can be made between propositions about mind or thinking and propositions about reality. The first relates to "wrong" thinking or to doubt or opinion recognized as question-

---

4. It may be suggested that the nearest we come to creative reasoning is found in "passing to the limit" in mathematical operations. This operation seems difficult to classify as between induction and deduction. "Extrapolative" reasoning has something of the same character and is especially important in natural science.

able. This is a matter of degree. To the extent that any proposition or idea is regarded as false or as affected with uncertainty, its contents are regarded as subjective, as being in somebody's mind rather than in the objective world. (In a real sense the theory of knowledge is the theory of error and illusion.) The second valid distinction, which is familiar in philosophy and which we have had more occasion to discuss at length, is connected with the limits of our power to postulate or to imagine deviations from reality as known. This also is more or less a matter of degree. The axioms of algebra seem "more certain" and unescapable and hence more mental than those of geometry, and the elementary laws of motion (the nature of mass and force) do not seem very far from the status of geometry as to inevitability. Again, the development of the relativity and quantum theories (discontinuity) has cast doubt on the reliability of what can or cannot be imagined as a test of truth.

All this is chiefly a long preliminary to a discussion of the third field of knowledge, in which lie the methodological problems of economics. The whole subject matter of conduct—interests and motivation—constitutes a different realm of reality from the external world, and this fact gives to its problems a different order of sublety and complexity than those of the sciences of (unconscious) nature.[5]

The first fact to be recorded is that this realm of reality exists or "is there." This fact cannot be proved or argued or "tested." If anyone denies that men have interests or that "we" have a considerable amount of valid knowledge about them, economics and all its works will simply be to such a person what the world of color is to the blind man. But there would still be one difference: a man who is physically, ocularly blind may still be rated of normal intelligence and in his right mind.

Second, as to the manner of our knowing or the source of knowl-

5. The reference is to interest in action, in contrast with the interest in knowing. It goes without saying that theoretical and practical interests are inseparably connected, though we can talk about them separately, by abstraction. Our theoretical interest in things as things centers in classification, which means the discovery of similarities and differences, including correlation and concomitant variation and probability. The significance of all this for action is obvious; we "predict" the unknown from the known (both in future time and in the present) and predict the effect of our actions upon materials. (All action ultimately reduces to moving matter in space by the use of our muscles.) Yet we unquestionably have purely intellectual interests which are not reducible to the production of desired modifications in the course of physical events.

edge; it is obvious that while our knowledge ("correct" observation) of physical human behavior and of correlated changes in the physical objects of non-human nature plays a necessary part in our knowledge of men's interests, the main source, far more important than in our knowledge of physical reality, is the same general process of intercommunication in social intercourse—and especially in that "casual" intercourse, which has no important direct relation to any "problem," either of knowledge or of action—which has been found to play a major role in our knowing of the physical world.

Hutchison, like other positivists, pretends that knowledge of people's minds is an inference, from the observation of their bodies, of their physical behavior.[6] The least critical consideration of the al-

6. ". . . Having examined by introspection the marginal utility of different amounts of money income to himself, [the economist] perceives that this 'inside experience' is correlated with a certain 'external' behaviour of his as regards money income. He arrives at the conclusion by 'external' observation that his 'external' behaviour regarding money is similar, in general, to everyone else's. He assumes or draws the analogy from this, therefore, that everyone else is 'internally' similar to himself.

"We again leave on one side the difficulty as to how this 'internal' assumption could conceivably be tested. This is connected with the crudity of the distinction between 'inside' and 'outside' experience. At this stage we want simply to emphasise the more obvious point that our economist cannot get any general results by introspection alone, but only by observation of 'external' behaviour (which may be so delicate as tone of voice, or facial expression), spoken and written words, etc., but which (to continue with this crude and misleading distinction) must be 'external,' whether further inferences or analogies as to the 'inner' experience are drawn or not" (p. 139).

And again: "Ordinarily, if one asks people how they know that a man gets utility out of a commodity, or . . . know that one man gets more utility . . . than another . . . one will probably receive as an answer something to the effect that 'This man regularly spends a greater percentage of his income on this commodity than the other,' or 'When I asked them how they liked this commodity this man exclaimed in one way, the other in another way.' *That is what is called in ordinary language* 'one man getting more utility out of a commodity than another'" (see pp. 147–48; his italics.) This statement might be labeled as a warning, to philosophers and others, as to the kind of thing a philosopher is likely to say under the urge to establish some theory which is far simpler than the facts; certainly, no one thinks that in speaking of an experience of enjoyment he means "exclaiming" or any physical act.

On p. 143 Hutchison enters an express denial that his analysis of "introspection" is in any way to be confused with doctrines of solipsism or behaviorism and says that he makes no assertion about the reality of consciousness or the existence or non-existence of anything. The clear meaning is that he has no philosophical position, and no theory of knowledge which is of any use in doubtful cases, where alone a theory is of any significance. The bare fact that Hutchison completely ignores intercommunication, while he makes all inferred or deduced truth a matter of "convention," means that the final precipitate is mostly confusion.

leged process of "inference" by which we are supposed to learn of the content of others' minds through observation of their physical behavior would show that it is so different from the inferences either of inductive science or of logic and mathematics that a different word should certainly be used. Cooley has used the phrase "sympathetic introspection," which, loose and "literary" as it is, goes deeper into the realities than the positivistic "simplism."

With reference to a given moment, it may be allowable to say that one "infers" another's thought or feeling from, say, uttered sounds and facial expression. But no brute fact is more familiar than the psychological datum that one does not hear or see much more than one understands. What we immediately, consciously, apprehend is the "meaning," and if called upon to reproduce the physical facts we should do so chiefly by "deduction" from the remembered meaning, not from any direct recall of sense data. Surely no one thinks that from any conceivable knowledge of the physical world it would be possible to predict what interests intelligent beings living in it would have, even if all conceivable knowledge of human psychology be thrown in.

What is really in question is the nature of intelligence, which can only be discussed by considering the process by which intelligence is built up in the individual, or by which an intelligent individual comes into existence. "We" undeniably live in a world where intelligence is the property of human beings who are born, live through a common life-cycle and die—both as biological units and as minds. And they are certainly born completely ignorant, without minds, and acquire knowledge and intelligence by a process about which the developed intelligence knows and can say a good deal.[7] Under the conditions of the only world we know anything about, knowledge and intelligence are completely "unthinkable" apart from a continuing and developing social process of learning. This necessarily involves for the learner intercommunication with other selves, including large numbers of selves who know (have learned) vastly more than himself and all of whom live in and react to a world of not-self, about which they habitually intercommunicate. Thus our knowledge of the world and our knowledge of one another and of "mind" in general form inseparable bodies of knowledge which must

7. Whether it is possible for human beings to conceive or imagine an immortal mind, which never learns but is eternally omniscient or at least eternally knows all that it ever knows (or to imagine a community of such minds), is a question which need not be argued here. The reader will be correct in inferring that the writer is very doubtful about it.

be studied in relation to one another, if we are to know anything about any of them or to talk sense about them. All are to be accounted for "genetically" in terms of a twofold historical evolution, in the individual and in the race.

Among the citations with which Hutchison prefaces his fifth chapter (and specifically its first section, on "The 'Psychological Method' ") is the following from Wieser:

"We can observe natural phenomena only from outside, but ourselves from within." The employment of this inner observation is the psychological method, "which finds for us in common economic experience all the most important facts of economy. . . . It finds that certain acts take place in our consciousness with a feeling of necessity. . . . What a huge advantage for the natural scientist if the organic and inorganic world clearly informed him of its laws, and why should we neglect such assistance?" [p. 132].

This position our author proceeds to annihilate—as nearly as one can tell what he means—or at least to ridicule. In the present writer's opinion it is essentially sound, though the analysis is admittedly not carried very far in a philosophical sense by Wieser or by most of those who advocate it.

Observing from within must be interpreted in the light of the social-mental, intercommunicative character of all thinking already insisted upon. It is obvious that knowledge based on such "observation" is intuitive in a special sense as compared with any knowledge of nature, or even with the very highest abstractions ordinarily treated as logical axioms or general forms of valid thinking as such. It is not conceivably possible to "verify" any proposition about "economic" behavior by any "empirical" procedure, if the key words of this statement are defined as they must be defined to be used with relevance and precision. To form the idea of economy or economizing, one must first know that the end of an action is in general more or less different from its empirical result. Economy involves an intention or intended result, which is not amenable to observation in any admissible use of that term.

As to the content, or "basic postulates," of economics, it is surely indisputable, to begin with, that the first of these postulates is the reality of economizing, or economic behavior, the general meaning of which is known to any possible participant in any economic discussion—"intuitively," in the sense already indicated. To repeat, it is not possible by any observation of any act to tell whether or in what degree it is "economic"; indeed, the subject himself rarely knows even approximately, until a considerable time afterward, and never very accurately. (The contrast with mathematical axioms may again be called to mind.) All discussion of economics assumes (and it is certainly "true") that every rational and competent mind knows (*a*) that some behavior involves the apportionment or allocation of means limited in supply among alternative modes of use in realizing ends; (*b*) that given modes of apportionment achieve in different "degrees" for any subject some general end which is a common denominator of comparison; and (*c*) that there is some one "ideal" apportionment which would achieve the general end in a "maximum" degree, conditioned by the quantity of means available to the subject and the terms of allocation presented by the facts of his given situation.[8]

We surely "know" these propositions better, more confidently and certainly, than we know the truth of any statement about any concrete physical fact or event, whether reported by someone else or made by ourselves on the basis of our own experience, and fully as certainly as we know the truth of any axiom of mathematics or of logic. We know them in the same way that one knows one is writing sentences and not simply making dark markings on a white surface, or is reading versus seeing such marks—by living in the world "with" other intelligent beings; we neither know them *a priori* nor by one-sided deduction from data of sense observation.[9]

8. This is one aspect of the intuitive or common-sense notion of economizing. The term refers also, and perhaps primarily, in everyday usage, to the more or less "correct" manipulation of the means employed. This manipulative aspect of economic behavior is treated in the sciences which make up the general body of *technology*, with which economics is not directly concerned. Everyday usage, and everyday thinking, are much confused as to the relation between economy in the allocative sense and "technical efficiency." In brief, the difference is that the choice between technical processes is not affected by the principle of diminishing efficiency and consequently does not give rise to apportioning and proportioning; the correct choice is one of all or none.

It is essential to understand that the concept of "physical" efficiency, as usually employed, is a misconception. It would be valid only in a case where only one physically described and measured result is in question, and where at the same time the means employed are at once limited and available for no other use. Such cases are certainly rare in reality; means are usually economized in any particular use because they are valuable for other uses. According to the most elementary laws of physical science, all the matter and energy which go into any reaction always come out of it quantitatively unchanged, so that efficiency as physically measured is always 100 per cent, which is to say that the conception is without meaning. Any efficiency measurable as a percentage involves evaluation of alternative possible results, the relative usefulness of the output alternative to any given result constituting the "real cost" of the latter.

9. The best illustration of apportionment and of the maximizing of desired results through correct apportionment is undoubtedly the individual's expendi-

A major problem in connection with the basic postulates of economics, and one which surely calls for notice in any serious philosophical discussion of its methodology (but which is not mentioned in Hutchison's volume), arises out of the habitual practice and usage in economic literature of treating the distinguishing fact about goods and services—the fact that they are the subject of economic decision —as a measurable quality in the things themselves. As every student knows, one of the first questions raised in modern philosophy, in connection especially with the transmission theory of vision, was that of what "qualities" really inhere in the object and which ones are in the mind of the observer. It is a familiar observation or remark that values (or some of them) are "tertiary qualities"—on the line of the famous distinction made by Locke between the primary and secondary. Closely connected with this topic is the vitally important matter of quantity and measurement.

The quantity or degree of variable attributes is fundamental for the interest in action, and the concept or feeling of objectivity itself, as against subjectivity, has come for the modern mind to be closely connected with the possibility of measurement and the accuracy attainable. This fact has also greatly influenced our notions of what constitutes "science," especially in English usage. (It is much less true in French.) Economic theory deals with interests as abstract magnitudes (intensities) and hence "naturally" considers them as inhering in the objects of interest, as attributes, and, also as measurable, which two considerations yield the familiar notion of "utility." This way of thinking is doubtless due in part to the fact that utilities receive a kind of measurement through the process of competitive exchange in the market, and in part it is due simply to the intellectual craving for objectification of any subject matter under discussion. Measurement and measurability present problems which cry for discussion, for it is obvious that measuring has a very different meaning in connection with different kinds of variables. The facts which are relevant for economic concepts present a paradox.

---

ture of a given money income in the purchase of "want-satisfying goods or services" (in general and accurate terms, exclusively services) available to him in a perfect market at given prices; but the principle can perfectly well be illustrated from a Crusoe economy.

For the purpose of the present discussion, the conception of economic activity may be limited to "stationary conditions," i.e., behavior relative to given wants, resources, and technical knowledge. Whether or in what cases activity deliberately aimed at changing any of these given conditions is "economic," is a question which raises issues of a higher order of difficulty than those in question here.

On the one hand, there is certainly no question of measuring utility as an objective quality of a good or service, and we apparently do not measure any sensation or feeling as such. For example, a thermometer does not measure temperature as felt but an inferential or theoretical "objective" state of things which is supposedly the uniform basis of the variable temperature sensation.[10]

On the other hand, it is indisputable that in the thinking of civilized man choices are very largely a matter of quantitative comparison. Apart from this fact, there can be no discussion of economics, for the concept of economy or economizing, or the synonymous term, "efficiency," literally loses its meaning. Yet a level of satisfaction, being a mental fact, is not measurable, in the sense in which any physical magnitude is measured. The question whether, or sense in which, the "general economic result," or "that which the individual strives to maximize," is a quantity, has been much under discussion since Edgeworth introduced the distinction between cardinal and ordinal magnitudes, and especially of late, since Hicks and Allen published their "Reconsideration of the Theory of Value,"[11] embodying the indifference-map approach. In the present writer's opinion, the magnitude in question is quantitative in the sense in

10. The saying often quoted from Lord Kelvin (though the substance, I believe, is much older) that "where you cannot measure your knowledge is meagre and unsatisfactory," as applied in mental and social science, is misleading and pernicious. This is another way of saying that these sciences are not sciences in the sense of physical science and cannot attempt to be such without forfeiting their proper nature and function. Insistence on a concretely quantitative economics means the use of statistics of physical magnitudes, whose economic meaning and significance is uncertain and dubious. (Even wheat is approximately homogeneous only if measured in economic terms.) And a similar statement would apply even more to other social sciences. In this field, the Kelvin dictum very largely means in practice, "if you cannot measure, measure anyhow!" That is, one either performs some other operation and calls it measurement or measures something else instead of what is ostensibly under discussion, and usually not a social phenomenon. To call averaging estimates, or guesses, measurement seems to be merely embezzling a word for its prestige value. And it might be pointed out also that in the field of human interests and relationships much of our most important knowledge is inherently nonquantitative and could not conceivably be put in quantitative form without being destroyed. Perhaps we do not "know" that our friends really are our friends; in any case an attempt to measure their friendship would hardly make the knowledge either more certain or more satisfactory!

11. See *Economica*, February and May, 1934. In reply to this, Dr. Oskar Lange defended "The Determinateness of the Utility Function," *Review of Economic Studies*, I (1933–34), 218–25, and a notable series of discussions have followed, chiefly in these two journals. See also Professor J. R. Hicks's *Value and Capital* (Oxford, 1939).

which any subjective state is quantitative and in very nearly the same sense as any objective quality for which we have no accepted technique of measurement and which must consequently be estimated. (The indifference curve corresponds to the use of the zero method in physical measurements.) The main point seems to be that in the absence of any technique of measurement, there is no clear differentiation between a subjective state and an objective quality, and the reference of an experience to the external world or to the mind is shifting and largely arbitrary. This may explain the somewhat anomalous fact that in literary usage the economic result which we attempt to maximize is commonly referred to as "utility," rather than as "satisfaction," though the former term means a quality of things and the usage makes grammar swear at logic.

But this is not the end of the paradox. The most embarrassing fact (which is indisputably a fact) is that actual exchange values certainly do not measure the satisfaction intensities (or "psychic income," or whatever it may be called) with which economic theory deals. These are "hypothetical," such as would be realized by the "economic man," who is postulated as knowing definitely and accurately all the facts and magnitudes, knowledge of which would influence his behavior in any way. These begin with his own tastes and the consequent psychological or subjective effects of consuming given quantities of any commodity, in comparison with all other commodities and also with all other possibilities, including "leisure" or the non-pecuniary values obtainable from the use of any resource outside the market organization. Perhaps the most interesting epistemological datum for economic theory is that we actually both know (everybody who understands the meaning of the proposition knows) that maximum efficiency is (would be) achieved through ideal allocation of allocable resources (that allocation which makes total return a maximum by making the marginal increment of return from the same small unit of the resource equal in all alternative modes of use) and also know that no individual achieves this maximum (or the chances are infinity to one against it). This divergence arises because ignorance, error,[12] and "prejudice" in innumerable forms affect real choices.

12. The economic subject would in many cases have to have perfect foreknowledge, as well as perfect knowledge. This foreknowledge might even have to extend to the infinite future, and, as Hutchison very properly emphasizes (p. 97), it is logically impossible for two individuals to have perfect foresight of each other's actions and to act upon it. More accurately, this is possible only if the activities of both are preconcerted.

Both of the facts just mentioned, the partial conformity of conduct to economic principles and the fact that conformity can only be partial, are really known with "absolute certainty"—in the sense already explained, that we are unable to think away the fact of deliberate activity of the sort described. If conformity were perfect, the behavior in question would cease to be either "economic" or deliberate, and would become a mere mechanical response to a stimulus situation, which is a categorically different matter.[13]

Superficially considered, economic knowledge presents a certain parallelism with our knowledge that a perfect circle has certain properties but that no empirical circle is perfect (or we could not know it if it were). But there is first the categorical difference already mentioned, that one can investigate empirically the imperfections of the circle, to practically any degree of accuracy worth the trouble, while this is possible for economic behavior only within the narrowest limits at best, and in a completely different sense of the word "empirical"—so different as to make it essentially a different word, if it is used at all. Methodologically considered, economics is a highly abstract "concrete deductive" science, similar to geometry or to mathematical mechanics; but in addition its data are intuitive in a far higher or purer sense than is true of mathematics itself (cf. p. 157). A closer parallel to the economic case from the physical world would be that of a law of physics involving a time sequence in phenomena, such as the law that the orbit of a body moving in a gravitational field is one of the conic sections.

The vital difference between the economic law of a maximum and the conic-section principle is that in connection with the former we have two independent sources of information, if not in fact three, which should be distinguished, and they do not agree. We know something about economic behavior and its motives in the same general way that we know about orbits and the "forces" which lie behind them, i.e., through sense observation and inference from

13. The known imperfection of correspondence between motive and result is further proof that we do not infer the former from the latter. Apparently it cannot be too often repeated that conduct cannot be interpreted in terms of positive categories. The phenomenal sequences of positive science cannot in any sense be problem-solving, while this is the most important fact about human conduct. Consequently any attempt to universalize positive categories involves denying the reality of the notion of a problem or solution, or question or answer. Of course it also involves denying the meaning of denial and asserts that illusion and error are themselves illusion and error. Limitations of the economic character of choice, in favor of factors still further removed from positive "factuality," will be considered presently.

observed behavior, in the physical sense. Motive in this connection is closely analogous to physical force.[14] We also, however, know about motive through the general process of intercommunication between our own minds and other minds, which is the fundamental basis of all knowledge, whether of the world or of mind (meaning human minds, primarily normal), and the basis of intelligence itself. The first difficulty of scientific method in economics is that the two main sources of information inherently disagree. Motives as inferred from their "effects" and motives as known directly by "internal observation" do not accurately correspond. (This fact is a condition of the existence of motivated behavior or conduct.) Perhaps it is more accurate to say that we know directly about the failure to correspond itself—due to error, prejudice, etc.—through the primary source or medium of knowledge, intercommunication. But if we raise the question of "testing" our knowledge of motivation in any particular case by an *ad hoc* investigation, in the only sense in which this is possible, it would appear that we bring in a third source of knowledge which probably ought to be distinguished from the general knowledge of mind derived from social intercourse. This is explicit questioning with answers based on explicit and critical introspection on the part of the economic subject making the choice.

We come now to another, and if possible even more essential, item in connection with the discussion of the basic concepts in economics—especially with reference to the positive or factual character of its data—which is entirely ignored by Hutchison. In the demarcation of economics, the interests of the individual (or those of the state, for the economics of totalitarian collectivism) are regularly and properly taken as factual data. It is usually made explicitly clear that in economics as a science no question is raised as to the "validity" of the "actual" scale of preferences of the economic subject. And our own discussion so far has accepted this view that preferences themselves are simply facts, the only question being as to how these facts are known. It must now be emphasized that this position is possible only for a treatment limited to the character of "pure" economics, completely divorced from any consideration of criticism or guidance of social action. In so far as any treatment of economics makes explicit reference to the merits of any social pol-

14. Force also—as every student or thoughtful person knows—is "metaphysical" and repugnant to the scientific intellect, and serious efforts have been made to build the theory of mechanics without it (without success!).

icy, some theory of value, beyond factual preference, is necessarily involved. This is just as true for rigorous laissez faire individualism as it is for any form or degree of interference or "control." Individualism, as a subject of approval or disapproval, is a social policy and an ethical category.

Moreover, a really thoroughgoing laissez faire individualism, accepting individual preferences as absolutely final, not only has never been either practiced in or advocated for any "society" (a political concept), but is even theoretically impossible under any conditions fundamentally like those of the real world. For, in a world in which individuals grow old and die and are replaced by new units who are born as "infants" and are necessarily reared and educated in the society in which they are to live and function as members, it is merely absurd to treat the individual as a datum for purposes of decisions regarding social policy. Any change in policy will affect the kind of individuals of which society in future time will be composed and not merely the relations between individuals, and these consequences cannot be ignored. And it is a fact, to be kept in mind and recognized as a condition of talking sense about human interests, that everyone, habitually and inevitably, makes a distinction which is vital, however vague it may be, between personal preferences and values assumed to be objective. (This means imperative but not absolute.) The social assertion of an individual preference itself rests on such a judgment of value; it is essentialy a "right" in so far as it has any significance whatever.[15] No discussion of group action can be carried on in propositions which merely state what "I want."

15. Hutchison appends to his book an eight-page discussion of economic policy, in the form of a destructive criticism of "Some Postulates of Economic Liberalism." It contains many good points and is characteristically notable for the citations in the footnotes. It certainly overstates vastly any claim ever seriously made on behalf of "classical economics" in alleging its position to be "that Economic Science quite definitely demonstrates that a Liberal, capitalist, *laissez-faire* economic policy leads to maximum returns for the community or to greater returns than any collectively planned economic policy" (p. 177). And Professor von Mises would hardly be generally accepted as "the leader of contemporary Economic Liberalism," unless this means the academic opponent of socialism most conspicuous for the extremism of his position.

The main defects of the Appendix seem to the reviewer to be two: First, the author does not recognize the obvious reservation for any defense of economic individualism (in addition to frictional limitations) that even in so far as the system "works" in accord with its theory, individuals—which really means families—share in the social product on the basis of productive capacity furnished (as measured by its sale value), which is perhaps never defended as having any close correspondence with ideal ethical desert, particularly for the dependent members of the family unit. More generally, he also takes the in-

But the value judgment has also a more immediate significance for the discussion of social policy. Judgments of value are also facts, data—and data of supreme importance. Social discussion has not only to be relative to some ideal of what policy ought to be, in the judgment of the parties to it; it also has to make a categorical distinction between what the individual members of any society affected by policy at the moment regard as right, or as rights, and what they, as individuals or as groups, sects, or what not, merely want. It is an indubitable fact that every normal individual makes this distinction in his own thinking with reference both to his interests and conduct and to those of other persons; and the fact that he usually does not, in the opinion of others, make it very accurately—especially in the sense that he tends to erect nearly every interest or wish of any importance into a right—by no means implies either that the distinction can be ignored or that it is possible to discuss group policy or the behavior of individuals in groups without recognizing that there is a valid though unprecise distinction.

The economic view is only one aspect of motivation and is usually severely limited in various directions by a number of other aspects. Activities conform only in part, and usually in a rather limited degree, if rigorously examined, to the economic principle that the motive is to realize given ends in the maximum degree possible with given means. The value of an action to the individual is only in part a function of the result achieved or to be achieved. To begin with, it is typical that the value is connected with the achievement of a result and yet not dependent on any value in the result itself. Perhaps the simplest illustration is that a "good" game must be good for

---

dividual as a datum and completely fails to recognize the point emphasized in our text above: that any approval or disapproval of any social policy must rest on ethical value judgments of some sort. (Also, as will be presently observed, human-social interests and values are at best only to a very limited extent covered by the conception of economic efficiency, even in the broadest possible definition.)

Second, he evades the main issue in formally declining to discuss "the relations of democratic authority and of experts to the general public" (p. 181), which in our view is wholly, and not merely "largely," as he says, "a political issue" and is virtually the whole issue in the problem of collectivism. But previously (p. 180) he has practically begged the question for collectivism by stating that its experts would be "chosen and dismissable by those who hired them," implying that this would be true in the sense significant for the individuals whose lives would be regulated by these experts. Moreover, his entire discussion relates explicitly to a "social-democratic Utopia," which experience and abstract reasoning both indicate is impossible—a practical contradiction in terms.

the defeated party, whose efforts are frustrated and fail, as well as for the winner, while even for the winner the concrete result—the score made in whatever form—is of no significance when achieved. This is as clear in the case of solitaire as in a competitive game. (The positivist might well ponder the fact that no objective definition can be give of "work" and "play," fundamental as the concepts are in any discussion of economics or of conduct in general.)

In addition, we all know that we generally do not know at all accurately what we want and in considerable measure act to find out. And our interests are to a considerable extent explorative in a more intrinsic sense; the motive of action is in part curiosity as to what the result will be and hence depends on partial ignorance of the result when the action is performed. It is undoubtedly a general principle that ends are more or less defined in the process of realization, and that the interest and value in an action center in this redefinition as well as in the achievement of any result given in anticipation.

The role of the value judgment in individual motivation constitutes a more serious limitation on the economic view of motivation. One commonly wants to do the "right" thing, without knowing what it is, in contrast with wanting to do any given thing. In this case the problem in action is to decide upon an end, upon what to want, as well as to achieve one's desire. And "rightness" has a variety of meanings; we want to be right in a mere conventional meaning and also in several "real" senses—aesthetically, intellectually, and morally. And the economic aspect of behavior itself has its own quality of rightness, beyond mere desire; it is within limits a "matter of principle"; "waste is sin."[16]

We have indicated only a part of the plurality of categories necessary for the interpretation of economic behavior. The same concrete behavior phenomena form the subject matter of all the social sciences, including psychology, and may be considered by the physical and biological sciences as well. A serious analysis of "social phenomena," oriented to the methodological controversies which have been rife in recent years (and more or less since the development of the Historical School), would have to be based on a quite complicated pluralism. The main types of categories in terms of which any

16. For a full discussion of this theme of the value judgment inherent in the notion of economy itself, cf. the admirable essay by Alex L. Macfie, *The Nature of Economy and Value* (London: Macmillan & Co., Ltd., 1937).

human act would have to be explained may be suggested by the following summary classification. This could be greatly expanded, and all the categories apply to virtually every conscious human action. It is particularly to be emphasized that even at the lowest factual level, truth and knowledge are inseparably related not only to interests but to values. Truth itself is a value.

I. Positivistic. (Causal laws in the sense of phenomenal uniformity, in contrast with motivation as an efficient cause, i.e., excluding deliberation and problem-solving; if consciousness is recognized, it is treated as "epiphenomenal.")

    1. Physical causality or behaviorism. To be applied as a matter of course, so far as it can be, so far as it can yield answers to our questions. Measurement and correlation (statistics).

    2. Historical causality. Linguistics is the type of a social science using the historical or institutional method, but it is also valid to a considerable extent for other departments of social behavior, including the "economic." (There is usually little question of deliberately changing a mode of institutional behavior, as the case of language adequately illustrates; also "observation" of meanings is a special problem.)

    2a. Biological interpretation, involving such essentially teleological concepts as competitive struggle and adaptation—as applied to plant or unconscious life—is an intermediate or hybrid category.

II. Motivated or deliberately problem-solving action. (Both "problem" and "solution" seem to be indefinable, doubtless the most important indefinables of our thinking.)

    1. Economic behavior. A subject uses given means to realize given ends, only the procedure being problematical. (Taken in the strict sense, this applies only to "stationary conditions," but all deliberative behavior is economic "in so far as," and in the sense that, ends and means are given and the problem is that of procedure.)

    2. Action in which the motive is abstract or social, such as interest in action or power as such, achievement, curiosity, conformity (to fashion or to law), distinction, co-operation, competition ("victory"), etc., but where no value judgment is involved.

    3. Action in which the evaluation of the end is the main deliberative problem. This category includes intellectual, aesthetic, and ethical activity, or the pursuit of the proverbial trio, "the true, the beautiful, and the good."

The positivist who would seriously try to be consistent and thoroughgoing would have to stick strictly to the realm of physical causality (uniformity of sequence) and deny the relevance of any other categories of interpretation. As we have seen, the validity of the notion of economy itself, or any interpretation of behavior in terms of motives, depends on the factor of error or uncertainty in numerous forms. But all such considerations—all conception of any process as problem-solving in any sense—are excluded by the pre-conceptions of positivism, are rejected as unreal, transcendental, or mystical.

It would hardly seem to call for argument that the methodology of economic theory should be worked out in relation to the function performed by the science or discipline in the education of the individual—the reason, apart from intellectual curiosity or general culture, on account of which most students will be interested in it. The first fact for emphasis regarding the relation between economic theory and action or conduct is that the activities for which it should furnish guidance are those of the citizen and statesman, not those of the individual as a *wirtschaftender Mensch*. Its practical problems are those of social policy. And the first requisite for "talking sense" about social policy is to avoid the nearly universal error of regarding the problem as in any sense closely parallel in form to the scientific-technological problem of using means to realize ends. The social problem, and the only problem which should properly be called social, is that of establishing a social consensus on matters of policy.

This is in no sense a scientific-technical or manipulative problem, unless we consider "society" under the form of a dictatorship over which the dictator is proprietor as well as sovereign, and as an enterprise which is to be managed solely in his interest. And even then the manipulative problem would be categorically different in form from that presented by the effort of human beings to exploit the objects and forces of nature. The manipulation—or "control," in the only proper sense of that word—of human beings (by other human beings) is almost entirely immoral and to be prevented; and when it is accomplished it is through such processes as coercion or persuasion, or especially deception, none of which has any meaning in connection with the control of natural objects by men. (The higher animals, especially those domesticated, are in an intermediate position.) If society is in any sense democratic or free, its problems are problems of group decision and group self-determination, in connection with which control is a misleading term.

The social action which the study of economics has as its function to guide, or at least to illuminate, is essentially that of making "rules of the game," in the shape of law, for economic relationships. The concrete form of such rules will be overwhelmingly that of taxes, or of prohibitions of particular lines of activity, subject to penalties. Consequently, the problem of prediction which is set for economics as a science may be said to be that of the individual re-action, as consumer or producer, to price data or, more specifically, to price changes. The problem of the role of general economic theory in such prediction is, then, to show what can be inferred from the general principles or axioms of diminishing utility and diminishing (technical) returns, both of which may be viewed as particular cases of the more inclusive principle of substitution.

The limitations of the possibility of prediction need all possible emphasis if the theory is not to be misused, and they are quite dras-tic. In the first place, it is evident that only the direction of the re-sponse, i.e., whether a given activity will be increased or decreased, can possibly be inferred from theory alone. The amount of response to a change of given magnitude (except reduction from the actual volume to zero) can in the nature of the case be known only from empirical-historical data stating the facts of past reactions to various price situations, or, conceivably, from answers by individuals to hy-pothetical questions.

And there are two other important reservations to be emphasized —in addition to the principle of *ceteris paribus*, which should hardly need to be mentioned. (It should hardly be necessary to remind any educated person that the effect of any one cause must be considered apart from the possible effects of other causes which may be operat-ing at the same time.) The first of the two important reservations is that the individual's satisfaction function or indifference-map must be assumed to remain the same during and after the change. (This obviously might be included under *ceteris paribus*.) The second reservation is that a person rarely acts exclusively on the basis of a satisfaction function. This means two things: (*a*) that the motiva-tion is not purely economic and (*b*) that the choice is not free from error. Both are excluded from the notion of behaving "rationally" in the economic sense.

The assumption of a stable satisfaction function is of course highly unreliable, but it has predictive value, in the absence of any dis-coverable reason for believing that it has changed. The point is im-portant particularly because of the difference between predicting human behavior and predicting the behavior of physical objects under changed conditions, in that the latter neither behave irration-ally or sentimentally, nor make mistakes, nor "change their minds" (and more or less correspondingly their reaction patterns), as hu-man beings are notoriously liable to do. This trait of human beings, in contrast with physical things, whose responses reflect an inner nature which is either invariant or changes only for objectively discoverable reasons, is admittedly embarrassing to the economist as a scientist, but there does not seem to be anything that he can do about it. It is particularly to be noted that change of mind upsets any positivistic prediction on the basis of observation of previous behavior to the same extent as it does predictions based on inference from the abstract economic laws.[17]

Economic positivists and empiricists have apparently given little thought to the manner in which we actually predict human behavior in everyday experience. The "law of large numbers" is applicable where large numbers of human beings behave individually in fairly standardized situations—the case of "insurable" contingencies or risks. In the prediction of individual behavior—one's own or that of an acquaintance or of a stranger—concrete records of past performance play a relatively small role in comparison with more subtle bases of insight into character and personality. If one wanted to predict the answer which an individual would get to an assigned simple problem in arithmetic, the first and principal basis would be to work the problem and see what is the "right" answer; and the next step would presumably be to inquire into his "competence." But arithmetic, be it noted, is the science of "right" answers, not a statistical study of those which men acually get. Where large numbers of human beings act as groups, and not individually, the basis of prediction is "social psychology," which even more than that of individuals is a matter of insight and interpretation, in contrast with statistical extrapolation.

In short: The formal principles of economic theory can never carry anyone very far toward the prediction or technical control of the corresponding economic behavior. But such a result, by any method, is both utterly abhorrent to all humane thinking and self-

17. A more fundamental weakness of inductive prediction in economics is that empirical (i.e., statistical) data never present anything like an exhaustive analysis of phenomenal sequences down to really elementary components, and the correlation of and extrapolation from composite magnitudes or series never can be very reliable. The real unit would be an invariant and measurable human trait, either an interest or a response independent of interests, a reflex. Mention of the effort and high-grade intellectual energy which has been expended in attempting to predict the course of various statistical economic series—and specifically the prices on the organized stock and produce exchanges—should be a sufficient reminder of the difficulties and limitations inherent in such projects; analytical studies of "forecasting" make it doubtful whether the results (so far) are much better than random guesses.

contradictory. The intelligent application of these principles is a first step, and chiefly significant negatively rather than positively, for showing what is "wrong" rather than what is "right" in an existing situation and in any proposed line of action. Concrete and positive answers to questions in the field of economic science or policy depend in the first place on judgments of value and procedure, based on a broad, general education in the cultural sense, and on "insight" into human nature and social values, rather than on the findings of any possible positive science. From this point of view the need is for an interpretative study (*verstehende Wissenschaft*) which, however, would need to go far beyond any possible boundaries of economics and should include the humanities as well as the entire field of the social disciplines. However, a sound investigation of problems recognized as economic, and of proposed lines of social action, would yield results surprising to the critics, as to the proportion of such questions which could practically be settled on the basis of a reasonable interpretation and application of sound economic theory.

All this negatively critical discussion of Hutchison's "position" does not imply that a student may not derive much useful education, in economics and in wider fields, from the study of his book. It is a very "learned" work, citing and quoting extensively, and hence is valuable as an introduction to the literature of its field. Its fallacies are rather those of omission—what it excludes rather than what it contains. But the exclusion is itself positive, not to say dogmatic; and in the reviewer's opinion its study ought to be accompanied by adequate warning of its limitations. It is perhaps the chief merit of the work that, as we have pointed out, the author ends up by virtually abandoning the "criteria" on which at first he lays so much emphasis.

From the very nature of conduct as problem-solving, and from the character of human problems, even at the level of relative simplicity considered in economic theory—and because no problem is purely economic except by abstraction from other and more important features of concrete human interests—it follows that "criteria" apply only superficially to statements about conduct. The limited part or aspect of human problems which can be treated in the form of positive science is the subject matter of the positive natural sciences, long since separated out and recognized as such—by abstraction from the complexity and waywardness of reality as a whole.[18] These sciences, indeed, include all the natural sciences of man and, specifically, all the branches of "sociology," in so far as their votaries have succeeded in developing these as positive sciences. In the nature of the case again, the limits to the development of positive sciences of human behavior are to be determined by "trying," and not by "theorizing." But there cannot possibly be any boundary with any degree of definiteness between the spheres of "determinateness" and of "freedom."

18. An ultimate limit to scientific explanation is of course set by the fact that the explanation of mental process is itself a mental process, so that any exhaustive explanation would have to explain both itself and the explainer. This not only starts a regress to infinity but contradicts the nature of thinking as an activity.

VIII

Statics and Dynamics: Some Queries regarding the Mechanical Analogy in Economics[1]

THE frequency and familiarity with which the terms "static" and "dynamic" are used in economic literature contrast somewhat strangely with the paucity of discussion on their meaning; and the comparative abundance of argumentation regarding the necessity for such a distinction throws into even stronger light the lack of effort at clear definition. Marshall's usage is typical; he constantly uses the terms "static" and "dynamic," and kindred expressions like "*ceteris paribus*" and "unchanging general conditions of economic life," and repeatedly insists on the importance of clearness in regard to them; but he nowhere offers a complete list of the static data, or "other things," or attempts a clear statement of the principles at issue. There are exceptions to this procedure of course; notably the work of J. B. Clark, Schumpeter, and the mathematical school of Walras and his successors. It is not the intention in this paper to go through the literature, or selected specimens of it, and give a detailed criticism. Neither is there any serious pretense of supplying in a positive, constructive way all that seems to be wanting. The aim is merely to raise certain questions, without attempting to give them final answers.

The terms "statics" and "dynamics" are of course borrowed from theoretical mechanics. Most of the writers who have used them were no doubt aware that the analogy of economic theory to mechanics is subject to limitations like all analogies. Schumpeter, indeed, explicitly remarks (*Wirtschaftliche Entwicklung*, p. 75) that there is no connection with mechanics, which we suggest is as far from the truth as an assumption of complete parallelism. There is a real and important relation, or the words would not have been taken over, and the constant use of the concepts of friction and inertia is additional proof that the analogy of mechanics exerts a large influence on the thinking of economists. It is from this standpoint that we ap-

1. First published in German translation by the *Zeitschrift für National-ökonomie*, Vol. II, No. 1 (August, 1930), this essay also appeared in *The Ethics of Competition* (New York: Harper & Bros., 1935) and is reprinted here by permission.

proach the subject; the mechanical analogy seems to deserve a searching examination and an effort to clarify some of the questions involved in its use.

The root idea in economic statics is clearly the notion of *equilibrium* and hence of *forces* in equilibrium. At the outset we are confronted with the fact that critically minded physicists have always felt the notion of force objectionable. From Newton down they have regarded it as metaphysical and unreal and have struggled to eliminate it from their conceptual systems. It seems to be unquestionable that for reflective common sense (if these more or less contradictory terms may be used together) there is a repugnance for action-at-a-distance and a strong urge to find explanations in the strictly mechanical terms of impact. Manifestly this question cannot be followed up here. We merely note that the "mechanical" theories of gravitation and other forces have never taken root in physics and that the role played by potential energy seems to make the elimination of metaphysical forces out of the question. The significance for thought of the new approach to the whole problem through relativity theory is not clear, even if the new theories receive such verification as is possible, and the analogy which is significant for economics is certainly that of the older Newtonian mechanics; indeed engineers will undoubtedly continue to use the old concepts, whatever may happen in a certain narrow realm of theoretical physics. Our point here is that in using the mechanical analogy the notion of force is involved and that it is a most troublesome one in its original context.

As compared with mechanics, the notion of force will be much more or much less troublesome in economics according to whether any particular thinker leans toward one or another type of psychology, which is to say one or another world view. The student with a materialistic and hence a behavioristic bias who cares about consistency had perhaps better give up at once such notions as force, tendency, and equilibrium, and restrict the matter of his discourse to statistical trends, correlations, etc., in the field of physically measurable magnitudes. That is, he will practically cease to talk of human beings and their wants, sacrifices and satisfactions, and deal exclusively with commodities and prices. This indeed is what a good number are doing at the moment—with whatever it may be of clearness as to the logical basis of the urge at the back of the movement. If terms like "equilibrium" and "tendency" are used in such a system it must be in the sense of statistical modes and mathematical limits, which is not the meaning they have in general usage. For the non-materialist, whether idealist, dualist, pluralist, or what not, so long as he considers it possible and important to speak intelligibly about mental life, the idea of force in human behavior is clearer and more real than in nature. For the human analogue of force is motive, and men do assume (when not trying to prove a contrary theory) that they have some knowledge of motives, from personal experience and intercommunication with their fellows, and this contrasts with the inaccessibility of any such knowledge regarding forces in inanimate nature.

In mechanics, change or process means motion, and analogically we speak of social processes as movements. The simplest case of mechanical equilibrium is that of the mutual cancellation of two or more forces (velocities?) giving complete rest. The economic analogue is the equilibrium of a market in which no economic process (exchange) is induced. As soon as we consider the process by which such an equilibrium is established, we enter the field of dynamics, and the basic problems involved in the use of the analogy of mechanics are forced upon the attention.

In an experimental setup to illustrate mechanical equilibrium, the forces unavoidably act through things having mass—weights or springs—and hence act upon these masses as well as upon each other. If friction could be eliminated from such a system, it would never actually come from any other position to a stationary equilibrium but would perpetually oscillate or move around some circuit which could be represented by an equation. With friction present, in addition to inertia, as it always is in an actual case, important distinctions have to be made, as there are different kinds of friction. With friction of the sort presented by solid bodies in contact, the system, released from any point other than that of theoretical equilibrium, may remain at rest, or if it moves it will come to rest. But the point of rest and nature of the movement toward that point will vary widely with the character of the friction (relation between standing and moving friction) and its magnitude relative to the inertia of the system and the degree of disequilibrium of the starting point. Details are irrelevant here, but damped oscillation is one significant possibility. The actual point of rest might be the theoretical equilibrium point, but that result is highly improbable.

Another type of friction is that represented by the resistance of a fluid to motion of a solid through it, which depends on its density and viscosity. If our experiment is performed with the whole apparatus suspended in water or mercury or molasses, the point of rest will be that of theoretical equilibrium, with or without oscillations, even though its motion may be indefinitely slowed down. A case more or less intermediate between solid and liquid is presented by sand or shot.

These cases suggest questions which it seems the economist might profitably examine. It is crude at best to attribute any continuing divergence of conditions from those of theoretical equilibrium to "friction" as economists generally do, since the theory of a frictionless system calls not for equilibrium but for perpetual oscillation. This, however, assumes the presence of inertia and raises the question of the relation between friction and inertia, or their possible analogues, in economics. It seems that the analogy in the mind of economists in discussing the tendency toward equilibrium is that of movement against a viscous friction, with inertia absent or negligible. The presence of a significant amount of inertia would mean a tendency toward oscillation, and a careful study in the light of this analogy of the tendency toward cyclical swings so common in economic phenomena might be both theoretically illuminating and practically significant. If the economic behavior of an individual has the nature of response to any condition which in turn responds to the behavior but only (for whatever reason) after a certain interval or lag, the first response will naturally go too far and set up oscillations. In the second place, the difference between viscosity friction and that between solid surfaces might well prove suggestive also.

Philosophically, the possibilities of inquiry along the line of a serious working-out and carrying-over of the mechanical analogy, and determination of its applicability and limitations, seem to the writer most alluring. Large results would of course depend on genius in the investigator or slow development through discussion. We should remember that it required roughly two and a half centuries (Galileo to Meyer, Joule and Rankine) for physicists to work out a clear definition of their fundamental concept of energy. In the background, of course, is the ultimate problem of psychology, especially the role of conscious deliberation and effort in comparison with automatic response. Traditional economic thought has occupied a sort of middle ground in this regard; it accepts deliberation regarding means as real but treats ends as given in the situation and argues that deliberation regarding ends (which common sense accepts without question) is "really" deliberation regarding means.

An objectively scientific view, of course, takes the further step and argues that all deliberation is "really unreal," at least as to making any difference in the process or result; in this view, conscious states are, at most, "events" in a certain time-space configuration, along with physical changes, but without any more dynamic quality. The question seems to boil down to the nature of error, and its correlate, effort. The scientific urge is against this notion, craving automatic exceptionless uniformity, i.e., an ultimately unchanging as well as passive nature of things.[2]

In the basic "economic law" of uniform price in a market, the assumption is perfect knowledge of conditions on the part of all economic subjects. It is surely conceivable that study might show to what degree the "resistance"—ignorance, prejudice, etc.—which prevents the facts from conforming to such obvious tendencies is really analogous to inertia or friction of the different types. The universal and unavoidable use of the terms "friction" and "inertia" in describing human responses shows that they have scientific and not merely analogical significance. The concepts, however, need to be sharply differentiated, as the law in the two cases is different; a force acting against (viscous) friction produces motion at a speed proportional to the force; acting against inertia it produces motion accelerating at a rate proportional to the force.

Whatever we conceive to be the "force" back of human behavior, whether conscious interests or "real advantage" (conceived biologically, hedonistically, aesthetically, or ethically) or merely the physical situation of the organism, the project of a proper mechanics of the process forces upon us a number of interesting questions. Mechanics runs in terms of three ultimate dimensions, time, space, and mass (which is supposed to have a more empirical standing than force), and to these must be added in application to reality the different types of friction as already noted. Only the time dimension seems to carry over directly and be available for use in such a field as economics. Yet it appears that we cannot reduce the economic process to quantitative terms unless we can give workable meaning to space and to mass and to space not merely in the aspect of measurable distance but in that of direction as well. We do constantly speak of direction in economic changes and even of degrees of op-

2. The working postulates of orthodox economics are those of British utilitarianism, given classical expression by Hume; it is assumed that men may be mistaken as to means but not as to ends. The question may be raised whether the notion of physical force does not like that of motive involve contingency, a kind of error which would explain its repugnance to the scientific intellect.

position or parallelism; when the notion is made precise it is that of "angle" between changes. Perhaps it will sometime be possible to use the notion of a "field" of social force and process in a definite sense which might be represented by co-ordinates. Perhaps the notions of momentum and energy and their respective laws of conservation, so vital to physical thinking, have real analogues in the competition of the market. In mechanics, action and reaction are equal; a force produces equal momentum (though not equal energy) in opposite directions. In mechanics, friction converts a measurable quantity of mechanical energy into an "equal" quantity of heat, though momentum is conserved. If such relations cannot be interpreted, it would seem advisable to find some way of avoiding the mechanical analogy and developing a less misleading terminology.

It will be observed that most of the discussion so far has really dealt with dynamics; not the abstract conditions of equilibrium (an equalization of forces acting in all "directions") but the nature of changes (movement) toward equilibrium has been considered. This procedure should serve to emphasize a fundamental contrast between the use of terms in economics and in mechanics. The discussion should have made it clear that no science of economic dynamics exists, as it could not exist prior to a definition of elementary magnitudes and units such as just suggested, and this is so far from accomplishment that the suggestion of its possibility probably strikes the reader as strained or fanciful. At best it may be said that the statistical economics now being prosecuted with so much zeal in various quarters might yield data for some of these definitions, though the inquiries are not consciously oriented toward any such general scientific aim. In actual usage economic dynamics, or dynamic economics, has become merely a critical and negative term to refer to the limitations of "static" analysis or more exactly to any particular author's objections to any other author's use of the equilibrium concept. Its least vague usage is that of a sort of catch-all for stressing changes in given conditions in contrast with adjustments to given conditions. In practice it suggests an insistence that there are no given conditions, which view if consistently maintained would mean that there are no predictable reactions and that science is impossible. This issue cannot be discussed here; the only answer in any case would be to point to the "history and prospects" of economics. Our concern is with definitions of concepts, and our present point is that there is no economic dynamics in the meaning the term should have if it is to be used at all. Economic literature includes no treatment of the relations between measured force, resistance, and movement. What it calls dynamics should be called evolutionary or historical economics. Mechanics, conversely, has no place for evolutionary categories; it assumes constancy in its ultimates, believing (until recently) that mass and energy are "really" neither created nor destroyed. In any case the general properties of materials are unchanged in mechanical transformations.

Our next task is to call attention to a certain relativity in the notions "static" and "dynamic" and to attempt to define with some care the important stages or terms in a series of economic processes in which relatively more stable conditions, i.e., conditions undergoing slower processes of change, serve for theoretical analysis as a framework or setting of given conditions with reference to shorter-period adjustments. These shorter-period adjustments, then, have the character of "tending" to establish equilibrium with reference to their respective given conditions at any given time, though with a certain lag due to the fact that the latter are also in fact continuously changing. Due primarily to the influence of uncertainty or ignorance of the future, which is associated with changes in the conditions in which economic subjects act, many other disturbances and maladjustments ensue in addition to the time lag. With regard to the final stage in the series, we shall have to inquire more particularly as to whether the longest-run processes which the economist has to consider have the equilibrating character, and hence whether the problem of economic evolution or progress can be given the form of a problem in dynamics. In the interest of clearness as to the nature of the relations and adjustments involved, we first call to mind some of the uses of the notion of equilibrium in connection with natural phenomena.

At first sight the idea of static conditions may seem to be merely that of *ceteris paribus,* but a little reflection will show that frequently much more is involved. It is true that the study of the causal relation, or correlation, between any two magnitudes which are involved in an interrelated system requires that the other be held constant. In the more precise language of mathematics, causality is a functional relation involving a large number of variables, and the relation connecting any two, when separable at all, is a partial derivative which is a function of all the others and at best can only be stated independently by giving each of the others some fixed value. In a general case, the relation of dependence may be mutual for all the variables in a function. But in real examples, the relation is not typically mutual, and elements which are to be treated as variable and those which are to be treated as fixed cannot be chosen arbitrarily. Equilibrium in nature is generally a phenomenon of adaptation in a real sense; factors in one group adapt to those in another group (as well as to each other); as between the groups, the adjustment is predominantly or wholly in one direction; rather typically, particularly in economics, the framework factors themselves are in motion independently, as already suggested, dragging the adapting group behind them instead of moving to meet the latter.[3]

The most common example borrowed from nature to illustrate static equilibrium in economics is that of water tending toward its level. Here there is no room for question as to the separation between the process and its setting, between the factors changing and the factors in relation to which they change. The "given conditions" are (1) the quantity and fluid properties of the water and (2) the shape and size of the drainage basin or system of interconnected containers in which it is free to move under the influence of (3) the force of gravity. What is variable is the position of the water or the various portions which make up its fluid mass. (The illustration is also of relevance in connection with the questions raised in the first part of this paper, the analogical meaning of gravity and inertia and the various sorts of friction and of the actual character of the process which might take place under slightly different conditions.)

What interests us here is merely the character of an equilibrating change. There is a fixed or presumptively fixed set of conditioning factors and a process which moves toward a state of rest by establishing equilibrium with relation to the given conditions. The prevalence of this general type of situation in the world is striking. The wind, for another example, results from a disequilibrium in the atmosphere, a difference in pressure corresponding to the difference in water level, and its blowing operates to equate the pressure and bring the process to a stop. Electric current is a similar flow from

3. All the possible types are met with in economics. The relation between price and cost illustrates an adjustment which is mutual as to direction of movement but with such a difference in speed and range that it is generally justifiable to say that cost of production "determines" price and not inversely. Changes in the cost of any one commodity reflect the relative movement of all competing industries using the same resources in production and hence are likely to be small in comparison to the change in price in the process by which the two are brought to equality. It seems inevitable and correct to speak of the relatively fixed magnitude as cause, as we say the level of the water in the ocean controls that in the bay, or that the earth attracts the falling apple, or that we tie the boat to the bank, even though the relation is mutual.

high to low "potential." All the movements and processes of ordinary observation seem to represent a flow of energy "down hill" and toward a level at which it would be at rest. Most of them are finally derived from the redistribution of the solar heat energy, which itself gives every indication of having the same character. Its flow perpetually maintains the disequilibria which cause the flow of water and air and hence the phenomena of life. The fundamental cosmic mystery is the origin and destination of a universe which science pictures as an irreversible reaction. (If the analogy of a frictionless system holds, the solar energy must complete a circuit sometime, in some way, but that is not our problem here.)

In economics we are chiefly concerned with equilibrium not as a state of rest but as a *process* in equilibrium, with a slower process forming the "given condition" within which a more rapid one takes place and tends toward a moving equilibrium. Thus the flow of solar energy and the form, position, and movement of the earth condition the complete circular process of evaporation of water from the ocean and its return flow thither through the streams. This circular process is in equilibrium when the amount of water reaching the sea is the same as the amount leaving it by evaporation and when, at every point in the complex circuit, the quantities arriving and leaving are equal, the flow neither expanding nor contracting. It is obvious that after any change in the solar radiation or any of the numerous other given conditions, all of which do in fact undergo changes, a considerable interval must elapse before equilibrium will be established. It follows that the system never really is in equilibrium ("moving equilibrium") at any point; but its tendency toward such a state is the main feature to be made clear in a scientific description of it. (The role of friction and inertia in producing a lag in the adjustment of processes toward a moving equilibrium with their given conditions is considerably different from the case of tendency toward stationary equilibrium, but the differences need not be elaborated here.)

In economics, as previously remarked, this general type of relation is exemplified in a series of stages. The notion of a series of "cases" in price theory, extending from short run to ultimate long run is especially familiar in the great work of Marshall, who recognizes four main "cases" in his price theory.[4] Some modifications of his results appear necessary in the light of a systematic survey of the material from the special viewpoint of the principle here under discussion;

4. *Principles of Economics*, Book V, chap. v, esp. sec. 8.

detailed contrast between our cases and Marshall's is not called for, but a few significant divergences will be noted in passing. There seems to be a hiatus in his series at the very beginning, at the short-run end. His scheme does not take sufficient account of the fact that, in the actual fixation of the prices of commodities which have a highly organized market and a definite price at a moment, the market is made and the price at any moment fixed, not by owners of supply and prospective consumers (as is assumed also in the mathematical systems), but by a class of professional traders who come in between these primary groups. This fact makes it needful to introduce an additional stage in price theory, with its own given conditions and position of equilibrium.

In the wheat pit of a grain exchange, for example, the given price-determining conditions at any moment are the opinions, dispositions, and financial power of the various traders. Actual demand by consumers and actual supply alike are outside of the market and operate only indirectly, through the opinions of traders as to what these facts are and are likely to be in the future as far ahead as they attempt to predict. The variables in the situation are the price and the distribution among the traders of claims against each other to deliver or accept the commodity. The total volume of such claims, or the amount in the hands of any individual, bears no determinate relation to an actual quantity of wheat or to any physical or human reality. The condition of equilibrium is simply that the price and distribution of claims be such as to make the total effective buying disposition equal to the total effective selling disposition, measured in bushels, relative to traders' attitudes as they are at the moment.

Over a longer period, roughly bounded by harvest time in the main wheat belt in the case of this commodity, the opinions of traders are no longer data in the price situation but themselves perpetually tend to "equilibrate," in relation to the facts of physical supply and consumers' demand, and to carry price with them. These facts therefore become the data for a different equilibrium or "normal," the price for the season as a whole. These data are properly separable, as those of the former case were not, into conditions of "supply" and of "demand." Producers or actual owners of wheat and its consumers are distinct if somewhat overlapping groups, and possession of wheat and need for it are distinct facts, which is not true of buyers and sellers in the speculative market or of the motives which determine their role one way or the other. Demand now includes the purchasing dispositions and purchasing power of all users of wheat, including present owners, measured for the season or unexpired part of it, while supply is the amount of wheat in the market as a whole, practically the wheat-consuming world. (Allowance for carry-over and for overlapping of seasons in different regions may for brevity be ignored.) For other things than agricultural crops, the "season" is indefinite, but there is a period within which relative unresponsiveness of supply to price changes is an important given condition in price fixation. The variables for this second case, of limited period with fixed supply, are the price and the distribution of the supply over the season and among the purchasers. The condition of equilibrium is that the price be such as to distribute the supply over the season and among consumers in accordance with the principle of equalization of marginal utility ratios with price ratios over the entire field.

Over a still longer period—in general a period of a few years—supply cannot be treated as a datum but is one of the chief variables in the situation, and the same is only less true of the incomes of purchasers. This brings us to the thorny question of what is more or less properly called the static economy, the problem of defining the conditions under which economic life will have continuity but not growth, production and consumption running along in a uniform volume and without change in general character. As remarked at the outset, the essential feature of such an economy, to make it most useful as a tool of analysis, has received surprisingly little intensive consideration. The task presents serious difficulties; in fact it is impossible to give a rigorously accurate definition for either unchanging volume or unchanging character of economic life without departing so far from reality as to make the significance of the treatment dubious.[5] Yet the notion may be both real enough and definite enough to be useful, even though a certain element of arbitrariness in definition must be accepted. We can only give our own formula-

5. Rigor would demand a community of immortal individuals who never learn or forget and never change their minds or tastes, absolutely standardized commodities and implements and processes of production, and resources which can neither be increased nor used up nor misapplied. In the mathematical treatment, one would expect such rigor. In fact these authors assume rather a sort of statistical uniformity which sacrifices realism without achieving the definiteness needed in deductive theory. Moreover, their systems of equations strive rather ineffectually to get beyond a general *a priori* instability for any position of the system other than that of perfect equilibrium. They are not seriously to be compared with the equations of mechanics which show the magnitude and direction at any point of stresses associated with disequilibrium and of their resultant.

tion with a brevity which must seem dogmatic but may serve for illustration.

The main given conditions of statically continuous economic life fall naturally, first, into the categories of (1) wants and (2) means of satisfaction, the latter meaning the ultimate resources of production.[6] Under productive resources, again, it is inevitable to separate (2A) actual "things," human beings and other physical agencies, from (2B) the general level of "culture" in its aspect of economic productive power. This latter in turn includes technology (2Ba) in the narrow, external sense of physical and chemical processes and the like and also (2Bb) in the human sense of the technique of business organization. This subclassification involves much overlapping, especially since technical development logically inheres in human beings, their traits and capacities; but such an enumeration seems necessary for clearness.

In addition to these main groups of data, certain further conditions have to be constant. Not merely the total supply of productive resources but also (3) the distribution of their ownership, including

6. This "Austrian" view that the quantities of the productive services are fixed under any given conditions cannot be defended at length here. It is not rigorously true to fact but is as nearly exact as any other general assumption in economic theory. The amount of any productive service forthcoming is theoretically affected by a psychological factor; relative irksomeness, odium, etc., must be taken into account when any productive resource is transferred from one use to another. But in the writer's opinion the classical economists seriously confused the "cost" to a nation or individual of its income as a whole, which is properly pain or sacrifice, with the "cost" of any particular unit of commodity which determines its price. The "pain" of labor and abstinence as a general fact has virtually nothing to do with price determining cost. In theory relative pain is an element in price, since it is an element in cost, but in fact labor is notoriously paid rather in inverse than direct ratio to pain, showing that the role of pain is insignificant. The supply of labor in any use is, like that of other factors, a matter of the relative attraction of competing uses and to a quite negligible degree a matter of the general supply price of the factor.

A more serious objection to the view taken herein relates to the unrealistic character of any classification of the productive factors. Manifestly the classes are not only indefinitely numerous, if one thinks of effectively homogeneous types whose units are really interchangeable, but shift their boundaries with the lapse of time. In the ultimate long run any human being or thing with productive qualities, practically without limit, has to be replaced or renewed and can be replaced with something else (a thing of other qualities) embodying the same "quantity" of abstract "investment," on the one hand, and "productive capacity," on the other. In a broad sense they are practically all capital. An examination which cannot be given in detail here would show that these facts do not essentially affect the argument. The productive factors are merely allowed whatever freedom of transformation they actually possess along with movement from one field of use to another. Any classification implied relates to the situation after equilibrium is reached.

both external goods and personal capacities, must be unchanging. (4) Monetary conditions must be specified in some form (which is hard to do very realistically, since a constant price level cannot be defined and under frictionless conditions any system "tends" toward indefinite inflation). (5) Finally, it must be remembered that in several regards an exchange system is incapable of standing alone; many economic functions have to be carried on or controlled by society as a unit, that is, by the government. Hence public policy in its various phases (which need not be enumerated—the whole political, legal, and moral system is involved) must be included among the constants of the economic system. In particular, the state must be assumed to exclude or set fixed limits to the creation of monopolies or the use of monopoly power.[7]

So much for the given conditions of the static economy. The variables in the process of establishing equilibrium are three: (1) The prices of final goods and services; (2) the prices of productive services (including a quasi-rent on intermediate goods somewhat in excess of maintenance and replacement charges passed on to other resources); (3) the allocation of productive resources among industries and among enterprises within each industry. (The "distribution" of final products among those who supply productive services is taken care of by the prices of the services and ownership.)

The conditions of equilibrium are all included under two parallel statements of marginal equalization—aside from the fact that all in-

---

7. Constancy in many respects would be secured for the static economy concept by assuming habit fixation on the part of the people. But this is hardly consistent with economic behavior.

One of the most interesting controversial points regarding the static economy can only be mentioned here. That is Schumpeter's view that all capital goods would be completely analyzed into land and labor and would as capital goods receive no income (interest or quasi-rent). It seems to the writer that under any realistic conditions as to wants and conditions of supply, goods requiring a longer time to produce must have greater value for the same expenditure of ultimate resource-services other than time. The supply of "time" in production is limited by the supply of consumable goods in general, and it must command a price unless all goods are free and the conditions of economic life consequently non-existent. Cf. Böhm-Bawerk's criticism of Schumpeter, *Zeitschrift für Volkswirtschaft, Socialpolitik und Verwaltung*, Vol. XXII; also article by E. von Beckerath, *Schmollers Jahrb.*, Vol. LIII. We agree with Schumpeter (and others—Pantaleoni and Wieser) that apart from the influence of interest itself there is no general preference of present to future satisfactions and no occasion for assuming such in the static economy. To make the conception realistic we must imagine a natural stationary equilibrium of the capital supply, such as the stationary state contemplated by J. S. Mill, the interest rate being sufficient to prevent the consumption of capital already saved without bringing about further saving.

come is expended in consumption, which is included in the definition of the static economy. These statements are: (1) prices of final goods and services are set at such levels that consumers in behaving economically (i.e., expending their incomes in such a way as to secure equal increments of utility from equal expenditures) exactly exhaust the supplies of all goods produced; (2) the prices of productive services are set at such levels that producers (entrepreneurs) in behaving economically (expending their respective productive outlays, i.e., costs, in such a way as to secure equal product increments of equal market value for equal outlays) exactly exhaust the supplies of all productive services (the supplies forthcoming at the prices offered, if one does not assume the supplies fixed).

Inspection will show that these two statements involve several other conditions. It is mere repetition to observe that production costs in money are equal to prices of goods, and productive resources receive (through "imputation") product increments equal (in price) to the productive increments they contribute at the margin. The phenomenon of "rent" in the ordinary meaning is taken care of, since it makes no difference in principle in the workings of the competitive process whether any type of productive service is used in making many products or in making only one—though it makes a difference no less than inversion in the causal relation between the payment for the service, as a cost item, and the price of the product. (If a productive resource is used in industries generally, its remuneration is a cause with reference to the price of any one product; if it is used in only one product, its remuneration is an effect of the price of that product.) Competition between entrepreneurs in the same industry (making a given product) fixes the price paid for the service at the value of its productive contribution just as effectively and in the same way as if the competition is spread over any number of industries. The only case not explicitly provided for is that in which the entire supply of a productive agency is a monopoly in the hands of a single entrepreneur, where in fact the distributive share would be a residuum merely. Other monopolies, of particular markets, of products and of productive processes as such, corners, etc., we exclude here for brevity.[8]

8. The static economy pictured here is one in which all economic processes are absolutely continuous without expansion or contraction. It may be observed in passing that the conception is not affected by cyclical periodicities in conditions, such as the succession of day and night or the seasons, alternation of productive activity, and consumption, etc., provided that ultimate repetitiveness is realized and all changes are fully foreknown and taken into account in the eco-

We now arrive at the fourth and final step[9] in the series of longer-run processes, each providing a setting or framework of conditions theoretically treated as given, to which shorter-run processes tend to adjust themselves so as to establish equilibrium. The first was price fixation by traders in a speculative market; the second price fixation by producers and consumers in a market where supply and demand are given for a limited period; the third was the case of continuous production and consumption of unchanging volume and general pattern; after this comes the problem of growth and change. (We may say simply "growth," assuming, according to custom, that both qualitative and quantitative changes represent improvement.) The particular question which concerns us in this connection has to do, first, with the "equilibrating" character of these longest-run, secular or historical, changes which constitute growth and, second, with the applicability of mechanical notions and terms to the treatment of these changes. We must see clearly what the changes are and what is their setting or given conditions—which now take us outside the sphere of economic phenomena—and inquire whether the correct scientific treatment of economic progress should view it as in its turn a move-

---

nomic behavior of all persons affected. In many connections the uncertainty which is associated with change is more important for economic theory than the change itself. This suggests that regular continuous growth might also be admitted in the static economy as such growth would not involve unpredictability (cf. Schumpeter). We raise no question as to the legitimacy or importance of studying a society in which growth is present but uncertainty absent and where consequently the ideal of marginal equalization of returns in relation to outlays of every sort is continuously realized. This admission does not affect the significance of the different separation made above, between a (perfectly adjusted) society with growth absent and with growth present. As to the term "static economy," it seems relatively more suitable to the concept pictured here—to the elimination of growth rather than the elimination of uncertainty. In strict conformity with the mechanical analogy, the term "statics" should relate, as suggested at the outset, to equilibrium in a commodity market.

9. It will be noticed that we come out with the same number of main "cases" as did Marshall (see above, p. 187), although we inserted at the beginning the stage of the speculative market. Marshall's distinction between short-run and long-run normal price is omitted because it seems to us misleading to draw a general demarcation between fixed capital (human and non-human) and that which moves freely from one industry to another. Moreover, there is a more fundamental difference of view. Marshall refuses to treat the shorter-period adjustments clearly as *transfers* of fluid resources from and to other uses. That is, he refuses, in this and other connections, to separate, sharply, productive changes under static conditions, i.e., changes compensated by inverse changes in other industries, from changes which affect the social aggregate. This refusal, in our opinion, leads him into a number of errors, especially the error of treating land as categorically different from other capital goods. Cf. p. 198 of this article.

ment toward a position of stability in relation to the (extra-economic) conditions which form its environmental setting.

That the processes of economic growth do take place inside a world of conditioning circumstances is a fact which does not call for argument. To make a detailed list, however, separating economic changes from surroundings which do not change or change independently of economic events, seems to be an impossible task. It is one of the problems of economic science itself to discover and mark out its own boundaries. The demarcation would not be excessively difficult on the side of the physical universe and its laws, or that of man himself in the physiological sense, but on the side of psychology and social institutions it is much more forbidding.[10] In any event, the general idea is clear, and that is all that is needed here.

As to the variables involved in the processes, it is enough to say that those which call for discussion are, as in the earlier stages of the argument, those which were the data for the preceding stage. This list—the given conditions of a static economy—also presented difficulties, as the reader will recall. With reference to the main factors, the fact of progressive change in the actual world is evident enough: the available supplies of (nearly all) the productive factors are increasing, technology and business organization are improving, and consumers' wants are expanding and, we assume, being raised to "higher" levels. Our question is, Are these changes properly to be regarded as resulting from "forces" which they progressively "equilibrate" and destroy, as the flow of water or air destroys the difference of level or pressure, thus advancing toward a condition in which the changes would cease? In this case we may be sure that economic growth is not being and will not be maintained by progressive change in the setting itself, creating disequilibrium as fast as growth removes it. If progress is a movement toward equilibrium, it must in the nature of the case be a stationary one.

The British classical economists, notably J. S. Mill, assumed economic progress to be an equilibrating process and thought that the

10. In this connection we have again to face the important factor of one's conception of man's nature and place in the cosmos. The "scientific" view assumes that changes in man can be completely accounted for in terms of external and prior natural conditions. A theory which recognizes ends and allows man real initiative in changing himself or his environment is in contradiction with a scientific conception of human nature and transfers the discussion to a different realm of discourse. In the writer's opinion the contradiction is insurmountable in the present stage of intellectual development. Philosophy and experience have not taught us concepts which enable us to think comfortably in the terms of what experience and common sense force us to recognize as real and valid.

equilibrium was near at hand. Among a large group of economists today we meet with the opposite assumption in a more or less clear form, namely, that progress is self-exciting and cumulative. It has even been argued by the historian Henry Adams that the law of economic advance is a geometric progression. The modern successors of the "classicals" have got away from the express assumption of the imminence of a stationary state, but we still find the discussion of long-run changes running in terms of a tendency toward equilibrium; the nature of the equilibrium and of the given conditions to which it relates is not clearly stated and when examined seems to imply the assumption which has been formally dropped. The remainder of this paper will be devoted to a brief survey of the main long-run adjustments or elements of progress from this standpoint.

For this purpose it seems best to adopt a somewhat different classification of the progress variables (formerly the constants of the static economy). All the elements are bound up in man himself, as consumer, laborer, owner, or entrepreneur, and in discussing growth it is not convenient to separate sharply the different capacities in which the same individuals function.

We may begin with the element of population, i.e., with man "in the abstract," the bare fact of numbers. This of course is one of the favorite topics of the older economics and one which has always been treated in a way to exemplify the equilibrating principle. Recent discussion has been more cautious and has reacted far enough from the assumption that a given psychological standard of living controlling the birth rate is a fixed condition which, along with a total production of necessaries increasing much less rapidly than numbers, determines a definite equilibrium population and wage level.

The case appears to be an instructive one in a methodological sense. There can be no doubt that the natural principle of biological increase under given conditions (as affecting individuals) is a constant ratio (which might be a rate of decrease) or that the capacity of any area to support numbers of human beings is finite. In more obvious senses, the increase of population involves a sort of equalization of "forces," both in the direct sense of birth and death rates and more indirectly as regards motives and conditions underlying these rates. But to admit that "there are limits" does not validate the treatment of population as "approaching a limit" in the sense that the condition of equilibrium may be stated in terms of other conditions taken as given. The essential fact for emphasis is the interconnectedness of all the growth elements involved in economic progress over against all those of the conditioning environment. Each changing economic element is a condition affecting the change of any other element, or its ultimate stability of position, just as the features of the non-economic environment are conditions; but the former cannot be assumed "equal." It therefore appears to be misleading rather than helpful to describe the growth of population as a tendency toward any describable state of equilibrium. An equilibrium must relate to economic progress as a whole, to every factor treated as given in the static economy, not to any single element, just as in the static economy equilibrium must apply to all the variable elements simultaneously. (For brevity we pass over the physical composition of population, age, and sex distribution, etc., where the notion of equilibrium has a special but familiar application.)

Turning to the psychological traits of peoples, we notice as the first growth element the expansion of wants. The common assumption is that this is a cumulative rather than an equilibrating tendency. The assumption need not be questioned as a fact under modern conditions, though it is easy to see how a wave of any of several kinds of social-psychological contagion might nullify predictions based upon it. Any careful discussion of wants should also place in the foreground the fact that it is commonly the social implications of goods that are wanted rather than goods themselves or their direct physical effects on the individual. Other psychic traits, such as knowledge, skill, personal energy, and morale, relate to man as producer rather than as consumer and in fact comprise the element of technology and business organization. Industry or energy and morale seem, like population, to be subject to an ultimate limit; they seem to approach a practical perfection (assuming that they do advance). Knowledge and skill present an interesting problem. There is surely a limit to what any individual can learn or learn to do. A group, however, seems to remove the limit by specialization; but specialization calls for co-ordination, which is undoubtedly subject to increasing cost. In the United States, the increasing proportion of the population which the census shows to be earning their living by telling others what to do is already a theme for viewers-with-alarm. In connection with the moral factor, the bearing of knowledge may raise questions; business management may yet have to take seriously the poet's dictum that a little learning is a dangerous thing.

Looking at these psychological traits from a more strictly economic standpoint raises the question of cost. Even if it is maintained that progress in this field is "natural" (in accordance, for example, with the Darwinian principle of selection of favorable spontaneous variations), it can hardly be denied that most of the change which we see taking place is the effect of deliberate effort and expenditure, partly by society and partly by individuals, and in both cases largely under the influence of the expectation of an economic return. Again it is difficult to see how an equilibrium analysis can be realistically applied. The cost laws involved in this branch of "production," and the closeness of association between bearing the cost and receiving the return, present interesting problems too complicated to enter upon here. The production of changes in human nature is also affected by an especially high degree of uncertainty, the human attitude toward which is difficult to rationalize or to discover empirically.[11]

Coming now to material productive resources (exclusive of man himself) economists have traditionally made a categorical distinction between the natural and the artificial, between land and capital goods. By definition, obviously, land would be fixed in supply for all time; in that direction there could be no growth; the land supply would be one of the permanently given conditions constituting the setting for progress, an extra-economic datum. However, the distinction between land and capital goods was never clear and has been more and more called in question. It is difficult to define any actual category of natural agents the supply of which, known and available for use, has not been produced at a cost in work and waiting or will not similarly be increased in the future (though this may not hold for a particular politically bounded area). The surface of the earth is ultimately limited, but is not and is not likely to be in itself a factor limiting economic activity or growth. It appears to us, moreover, that on the one hand it is both impossible and futile to go back in time to the origin of resources, that is, to the advent of man on the earth, while on the other hand at any given time all resources are equally "ultimate" except in so far as they are known to be perishable and to require replacement.

11. Theorists generally assume that uncertainty is a psychological cost, but the evidence from gambling, gaming, and the like and that from "risky" types of business also seems to the writer to run in the contrary direction, other things being equal. If it is attractive on the whole, in comparison with a fixed, known reward equal to the true actuarial value of the contingent one, then the average return to investment in advertising, for example, should be below the general average rate.

To state our own position briefly, the facts seem to be that while most of the productive agencies in use at any time require maintenance and replacement, there are some which require only maintenance and a few perhaps which do not require even that. If the service of agencies which wear out are to be continuously available, a part of their earnings has to be set aside as a replacement fund. Under static conditions, as intimated above (n. 8), the matter would take care of itself. Every agency (i.e., its owner) would receive its current imputed product, out of which would be paid to "other agencies" whatever might be necessary (if anything) for permanent maintenance and replacement, only the residue being net income available for consumption. (Ultimately, the net residue is a payment for waiting or more accurately for time itself.) The distinction between maintenance and replacement really has no particular significance and would practically disappear in a static economy. In a progressive economy, the supply of productive agencies is increased by saving and investment, in accordance with the principle that equal investments yield equal increments of perpetual net income (or actuarial probabilities of such, or more, or less, depending on one's theory of uncertainty). It is true that some productive agencies may be more freely multiplied than others, and there are various degrees of uncertainty, and other differences. At the growing point or margin, natural resources analyze into two elements, a cost of discovery, which is essentially the "production of knowledge," already discussed, and a cost of development, which is the same as any other investment of capital in the production of things under known conditions.[12]

This brings us to growth of capital as a general fund, embodied in particular goods or ideas, but contrasting with any particular example of the latter. This is of course the problem of saving and investment, to which frequent reference has previously been found necessary. Avoiding the general problems of the theory of capital and interest, our question is whether accumulation is to be treated as an equilibrating process, and, if so, what are the conditions of equi-

12. This analysis of land into knowledge and capital goods may be contrasted with Schumpeter's analysis of capital goods into land and labor services, referred to previously.

The only peculiar condition is that this particular field of knowledge seems to be in a somewhat special sense exhaustible; there is a theoretical limit when the resources of the earth would be fully known, and in that sense this line of growth is equilibrating. (Nearly any scientific discovery is really and in economic significance an addition to the known resources of the earth as in another view it is an addition to technology, a human quality.)

librium. The neoclassical treatment of the interest rate typically proceeds from the proposition that it is a price and like other prices expresses equilibrium between supply and demand. This may have either of two meanings, referring to equilibrium under the given ("static") conditions or implying that the process of economic growth really moves in time toward a condition in which the interest rate would be permanently stable. Not uncommonly the two views are confused in the same statement, especially in the sense that supply is assumed to be subject to growth while the demand (general conditions, not absolute amount demanded) is assumed to be constant. An intersection of a demand curve with a curve of rate of increase in supply is of course meaningless.

Moreover, both the short-run and long-run equilibria, when clearly formulated, are in our opinion misleading and practically fallacious. This is so in the short run because the supply of capital at any given time, like that of concrete factors, is virtually fixed (and variations to which it may be subject are dependent on other things than the interest rate), while the amount demanded depends upon the rate and may vary substantially from zero to infinity if the rate is high or low enough. Hence the interest rate at a moment in a perfect capital market is a matter of the demand, the demand price for the given supply. The long-run case is more properly in question here and more important. We may illustrate by Marshall's statement: "Thus then interest . . . tends toward an equilibrium level such that the aggregate demand for capital . . . is equal to the aggregate stock forthcoming . . ." (*Principles of Economics*, p. 534). His reasoning apparently is that saving is motivated by interest and that the accumulation of capital must bring down the interest rate (diminishing returns) and hence that the process will finally come to rest at a point at which the return is inadequate to induce further net saving. The essential fallacy we find in the argument is that other things which must be assumed equal not merely are not but cannot be, that accumulation itself has other effects than the equilibrating one, some of which work in the opposite direction. One such effect is that as new savings are invested, the income derived from them reduces the difficulty of saving at the same time that incentive is reduced. It would seem to be impossible to say, a priori, which effect would predominate or to assert that if everything else remained unchanged saving would cease before capital became entirely a free good (which, as already observed, could not happen until all goods became free). In addition, we must note a further, less direct effect, that abundant capital and low interest rates stimulate invention, the general tendency of which is to elevate the demand curve for capital. Moreover, the activities of invention and discovery themselves absorb capital (apart from that used in constructing and developing the results), and in this employment the law of decreasing returns seems to work in a slow and uncertain way.

In connection with these reverse influences must be noted the high rate of accumulation which we actually find in the contemporary world, with the absence of any clear tendency either for accumulation to slacken or the interest rate itself to fall. These facts alone would make the theory of a tendency toward equilibrium questionable and prove that at least that condition is indefinitely remote in time, giving "other things" indefinite scope for action.

For methodology, the point is that the "other things" or "given conditions" assumed as the setting for any particular process form an interconnected system, while the process is also one of a number forming a similar system. For very small changes it is admissible to assume that while any element or condition changes, the others in the same group remain fixed. But in discussing trends over any considerable period of time this must not be done. The greatest caution needs to be exercised in determining and specifying the systems of constants or long-period processes and of variables adjusting to them (and to each other), if the notion of tendency toward equilibrium is to yield sound results.

In regard to the distribution of ownership of productive capacity, specified as a constant in the static economy, the long-run tendency would appear to be, as in the case of the expansion of wants, definitely cumulative as opposed to equilibrating. Ordinary economic forces tend toward a progressive concentration. Wealth does breed; "to him that hath shall be given and from him that hath not shall be taken away." If such a trend is not empirically prominent, it is because of various sorts of deliberate social interference, equally numerous "accidents," and perhaps factors analogous to those which make any large mass unstable. However, beyond a certain point again, other things cannot be equal; the possessor of a vast fortune, especially if it has been inherited, can hardly have the same motives and interests as one just achieving business success.

Our general conclusion must be that in the field of economic progress the notion of tendency toward equilibrium is definitely inapplicable to particular elements of growth and, with reference to progress as a unitary process or system of interconnected changes, is of such limited and partial application as to be misleading rather than useful. This view is emphasized by reference to the phenomena covered by the loose term "institution." All speculative glimpses at trends in connection with price theory relate to a "competitive" or "capitalistic" economic system. But all the human interests and traits involved in this type of economic life are subject to historical change. Moreover, no society is or could be entirely and purely competitive. The roles of the state, of law, and of moral constraint are always important and that of other forms of organization such as voluntary co-operation may be so. Business life in the strictest sense never conforms closely to the theoretical behavior of an economic man. Always history is being made; opinions, attitudes, and institutions change, and there is evolution in the nature of capitalism. In fact evolution toward other organization forms as the dominant type begins before capitalism reaches its apogee. Such social evolution is rather beyond the province of the economic theorist, but it is pertinent to call attention to the utter inapplicability to such changes, i.e., to history in the large, of the notion of tendency toward a price equilibrium. Probably we must go further and reject entirely the use of the mechanical analogy, the categories of force, resistance, and movement, in discussing basic historical changes.

IX

The Business Cycle, Interest, and Money
A Methodological Approach[1]

ONE of the most important criticisms of a mechanical sort[2] which is urged against the "capitalist system" (as it is familiarly misnamed) by its attackers centers in the phenomenon of unemployment and, specifically, in business depression. In serious economic discussion, depression is of course the correlate of "boom" conditions, and the real underlying phenomenon is the tendency for the control of economic life by market competition to give rise to oscillations, or fluctuations, of a more or less rhythmical or cyclical character. An argument frequently urged against economic theory, in its aspect of apologetic for free enterprise (which a functional description inevitably gives the impression of being), is that it has overlooked or ignored the existence of cycles and depression which the critics assert is inherent in such a system.

The question of theory, the nature and causes of economic cycles, will be our chief concern in this paper, which will refer to the problem of policy only briefly, in conclusion, for the purpose of clarifying the explanatory argument. Economic theory, as expounded in the orthodox tradition, down until very recent times has been criticized validly because it failed to recognize the business cycle as a reality and to inquire into the causality of the cycle. However, this criticism does not, as frequently contended, involve repudiation of the deductive-theoretical method of attack upon economic problems if correctly used, as the following argument will make clear. On the contrary, in the present state of economic analysis, little argument should be required to show that purely abstract theorizing about the free-market system of economic organization should long ago have led students to expect cyclical changes as a matter of course, even if

1. Reprinted by permission from the *Review of Economic Statistics*, Vol. XXIII, No. 2 (May, 1941).

2. Mechanical criticisms are to be distinguished from ethical. The former allege that the enterprise organization is bad because it does not work in accord with the "theory"; the latter, that it is inherently vicious even if competition were always perfect, etc.

the occurrence of these changes and the evils which they involve did not force them upon the attention of students.

The issues go back to methodological considerations. Economic theory, as an abstract logical system and as a functional and hence more or less apologetic account of the free-market economy, has always pictured the free-market economy as an "automatic" mechanism—assuming voluntary exchange or the absence of force and fraud. Its nature is that of a machine self-regulated by a governor. A little reflection about the workings of any mechanical governor suffices to show that such a device always controls the regulated phenomenon—the speed of an engine, the temperature of a room, etc.—within some limits, between which it oscillates in a more or less regular or rhythmic cycle. This follows from the inevitable presence of "lag" in the working of the mechanism. The shape, amplitude, and periodicity of the oscillations to be expected depend on the nature and amount of the lag in the response of the mechanism. In fact, under conditions which are both quite simple and fairly common, the first response of a governor may be "perverse." The analogy of a thermostat regulating the temperature of a house by controlling the flow of fuel upon a coal fire has long since been suggested in connection with economic cycles. The immediate effect of the thermostatic call for more heat will be to cool off the fire appreciably; and, conversely, the fire will burn more intensely for a time after a rise in temperature lessens the flow of fuel.

Application of such simple mechanical principles to the price system, with recognition of its obvious factual characteristics, should have led economists to recognize the inevitability of a tendency to oscillations in practically every economic adjustment or response. Consequently, they should have recognized not merely the unreality of the notion of a tendency to establish stationary equilibrium but also a limitation amounting to a degree of falsity in the logical method of simultaneous equations. In the presence of a lag between cause and effect, the function-and-variable conception of cause and effect itself is valid only for long-run tendencies; it applies to the equilibrium situation only, giving no information as to the quantitative relation between the cause and the effect (the independent and the dependent variable) at any moment of time.

Variations in an economic cause can never be expected to produce strictly simultaneous variations in its effect. The functional relation between, say, the price of a particular commodity and the quantity consumed, as depicted by a demand curve (the simplest and most reliable case of economic causality), tells us nothing about the relation in time or even in magnitude between changes in the one and the responsive changes in the other (assuming such relation is accurately known). The response may be delayed by an indeterminate interval and may at a given moment have a magnitude indeterminately divergent in either direction from that of the new position of equilibrium.

Two special cases of economic cause and effect are particularly important. On the one hand, even when the causal relation at equilibrium is simple and monotonic, perpetual oscillation of the dependent magnitude may be the natural reaction to a constant value of the independent variable. A perfectly constant air pressure in an organ pipe sets it into vibration. On the other hand, changes in one variable may produce change in another, which may or may not include oscillations, in situations in which at equilibrium the magnitude of the second is completely independent of the magnitude of the first. This phenomenon of "disturbance" is especially important in monetary theory, which will presently be our main concern. A monetary change may be expected to produce a temporary change in any price ratio—to be followed, after a varying course of events, by a return to the original value.

For a simple mechanical example of the phenomenon of disturbance in the absence of any long-run causal relation, we may think of a dam across a stream, with control works of any sort, backing up a substantial quantity of water on the upper side, and we may consider the relation between, say, the amount of opening in a spillway and the flow of water at the dam and in the stream below it. Any opening or closing of sluices will produce a temporary change which may be of very great magnitude in the level and the rate of flow of the stream below the dam, *but no permanent change*. After a period of adjustment, the flow below the dam will be the same as the flow above it, which is not affected at all by the control exercised at the dam itself. The flow below the dam is not a "function" of the size of opening in the obstruction, or of the height of the latter, whether at equilibrium or at any moment during readjustment to a change in the effective height of the dam.[3]

3. In this case the effect-magnitude would not be thrown into oscillation to any important extent, but mechanical situations in which the result would be of this character can be invented without difficulty. It is to be noted that in relation to such a situation there is no meaningful short-period equilibrium. Most of what is said in economic literature about what happens "in the short run" involves some confused reference to some phenomenon of disturbance, but further inquiry into the topic is not called for here.

It should be emphasized that none of these special considerations invalidate the concept of equilibrium or the necessity of using the concept in causal analysis. Even in a simple mechanical situation, where the result to be expected from a constant cause would be perpetual oscillation in the effect, as in an organ pipe or other vibrating systems, the notion of equilibrium is necessary for analysis and explanation. This is also true of a system which does not convert energy, such as a pendulum oscillating without friction in a vacuum. The attraction toward a position of equilibrium is the vital point in the theoretical explanation.[4] And, in practice, the problem of action is to construct or modify the mechanism—in so far as steadiness in operation is desired—so that oscillations will be held down to whatever extent is justified by the cost involved. A thermostatic regulator or speed governor can be built so as to operate with a degree of accuracy to which no definite limit can be assigned, short of absolute perfection.

MAIN "CASES" OF ECONOMIC OSCILLATION

In practically every economic adjustment or cause-and-effect relation, conditions are present which clearly involve a tendency to oscillation. Three main cases must be briefly considered.

First case: the demand relation.—The first and simplest case is the demand relation, the adjustment of price in a speculative market for a product, under the assumption of an approximately constant flow into the market on the supply side.[5] We may think of a commodity such as wheat. Price is assumed to be unaffected by monetary changes, to be an ideal relative price, measured in "neutral" money or any ideal *numéraire*. At any moment of time, such a product ex-

4. Incidentally, it is interesting to note that economic theory has generally treated the absence of friction as the condition requisite for establishing and maintaining equilibrium. Pure mechanical theory generally has the opposite implication, that only the presence of friction will put an end to oscillations, and only a particular kind of friction (fluid viscosity) will result in a position of rest coincident with the position of theoretical equilibrium.

5. All markets are speculative and, in fact, approach the character of an ideal market more or less in proportion to the degree that they are explicitly and effectively speculative, i.e., to the degree in which there is organized speculation. Of course, direct, explicit speculation is possible only in connection with a commodity which can be stored and which regularly exists in stocks; but the reasoning will apply in a more complicated form to the prices of most services. For services which do not become embodied in products and get marketed as products are in practically every case the services of things or agents (including human beings) which can be accumulated and "produced" by services of previously existing agents.

ists in some quantity, held in stocks which are more or less constantly drawn down by consumption and replaced from production. The effect of, say, a reported prospective increase in demand or reduction in the supply (whether the report is true or not) is an upward movement in the price, in accord (here) with general demand theory. The next step called for by general theory is a reduction of purchases and stimulation of sales and the establishment of equilibrium at the "correct" level. But, in the first place, if there is an appreciable lag in the response of consumption to price change, the response will be "overdone" and will reverse itself, since in the meantime the rise in price will go beyond the point at which it would have stopped if the decline of consumption had simultaneously kept pace with it.

The tendency of such a change to be overdone is accentuated by another factor. A well-recognized psychological phenomenon is that an upward movement in price tends to create a belief in an upward trend, and the effect of this belief is to stimulate purchases and retard sales, leading to a cumulative rise in price. This effect, of course, is the opposite of the theoretical effect of the price movement. But this cumulative tendency can operate only within fairly narrow limits. The buying which is stimulated by the rise in price will be speculative buying to hold, not buying for consumption, even if it is done by consumers. Its effect is to hold more "wheat" out of consumption and so to increase the stocks speculatively carried. In a well-organized market, this situation must soon be recognized by professional speculators and will lead to a reversal in the direction of movement, which will then similarly tend to go to an extreme in the opposite direction. Thus the general result to be anticipated is more or less regular oscillation within more or less definite and fairly narrow limits.[6]

The question arises whether, even in the absence of any definite change in either supply or demand conditions, price in a speculative market could be expected to remain constant. The answer would seem to be in the negative. It is a case of *unstable equilibrium*, and any small accidental change will upset it and start oscillations. Such phenomena are not explained in terms of what happens at the turning points. If a cone is balanced on its point, we do not inquire as to what particular "cause" makes it tip over. The situation of a market

6. The range will be fairly narrow, except in so far as the completely irrational psychology of a "boom" may become operative, in which traders bet on the behavior of other traders rather than act on estimates of the economic facts.

is far more complex than that of the balanced cone, due to the time dimension and the role of energy flow. A closer analogy is the flow of water through a channel. However smooth the surface over which the water flows, there will always be ripples of some amplitude, their detailed character depending on conditions which, as in the case of the cone, could not be accurately determined. In the case of a market, however, psychological factors create vastly greater complexity, sensitiveness, and uncertainty in the result.

Second case: the supply relation.—The second case is that of supply, the regulation of production by the price of the product, this time assuming an approximately invariable demand function. Price, as before, is assumed to mean relative price in terms of an ideal measure of exchange value. Here the natural tendency to oscillation is enormously aggravated, since the lag of productive adjustment behind a price change is typically much greater than that of consumption. The technical reasons for delay in the adjustment of production to prices need not be developed; and to simplify the analysis, we assume "constant cost" in the long run. The fact that cycles occur in particular industries and the reasons for their occurrence are well known. During some interval before an increase in price becomes reflected in an increased flow of the good into consumption, commitments in the direction of increased production may go forward without producing any effect in the way of reducing price —and reciprocally for a decline.

The situation may be illustrated by an aggravated case, a product with a very long "production period," such as apples. If at a particular time the production of apples is profitable, a period of some ten years—the time required to plant trees and bring them to the age of bearing—may elapse before an increased flow of the product into the consumption market acts to reduce the price. In the meantime, the extent to which the development of productive capacity may be overdone might go virtually beyond any assignable limit. The production of apples has been chosen for illustration because the construction period for the chief item of specialized productive equipment used—the growth period for orchards—is especially familiar and definite. But the same argument applies to any product whose production calls for specialized equipment which itself requires a considerable time for production, so that a corresponding interval is required to expand the output of the final product in response to an increase in the demand.[7] It should be emphasized, again, that the situation is likely to embody unstable equilibrium to such a degree that fluctuations in production, of a more or less rhythmical sort, are to be expected, even apart from any such change as would attract attention in the demand or the supply. Where this is the case, the productive fluctuation or cycle does not call for any concrete causal explanation beyond the fact of unstable equilibrium itself— as, similarly, we do not need a specific explanation of why an object resting on a point does not remain balanced.

Those phenomena also are due to speculative conditions, to the absence or imperfection of foresight. The development of an active and well-organized market would contribute substantially to the stabilization of the industry. The existence of such a market would stimulate investigation and the dissemination of information. (If the product can be standardized, sale for future delivery is possible, even beyond the period for which storage is feasible.) Even an active market for the specialized capital goods (orchards) should contribute to stabilization if it is not too much influenced by the "sucker" mentality. But we should always keep in mind in economic reasoning that perfect foresight is theoretically as well as practically impossible, unless all the parties plan collusively in advance all details of their procedure and adhere to the agreed plan. The resulting situation would be the antithesis of individualism—the ultimate communistic-anarchistic collectivism, as impossible as a perfectly competitive system. But lack of knowledge by one individual (or unit) as to what others are doing and planning is mentioned as one form of uncertainty in economic life.

In this case also, the first effect of a primary change, such as an accidental shortage or an increase in the effective consumption demand for the product, may be perverse. This result appears in such a case as livestock, where a rise in the price may cause a withholding of animals (females) from the market for breeding purposes and so may lead to a temporary reduction instead of an increase in the flow of the product into consumption. The "corn-hog" cycle is a familiar illustration of an oscillation which is no doubt aggravated by

7. The time required for contraction, it will be noted, depends on the durability of the specialized equipment—within the limits beyond which the plethora of capacity may justify outright destruction. Hence the expansion and contraction phases need not be approximately equal in time length; the histogram of the cycle may be quite unsymmetrical. But there probably is in fact a general correspondence between the time required to produce specialized equipment and its service life.

this factor. Similar effects might arise with a grain like wheat in a poor region where the yield was a small multiple of the seed. In this general case, also, as in the first, we should no doubt expect oscillations of appreciable magnitude even in the absence of noticeable changes in the underlying conditions.[8]

Third case: the theory of the "business cycle."—The third case is the main phenomenon mentioned at the outset, the tendency to oscillation of production and of general prices in an economy as a whole, i.e., the phenomenon of the business cycle. Discussion within the limits allowable here must be considerably oversimplified. The position to be argued is that the cause of fluctuation or oscillation in an economy (in contrast with a particular industry) is found in a combination of the two general principles already considered—the first reinforced by the second. In the argument for the economy as a whole, general product prices and cost prices, in money, take the place of relative price and cost for a particular product in some ideal *numéraire*. That is, we are concerned with general prices, or the price level, which is another way of referring to the "value of money." The basic phenomenon of the cycle is, then, speculation in money, combined with lags in the actual output of final products

8. Discussion of oscillations in the production of a single commodity seems to call for some mention of the so-called "acceleration principle." But the reasoning underlying this principle, or relation, seems to the writer to be interesting chiefly for the confusion which it involves, specifically with reference to that notorious source of difficulty, the "time dimension." It is argued that if a new demand for a product equal to a certain fraction of the replacement demand is added to the latter (in an industry in equilibrium), the effective demand may be increased in a much greater ratio, in consequence of the durability of the product. For illustration, if the service life of a product is ten years, the replacement demand at equilibrium will be ten units per year for each hundred units in service. Then satisfaction of a new demand for ten units within one year would call for production of twenty (for each hundred previously in use) instead of ten units, an increase of 100 per cent instead of 10 per cent.

Such reasoning rests in the first place on the selection of an arbitrary period of time. If the latter is assumed to be sufficiently short, the multiplication of demand can be raised to any ratio, while after the "year" is ended the number required for replacement goes back to the old figure for the rest of the ten-year period. The tenth "year" again, and every tenth year, would see a demand for double production. Enough has been said to show the unreality of the reasoning. That "demand" is also taken as an absolute quantity, as well as a quantity for an arbitrary period, is evident. As soon as the correct view of it as a function is substituted, the argument seems to become practically meaningless. But a change in the rate of growth of demand for a product may cause an absolute decline in the "apparent demand" for a durable means of production (a new curve at a lower level) if there is a sufficient lack of foresight back of the apparent or empirically actual demand. The subject is important and cries for thorough and careful investigation as to both the theory and the facts.

behind planned changes or commitments in production. This third case, however, is further complicated not merely by the heterogeneity in the "commodity" and the conditions of production but especially by the behavior of money costs of production in relation to product prices, as a consequence of induced changes in stocks and flows of money.

Cycle analysis properly begins with the fact that the general price level, the reciprocal of the value or purchasing power of money, is subject to the same psychological tendency already pointed out in connection with the price of a particular product such as wheat. An incipient tendency of prices (of products in general) to rise creates the impression of an upward trend (a downward trend in the value of money). The root of the phenomenon in this case is the fact that money, while not literally consumed, is in part effectively "used"— i.e., employed in a real, technical, or quasi-technical role in organized production and distribution—and in part it is held "idle." The motive for holding money idle, or especially the main variable motive, is speculation for a rise in its future value. The fact that men commonly do not think of the activity in these terms operates as an aggravating condition. Since cash holdings yield no return in any other form, any cash held longer than necessary to bridge over the regular non-coincidence of receipts and disbursements must be expected to increase in value (relative to other wealth) at a rate equal to the yield of any property to be had in exchange for the money, at existing prices—with allowance for the uncertainty in both alternatives.

The economic process in a pecuniary economy involves the holding or owning, by somebody, of wealth—all the wealth of the economy—and also the entire stock of money. Hence every property owner has the alternative either of holding money up to the amount of his fortune or of choosing the concrete kind of wealth other than money that he will hold. The existence of claims against wealth, bearing "interest," specified as a periodic amount of money, and (usually) promising redemption at a specified money value at a specified future date, is a further complication which will be dealt with later. Any belief that the value of money will rise in the future, relative to real wealth, tends to lead men to hold money (or such "bonds") instead of real wealth, the natural effect of which is a fall in the money value of wealth (and a rise in the value of bonds), which tends to confirm the belief and aggravate the tendency and so on cumulatively. (And conversely, of course, for the opposite movement if it is once started.)

For reasons which are fairly obvious, the tendency to accumulation of idle money held speculatively, thus lowering the price of wealth (and raising the price of "bonds"), does not reverse itself before the movement gets far from the equilibrium position, as does the similar movement in the case of a particular product. On the one hand, the "real" demand for money, for use in effecting transactions, is not of a comparably definite character. This real demand depends on two factors, the price level and the volume of trade, and both factors are largely dependent upon changes in the demand for money for speculative holding. Thus the concept of an equilibrium value of money is extremely vague at best. But it is nonetheless necessary for analysis and nonetheless real; and the knowledge of its reality as a center of oscillatory tendencies is an essential factor in the situation at any point in the cycle. To this vagueness must be added the absence of any basis for accurate knowledge, or any general consensus in the minds of wealth owners as to what the "true" value of money, the "natural" price level, is in any momentary situation, even in so far as such magnitudes exist or are believed to exist. This aspect of things is further aggravated by the peculiar psychology of money already mentioned, the tendency of men generally to think of it as "absolute" in value and to believe that other values are changing, instead of realizing that they are speculating in money when they are actually doing so. (The exigencies of accounting probably have much to do with this attitude.) In short, in the case of money, the speculative demand predominates over the real demand, while in the case of a commodity the opposite relation holds. Thus the tendency for increase or decrease in speculative holding of money (i.e., disposition to hold which reflects itself in general prices, the quantity of money being constant) to feed upon itself cumulatively is subject to no such effective check as results from the accumulation of a consumable commodity with a fairly definite demand curve which is fairly well known, like the stock held speculatively. Indeed, in the case of money, just what does set a boundary to a movement of general prices in either direction, and especially the downward movement, becomes something of a mystery.

The general condition of instability is further accentuated by the role played in economic society by the banks, which function as central depositories or storehouses for idle money or lending power. Two facts are important. The first is that in real life the banks are the primary agencies through which "money," including circulating deposits, is "created" or put into and withdrawn from active circulation. The second is that these changes are effected mainly through the making and cancellation of loans for production purposes, i.e., for investment in productive equipment (or for holding such assets, including all inventories). For reasons which are familiar, the consequences of short-period lending are peculiarly serious.

This discussion brings us to consideration of the role of the second of our two primary tendencies to oscillation, namely, oscillation in production, which has already been noticed in connection with a particular industry but is now to be considered for production as a whole. Even in the simpler case, the relation between the demand price for a product and its output was noted to be one of unstable equilibrium, so that cyclical fluctuations in production will be the rule, quite apart from periodic changes (or any notable changes) in demand. The relation between changes in production plans and actual output placed on the market may, as was also noted, be inverse instead of direct for a time after a turning point in the cycle.

When we turn to production in an economy as a whole, these factors may be expected to be present and operative, but operative in a somewhat different way. Producers' decisions are, of course, based on the relations between money prices and money costs. In connection with a single product, we could assume that variations in the price would not appreciably affect the prices (rent) of ultimate productive capacity—labor and fluid capital—i.e., that the incentive and the resistance to expansion or contraction would be a matter of mobility, meaning conversion into and out of specialized forms.[9] In relation to production as a whole, this principle of price constancy for ultimate productive capacity cannot be assumed; or, more accurately, like the mobility of "capacity" between industries, it now has meaning only with reference to the different "stages" of industry in general. These stages may be simplified into two, the creation of new productive equipment and the operation of equipment already existing in the creation of the final product for consumption. The essential fact now is that the prices of final products are more responsive to those *monetary* changes which fundamentally operate upon general prices and manifest themselves in changes in the price level.

Speaking in concrete terms, the ultimate cost of production, for industry as a whole, consists largely of wages—excluding agriculture, which plays an extremely small role, and probably on the whole an

9. In the case of labor, this means retraining or different training of the youth coming into the ranks of labor and involves no real substantial difference in principle in comparison with other forms of capital.

inverse or stabilizing role, in the cycle. Especially with reference to moderately short-run changes, the *variable* costs of productive enterprises, as they are actually organized and financed, consist overwhelmingly of wages.[10] Wages are notoriously sticky, especially with respect to any downward change in hourly wage-rates, which is the important fact in the unit cost or marginal cost of products.

BEHAVIOR OF MONEY

To sketch in an explanatory way the course of events to be expected in the competitive adjustment of production to demand, we require a simplified picture, or "theory," of the behavior of money. For present purposes, the following assumptions seem justifiable: (*a*) The total quantity of money (M in the Fisher equation) is constant, including both "cash" and the lending (deposit-creating) power in the hands of the banking system. (*b*) The transactions-velocity of circulation of money in effective use (we may call it "active V") is also constant. This means that changes in "total V" reflect transfers from idle reserves or hoards (where $V = 0$) to active use, or in the opposite direction (hoards, including idle lending power of the banks). In consequence, finally (*c*) changes in general prices (P) reflect changes in "active M." That the division between active and idle funds is not definite or determinate goes without saying, and the other assumptions are more or less unrealistic, but the whole group of assumptions seems to be a close enough approximation to the facts to function as a hypothesis for a general explanation of the cycle.

SEQUENCE OF EVENTS IN THE BUSINESS CYCLE

With respect to production, the course of events expected will be virtually the same in principle as in the corn-hog cycle, or the apple cycle, but will rest upon a tendency of general prices to fluctuate and will be aggravated by the concentration of this effect upon final products while cost-prices are sticky. Let us begin our discussion with a condition of depression, involving unemployment of labor and equipment, especially in the production-goods industries. Any incipient upward tendency in business conditions—or even a belief that such a tendency is in prospect—naturally tends to act cumulatively as a stimulant to operations. Re-employment will re-

10. Stickiness of the prices of intermediate products at various stages in production, or of dealers' margins, and the role of ownership, would have to be considered as important in an exhaustive analysis.

sult in increased disbursements, especially to labor, which will increase the demand for consumption goods, with a further reaction upon production-goods industries, and so on cumulatively. The increased disbursements are assumed to come out of idle money, either cash (or deposits) in the hands of enterprises, or deposits newly created through loans or perhaps resulting from governmental action.

As unemployment of heavy-industry equipment is absorbed, a wave of investment in these industries will naturally follow, with a still greater increase in disbursements but, during some period of lag, without any increase in the output of consumption goods. Hence the investment tends to be "overdone" and/or to be made at "excessive" cost. This last feature is connected with the absorption of unemployed labor, and perhaps with a drawing-in of "inferior" workers, but especially with a rise in wages, probably gaining upon the rise in prices of consumption goods.[11] The interval of "inflation" may continue until idle funds (including lending power) are exhausted. This situation will certainly lead to a "crisis" and the reversal of the whole process. But reversal may come about from other causes, such as the overtaking of prices by costs, a crop failure or any calamity in the business world, or mere "psychology." Too much attention has been given to this problem of the cause of the collapse. The essential fact is merely the unstable equilibrium. As already noted, we do not try to find out what particular cause upsets an object balanced upon a sharp point.

For reasons which are not very mysterious, the declining phase of the cycle tends to be relatively precipitous and catastrophic in comparison with the ascending phase. And the turning point at the "bottom" is also a more obscure phenomenon than that at the peak. The essence of the matter presumably is that investment reaches an effective minimum, actually with a substantial amount of under-maintenance or disinvestment, for a time.[12]

11. If there is a notable "perverse" reaction, it is because of diversion of productive capacity, specifically labor, from the consumption-goods field to that of investment, so that the flow of final products is actually reduced until the new "crop" of capital goods comes into bearing.

12. The most serious problem in the cycle is undoubtedly the occurrence of a condition of relatively stabilized depression, after recovery has proceeded to approximately the point where heavy industry is being maintained at a level which will permanently supply the existing consumption demand, but without the growth in total investment which must be regarded as a normal feature of "capitalist" economy. (And for obscure reasons a considerable growth of invest-

BEHAVIOR OF INTEREST RATES

In the argument so far we have said nothing about the course or the role of the interest rate or rates. This topic involves two questions: first, the effects of interest rates on the course of the cycle itself and, second, conversely, the effects of the course of events in the cycle on interest rates. To the first question, as to what interest rates have to do in an effective causal sense with the course of events of the cycle, the answer undoubtedly is "very little"! To be sure, interest is an element in cost of production, and interest rates, as well as wages, show an important lag. But, clearly, in view of the way in which enterprises are commonly organized and financed, the borrowing rate on money, including the rate of yield at which bonds can be sold and the bank rate, is relatively quite unimportant in comparison either with the effects of wage changes or with the role of speculative considerations. Its effects are important "in the long run" but not for the periods for which businessmen can or do make plans in a depression.

It is no doubt hypothetically or theoretically true that if interest rates were to rise high enough, and soon enough, on the upswing, they might put a check to the boom before it reached a point involving the inevitability of collapse. But in fact they do not rise to any such level or at any such speed.[13] In the other direction, an effective stimulus to recovery might occur if money could be made available at rates low enough (or at negative rates "high" enough) in the time of depression. This situation, however, would probably require either enormously high negative rates for the short term or lending on long term at very low rates and without critical scrutiny of the security of the loan. Negative rates can hardly prevail naturally, because of the negligible cost of storing money, and the second possibility is also excluded for private lenders. Thus, apparently, any action operating through interest rates can only be

---

ment may be necessary to make a free-enterprise economy operate at a level near its capacity.) We have seen in England in the twenties and in the United States in the thirties such a relative stabilization, with a considerable amount of unemployed labor, some excess plant capacity in industry, and a great plethora of idle funds. In the writer's opinion, this may be explained by political conditions. In view of these conditions—notably the aftermath of one world war and preparation for another, and, perhaps worse, the reformist activities and especially the reformist talk of governments which have worked directly against recovery—the phenomenon is not really very mysterious.

13. The momentary "crisis" rates, for funds to meet payments for which commitments have already been made, are not really in point.

effective for moderate fluctuations (cf. Hawtrey's earlier views) or as a detail in connection with those of major proportions.

We turn now to the second question, concerning the effect of the events of the cycle on the interest rate, which is a more interesting question for general economic theory. The first fact to be noted is another way of stating what was commented on above, i.e., that a relatively moderate decline in speculative conditions may suffice virtually to kill all demand for loans for new real investment (at rates above zero) or even for the maintenance of existing investment, beyond that which may be loosely designated as "necessary." Such a situation, reducing the effective demand for capital for real investment to zero, completely changes the ordinary meaning of the interest rate and the causality affecting it. As already noted, capitalistic economy is "normally" progressive, in the sense that total investment is growing at a substantial rate. This point deserves the utmost emphasis. We do not know whether a free-enterprise economy is permanently possible under any other conditions. Under the assumptions of rational behavior and foresight, a stationary condition or even retrogression should not interfere with efficiency. But growth is clearly required for a high degree of effective mobility. For other reasons—of a psychological and institutional character— and in the absence of historical experience, speculation as to what would actually happen under an established expectation of stagnation or decadence becomes unrealistic. (The concept of a stationary society is nonetheless necessary for analytical purposes.) In any case, under "normal" conditions, with a substantial amount of net real investment going forward, the loan rate on money must approximate the expected rate of yield on such investment. Allowance must of course be made for risk, and also, in connection with long-term loan contracts, for foreseen changes in the value of money and for this particular form of risk, since loan contracts usually call for payment of interest and repayment of principle in lawful money.

The contract for a loan of money is always equivalent to a sale of an interest or equity in some assets owned (or to be created or acquired and owned) by the borrower, plus a lease of this equity interest to the lender, plus, usually, a contract for the repurchase of the equity at the terminal date for a money sum (usually) equal to the principal of the original loan. Any typical loan contract could be replaced by such a combination of contracts, effecting exactly the same result. It could also be replaced by "co-partnership" arrangements of various forms. Under ideally perfect competition and perfect foresight, all these forms of contractual arrangement would be a matter of complete indifference to all parties. In fact, under these ideal conditions there would be no occasion for "contracts" at all! Choice among the possible arrangements by the parties in question is purely a matter of the specialization of the bearing of risk or uncertainty in various forms. In fact, all contracts, or commitments over future time, are essentially of this sort; the typical contract relates especially to the uncertainties due to market imperfections.

While the rate of interest stipulated in long-term loan contracts will naturally be affected by any anticipated change in the value of money over the period of the loan (the loan being made in money), monetary phenomena have absolutely nothing to do with the theoretical nature or causality of the rate of return on real investment. A Robinson Crusoe would have to calculate this rate of return as a condition of making rationally any plan for the future. In the same way, in all essentials, the rate of return is involved in the plans and decisions of individuals or enterprises in the most complex organized enterprise economy, using a money unit of value in any form whatever. All plans involving any commitment for the future include, or essentially are, plans for investment or disinvestment, or for both together (i.e., for the transfer of investment from one field to another). This would be true even in a Crusoe economy using no "goods" other than those which were superabundant and free. In all essentials, the training or retraining of a laborer—of a Crusoe or a worker for wages in contemporary society—is a matter of investment or the transfer of investment; and the economically rational management of such activity involves the same kind of investment-yield calculation as the production of any material instrument or the replacement of one such instrument by another—presumably in response to a change in the form of consumption demand.[14]

14. A logically simpler way of looking at the problem of the rate of return on invested capital under ideal conditions—in a Crusoe economy or an organized economy, considered as a unit—is to think of the present worth of a future income stream. The decisive fact is that "sources" of future income can be produced at a cost which (apart from disorganization and blockage) consists of the sacrifice of a consumption-income stream during the interval required to make the investment, i.e., to construct the source in question. If the new source will be productive at a known and uniform income rate for a very long period, and if the construction period is very short, the calculation of the cost as a multiple of the perpetual annual yield (assumed to be known in advance) is a matter of simple arithmetical division. Under more realistic conditions, the interest rate itself is a factor both in the calculation of the cost and in the conversion of the time-limited yield-stream into a perpetual one. The problem becomes mathematically more complicated, but still not difficult, and the principles are identically the same.

In a capital-using economy, with effective freedom to invest (and specifically with new investment going forward in substantial volume), it is (to repeat) self-evident that if loans of money are made, the effective rate must tend to be approximately equal to the rate of return on investment, regardless of the value unit in terms of which computations are made. In long-term contracts involving any stipulated exchange ratio, this contractual price will of course be influenced, in a mathematically simple way, by the general market anticipation of future price changes and the prevalent attitude toward any recognized risk of such changes. And if any contract calls for payments of "money" at future dates, the amounts will be affected in the same way by any expected change in the value of the money unit. The loan of money at interest is such a contract.

If loans are made for some entirely different purpose than that of constructive investment, they will be made at the same rate, if men act "sensibly," since no one need pay more or take less. The only "other purpose" which comes to mind is that of the consumption loan. A little reflection will show that only a net change in the whole volume of such loans outstanding can be counted either as demand or as supply in the loan market and then it must be counted on both the demand and the supply sides. The logically correct procedure in loan-market analysis is to take account of consumption loans only by allowing for any increase or decrease in the flow of capital into investment which may result from a change in the total demand for and volume of such loans. That is, if the actual net saving in any period is correctly stated, borrowing for consumption need not be explicitly mentioned at all. Where there is an effective investment market, the rate on other loans is set exclusively in the competition for real capital for real investment.

Speculation as to what the rate of interest would be in a society or world with its stock of productive capacity fixed, and with consumption loans the only ones being made, is practically pointless. Assuming an ideally perfect market, the rate would undoubtedly fluctuate "wildly" over a wide range of positive and negative values between winter and summer and over holidays, etc. This is the situation in which the interest rate would be determined (à la Fetter and one of Böhm-Bawerk's theories) by the general market comparison between present and future consumption. In the actual world, the comparison between present and future is reflected in the volume of saving—or eventually of dissaving—and not to any extent in the rate of return. The rate of return can be affected only indirectly, and very slowly at best (and under *ceteris-paribus* conditions which are contrary to the facts). Also, a change in the rate of saving may produce a disturbance in the market rate of interest, followed by re-establishment of the original rate after the period of time required to adjust the speed of new capital creation to the changed flow of saving into the capital market (or, eventually, to adjust the rate of obsolescence to the planned rate of dissaving).

Correctly interpreted and applied, this hypothesis of a world in which no investment is taking place is of the greatest importance for understanding the behavior of the loan rate during a depression. In a severe depression that formal situation is approximately realized, because, as already noted, only a relatively moderate decline in business prospects is required to stop the growth of investment. However, the differences between the real world in a depression and the world of our hypothesis are fully as important as the common characteristic of the two, the bare fact that net investment is absent, total investment stationary.

Under depression conditions, everyone concerned knows, or normally assumes, that the suspension of investment is not due to physical conditions (no possibility of productive investment). Nor yet is it due to any unwillingness of savers to offer a considerable supply of new capital at a real rate equal to what the investment would yield, correctly measured in value units, if economic equilibrium could be restored and freedom and flexibility re-established, along with ordinary foresight and confidence. Finally, everyone knows that the situation is not caused by any lack of persons able and willing to function as entrepreneurs. The condition is known to be one of "accidental" disorganization of price relations and foresight of the future. Men know, in a general way at least, how such a condition came about; or at least they know that the economic system has got into such a state many times before and has got out again, in a fairly short time compared with the human life-span. Hence they naturally assume that the state of suspension of net growth of capital and of investment demand is temporary.

There is another vital difference between the real condition during a depression and the hypothetical one of a world in which all productive agents are physically given ("original and indestructible," and without any possibility of adding to supply—like the mythical Ricardian land). This difference lies in the fact that, as a survival from the preceding relatively normal condition of affairs, a very considerable volume of long-term "gilt-edged" bonds exists—and a few such issues may also be floated during the depression itself, especially by governments.[15]

The course of events under these conditions is what would be expected from simple, general considerations. The loan rate for very short periods falls to "zero," i.e., to a figure which in any instance is a measure of the estimated risk and the cost of making a loan, without any actual interest. The rate as reflected in the price of long-term evidences of debt substantially free from risk does not, however, fall to anything like this level, for the simple reason that men do not expect the depression to last forever. This rate on long-term and highly safe loans measures the speculative anticipations in the economy as a whole as to the future course of events in the depression and especially the course of the rate of return obtainable on loans for real investment after recovery is expected to set in, reviving effective opportunity for such investment. This speculation is also, as goes without saying, affected to an important degree by speculative anticipations of a "fall in the value of money" in connection with recovery, which is a very important factor in offsetting the plethora of idle funds as a force that raises the price of bonds and reduces the long-term rate of interest.

If, for some special reason, men should come to expect an indefinite duration of depression conditions, the absence of real investment opportunity, present or prospective, would become the predominant condition, and ultimately society would approach the condition mentioned above, in which saving and borrowing and lending would be purely a comparison of present and future consumption. The form taken by any accumulations made would then be a pure speculation in future values of the various forms of (nonproductive) wealth, for storage, including money. In the conditions of our own real world of today, such a state of expectations is hardly so remote as to be summarily dismissed from serious consideration; but the more probable eventuality is a taking-over of the investment and entrepreneur functions by government, i.e., the establishment of some kind of collectivism.

15. These are referred to as "securities" by the currently popular romantic school of interest theorists (Mr. Keynes and his followers), making use of a "metonomy" convenient for their argumentative purposes.

KEYNESIAN THEORY OF INTEREST

The considerations just set forth indicate the amount of validity or weight which is to be attributed to a "monetary" theory of interest. It is possible for a monetary disturbance to bring investment to a stop for a time and/or for anticipated change in the value of money to be so great as largely to predominate over the real forces which "normally" determine the interest rate—i.e., the productivity of investment. The effects of such factors on the terms of contracts of known duration are easily calculable. But the primary datum in interest contracts is the expected real rate of yield on investment, even during severe depression—as long as this condition is not expected to be permanent. Monetary and other derangements act only as distorting forces. It ought to be unnecessary to expound to competent students of economics the general relations between these various factors affecting the loan rate or particularly to point out the necessity of considering all of them and of separating them. The stipulated rate in loan contracts becomes a monetary phenomenon precisely to the extent that prospective changes in the value of the unit in which such contracts are drawn is the predominant (eventually the only) factor in the calculations of borrowers and lenders. It goes without saying that the price of bonds must equalize the attractiveness of bonds and of money for holding. As to the first part, the grammatically positive part, of the liquidity-preference theory of interest—with an important emendation—there can be no argument: ". . . the rate of interest at any time, being the reward for parting with liquidity, is a measure of the unwillingness of those who possess money to part with their liquid control over it"—in exchange for bonds. In other words, the rate of interest *is* the premium on present money over future money. The substance of the theory is in the negative part of the statement, the denial that other things need be considered, making the positive statement an *explanation*. By the same reasoning the price of eggs—of hens or of dodoes—would be explained by the relative preference for the commodity and for money or "liquidity." But there is a vital difference in the application; a· change in the quantity of money would in fact tend to change the price of a "good" in the same ratio; but it would *not* change the price of bonds—future money—beyond a possible temporary disturbance.[16]

16. The quotation is from J. M. Keynes, *The General Theory of Employment, Interest, and Money* (New York, 1936), p. 167. Beyond reasonable doubt, if the conventional monetary unit became *too* uncertain, but other features of a free-

In a discussion of the influence of speculation in the future value of money on the rate of interest on loans—under any possible conditions—the most essential fact is that there is no functional relation between the price level and any rate of interest. Consequently, no monetary change has any direct and permanent effect on the rate. On this point such writers as Keynes and Hicks fall into the simple methodological fallacy dealt with in the early part of this paper— confusion of the power to "disturb" another value magnitude with a real functional connection of causality. Keynes bases his whole argument for the monetary theory of interest on the familiar fact that open-market operations can be effective.[17] Hicks makes the error more palpable by saying explicitly that new currency injected into an economy "at first" and "in the first instance" lowers the rate of interest, or discount, but afterward raises prices and *"therefore* tends to increase discount."[18] But in his entire subsequent argument, Hicks assumes without qualification or reservation a definite (inverse) functional relation between the quantity of money and the interest rate.

It is a depressing fact that at the present date in history there should be any occasion to point out to students that this position is mere man-in-the-street economics. The position is analytically absurd, and any respectable textbook in economics explains why. The rate of interest in its normal aspect as the rate of return on investment is the ratio between two value magnitudes, income and wealth. A change in the unit of value can affect this ratio only as it affects one of its terms *more* than it affects the other. There may (or may not) be such a differential effect for a time, after a monetary change. Of course if created currency is used exclusively to buy bonds, or

---

contract economy were maintained and the disposition to save and invest and to make loans for this purpose also continued to prevail, men would cast about for some other value unit in which to make loan contracts.

17. *Ibid.*, p. 197.

18. See *Econometrica*, V (1937), 151. All this is quoted by Hicks from Marshall. I have italicized the word "therefore" but will not discuss here the question raised. Without more explanation than is given by Hicks, or by Marshall, the statement is fallacious; only the expectation of a future rise in prices, during the term of any loan, will operate to raise the contractual loan rate. Hicks's *Value and Capital* (Oxford University Press, 1939) does not seem to give a quotable statement of a liquidity-preference-function theory of interest. His "imperfect moneyness" (p. 166) theory involves an even more palpable fallacy, since if all wealth were "ideally" money the price level would approach infinity, but at equilibrium the rate of interest would still be the productive yield of wealth-creating investment. But present purposes do not call for an examination of the manifold confusions of which unfortunately this book largely consists.

even to construct new equipment, it can temporarily raise the relative price which the principal, or source, will yield. Such an occurrence is a temporary disturbance only. As a monetary change diffuses through the economy, it comes to affect all classes of prices in the same way, and at equilibrium any relative price will be the same as before the monetary change occurred—except in so far as in the meantime changes may have occurred in the factors which really control the price relation in question. For the interest rate, the controlling cause is the income-cost of producing capital goods, per unit of expected income-yield. Beyond the phenomenon of disturbance, any expected change in the future value of the unit in which payments (of interest and/or of principal) are made will affect the nominal rate in long-term contracts in the same way for loans as for any contract to make any payment (in the same unit) in the future.

That a monetary theory of interest should be defended by economists of repute is especially mysterious in view of the facts, which are directly contrary to what the theory calls for. There seems to be no defensible way of defining or measuring the esteem value of money for holding ("liquidity preference") such that its magnitude is not high in depression (relative to anything but monetary obligations) when interests rates—by any possible definition—are low, and vice versa. But, as we have seen, the facts accord with common sense. Short-term rates are low or zero in a depression because opportunity for real investment is temporarily cut off, and such loans do not require the lender to part with his money, or his command over money, for a period significant for changes in its value. The decline in the rate of long-term loans (bond values) is much less and is easily accounted for in terms of an expected recovery of opportunity for investment on the one hand and of the value of the unit in terms of real wealth on the other.

THE QUESTION OF POLICY

We turn now to a very brief consideration of the problem of action in connection with the business cycle. The sketch of the theory which has been given is sufficient to indicate the general character of the problem of action set by the phenomenon. Some means must be found for preventing individuals, business units, and banks, acting separately or in conjunction, from behaving in such a way as to change drastically and rapidly the amount of effective money in active use—or the velocity of circulation of the total stock of monetary medium, actual and potential. Such a change causes not merely a movement in general prices (*ceteris paribus*) but more especially differential changes in the prices of (*a*) consumption goods, (*b*) capital goods, and (*c*) productive services, especially wages, which are the entrepreneur's costs of production. In a free market these differential changes would be temporary, but even then they might be serious; and with important markets as unfree as they actually are—and prices as sticky and labor and capital as unmobile—the results take on the proportions of a social disaster. Hence it is "necessary" to prevent speculation in money, or hoarding, i.e., important changes in the amount of money held idle. General prices and the more sensitive prices of final products and regularly marketed capital goods must be maintained at a relatively stable level, and the public must be given confidence that this action will be taken.

Such action can be accomplished only by positive monetary control. Up to a point, socialistic critics have been right in regarding cycles and depressions as an inherent feature of "capitalism." Such a system must use money, and the circulation of money is not a phenomenon which naturally tends to establish and maintain an equilibrium level. Its equilibrium is vague and highly unstable. Its natural tendency is to oscillate over a fairly long period and a wide range, between limits which are rather indeterminate. Turning for illustration to the field of mechanical analogy, we may think provisionally of the difference between the behavior of a balloon in the air and any object whatever which is released in water as a surrounding medium. The balloon, lighter than the air at the ground level, will find its position of equilibrium at a height where its specific gravity is the same as that of the displaced air and will remain at that level. But any object released in water (which is practically incompressible) will go either to the bottom or to the top. It will never remain naturally stable at any intermediate position between the two. Consequently, either a fish, or a submarine boat built by man, must constantly expend energy to keep from rising to the surface or sinking to the bottom and cannot maintain a stable position at any point. The best that is possible is to keep correcting the tendency to move in one direction or the other, upward or downward.

This analogy is oversimplified, particularly in that the movement of the fish or boat will not ordinarily reverse itself and give rise to oscillations; but it does indicate the nature of the problem involved in monetary control. The monetary system can never be made automatic. An approximate constancy in general prices, or in the relation between product prices and wages, can in the nature of the case be achieved only by deliberate action, based on constant attention, correcting or offsetting incipient tendencies to expansion or contraction. More detailed analysis must be left to the study of monetary theory as a special branch of economic analysis. Serious problems are involved in finding a reliable indicator of the actual monetary position and its changes, in devising a prompt and effective mode of action on the monetary situation, and especially in the political and administrative field, in safely delegating the necessary authority to any human political agency for exercise on behalf of society.

With reference to the use of the cyclical tendency as an argument for collectivism, however—or any sweeping action by government outside the monetary field—two very important sets of facts should be pointed out. In the first place, with negligible exceptions, the business cycle does not work to the advantage of any significant group or interest in "capitalistic" society. On the contrary, practically everyone suffers heavily from it, incurring serious economic loss, if not privation. Hence the problem of cycle analysis does not arise out of and does not involve conflict of interest. This means that remedial action is a matter of economic understanding and of political intelligence and administrative competence, in matters of an essentially technical character. The situation would hardly seem to call for solution along lines which would involve the most intense conflicts of interest and would raise the most serious political problems in that regard, while, in addition, the technical organization problems in connection with establishing and operating a collectivist economy would presumably be of infinitely greater magnitude than those involved in the control of one detail of it, the monetary system

The second set of facts relates to the nature of the problem as it would present itself to the government of a collectivist society. If a collectivistic, or socialistic, state is to preserve any of the traditional economic liberties of individuals, it also must operate on the basis of money and market transactions, with prices of products and of productive services controlled by competition, in essentially the same manner as in the enterprise system. The fact that the government would be the chief owner of productive wealth, and the "entrepreneur" in the great bulk of economic activity, would not change things in that regard. The totalitarian-communistic regime in Russia, if it ever seriously tried to get away from the pecuniary market structure as the general framework of economic organization, certainly did not succeed, but ran into disastrous consquences and soon gave up the attempt. Serious realistic contemplation of the problem of administering the economic life of a modern nation, using modern technology, surely makes it clear that effective administration would be impossible by any other method, even if the government possessed unlimited power and took no interest whatever in the liberties of citizens. In particular, the lending and borrowing of money (or credit) would have to be the chief medium of control between the government and the managers of concrete enterprises.

In short, the monetary situation in a collectivist economy would have the same character that it has in an individualistic or free-enterprise system, and, in particular, the same tendency to cyclical oscillation would manifest itself and would present essentially the same problem of control. Though private individuals would not own productive wealth, productive enterprises would in effect do so and, at any rate, would have to decide when and in what volume to borrow and invest, or to disinvest and pay off loans. Both would be free to accumulate and decumulate money—unless prevented by measures designed and implemented for the purpose. It does not seem that the technical and administrative problem would be substantially simplified under collectivism or that there is any ground for assuming that government would be much more likely to be successful in solving the problem. Certain kinds of remedial action would be carried out more easily in a collectivist state, under the conditions which would have to be present for the state to exist at all, but on examination these conditions will be found to root in arbitrary power over the activities and lives of individuals. As has been remarked before, there is no problem of unemployment in a penitentiary. In any other sense, the argument for collectivism from the standpoint of the problem of the business cycle does not seem to have much force. The general presumption is that, as already suggested, the control of all features of a national economy by a central authority would present much greater difficulty than the control of one feature.

X

Salvation by Science: The Gospel According to Professor Lundberg[1]

IN THIS small volume, based on university public lectures, a prominent sociologist develops the "scientistic" doctrine for which he is fairly well known through articles in professional and popular journals. The work represents about the "last word" in simplism of this species, that is to say, empiricism with a minimum of implicit rationalism. Those who like such literary and intellectual entertainment are, as a rule, already ardent adherents of the doctrine; but the argument is dangerous for several reasons. While the style is mediocre, it is confident and persuasive. More important, Lundberg's view actually rests on very strong evidence and is very largely true; but this fact obscures equally important limitations, the human mind having a "tropism" (or intellectual original sin) which inclines to oversimplification and easy solutions for the hardest problems.[2] For these reasons, it seems justifiable to examine the book at a length beyond the ordinary review. On the subject of methodology in the study of man and society, even an article must be only a sketch; but the philosophical naïveté of a work such as Lundberg's, dealing with the most profound and serious problems, should be reasonably exposed.

A critique of a polemic for scientism in the social field may begin by noting the fact, as important as it is obvious, that, if simplicity is

1. A review article, reprinted by permission from the *Journal of Political Economy*, Vol. LV, No. 6 (December, 1947), on the book, *Can Science Save Us?* by George A. Lundberg (New York: Longmans, Green & Co., 1947).

2. For two other recent examples of the type, by a neurologist and a psychologist, both of high standing (C. J. Herrick and J. Kantor), see the April, 1946, issue of *American Scientist*. In philosophy, this position is known as "positivism" and is associated with the name of Auguste Comte. (On Comte and his antecedents see especially F. A. Hayek, "The Counter-Revolution of Science," *Economica*, February, May, and August, 1941; see also the same author's scholarly critique of the position, *ibid.*, August, 1942; February, 1943; and February, 1944.) The same general view is familiar in this country in the work of John Dewey and his "pragmatic" school of philosophy and ethics. Dewey is mentioned casually in Lundberg's book, Comte more approvingly.

what is wanted, a similar result can be reached as easily, and at least as logically, on the basis of opposite assumptions—i.e., by way of idealism in any of its forms.[3]

3. Lundberg refers at the outset (p. 2) to the work of Chancellor Robert M. Hutchins, of the University of Chicago, who expounds a moralistic simplism and is currently popular as an opponent of Dewey. A moralistic view naturally leads to the opposite practical conclusion; since the ills of life are due to personal sin, the remedy is precisely that preaching against which Lundberg preaches. To be sure, such a program soon runs into one of punishment, administered by the "proper" authority. But, as we shall see, this is true of scientism also—with a difference only in the proper authority. Under either system, as in choosing between them, it is all a question (in the words of Humpty Dumpty to Alice) of who is to be master, specifically (as in the same classical context) of who is to decide the meaning of words; for such words as "freedom," "democracy," and "truth" can readily be defined to beg nearly any serious question in favor of any desired answer.

An especially interesting assimilation of science and social discussion from an idealistic direction has recently appeared in Michael Polanyi's Riddell Lectures for 1946, *Science, Faith and Society* (Oxford University Press, 1946). His theme is the moral and social character of scientific activity and an implicit identification of the "reality" studied by science with that which, according to the author, underlies all seeking of answers to questions, in contrast with the reduction of all behavior and mental life to empirical and mechanistic terms. There is also much truth—and terribly important truth—in this view, and the emphasis is badly needed as a counterweight against the vogue of naïve, positivistic scientism. Yet this position is at least as dangerous as the other if its limitations are not kept in mind. It tends strongly to run into a sellout of science and hardheaded thinking to emotionalism, wish-thinking, and mysticism. (In his attitude toward "occult" phenomena Polanyi himself stops little, if at all, short of this point: he makes no reference to any of the social sciences or to the claims of scientific method as usually understood in dealing with social problems; he ignores the fact that agreement is reached without formal coercion in natural science and certain aspects of social science but not in the field of law and morals, which is the factual root of the whole social problem.)

Of the two approaches, scientism is probably the more dangerous, especially in the English-speaking world, the first and last home of liberalism; for this is also the home of "Baconian" science and modern technology and in moral philosophy has typically embraced a naïve utilitarianism. It is of some import that accidents and ineptitudes of international politics have removed the "Fascist" form of totalitarianism, based on German idealistic philosophy and romanticism, and immeasurably strengthened the "materialistic" Marx-Stalin brand. But the main danger is that scientism contains so much more of the truth, particularly of "demonstrable" truth and the kind of truth that is mainly involved in intelligent guidance of action. The effective role of mind in human behavior is small, especially as regards ends (where the main problem arises); most of it is mechanics, which is to say that it is to be described and accounted for scientifically. The truth of idealism is interstitial, limitational; and it is equally a disservice to the cause of "freedom" to deny it altogether and to pretend that its role is or could be large. But its reality is proved by mere mention of the behavior of the scientist himself or of the lecturer on methodology! (Lundberg says [p. 67] that scientific method is a form of human behavior, but he is blind to the obvious implications [see concluding part of this article].)

It is no surprise that our author devotes much of his effort to inveighing against the oversimplification of social problems—by other people. Thus his book is anything but an example of the unemotional scientific attitude which it urges upon others in language charged with enthusiasm, scorn, and other emotions. It contains little or nothing in the way of definite philosophic criticism or construction. No serious attempt is made to define "science" by concrete distinction from other forms of discourse or human activity or to show the difference between "good" and "bad" science in the treatment of social or other problems. Only by laudatory references to the "older sciences" and the triumphs of modern technology, in contrast with the confusion prevailing in the social field, is it made clear that all discussion of the latter must follow the model of physics and chemistry and biology.

It is assumed, rather than argued or explicitly stated, that the problems of personal life, social relations, and political and economic organization are of the same kind as the prediction and control of events in (non-human) nature and so will similarly yield gradually to the same mode of attack. All that is needful is that intellectual leaders hearken to the evangelical message, renounce "vested interests," "romantic star-gazing," and traditionalist or obscurantist prejudices and be converted to the scientific point of view.[4] This means, of course, that the problems of life and society are exclusively problems of means and ends. Both means and ends are taken as purely objective, requiring merely to be ascertained by scientific investigation. Such discussion as the book contains—mixed up with preaching, denouncing, and exhorting and the argument from analogy—centers in the nature of ends. Its "contribution" is, or should be, the negative one of making it clear to any careful reader—by its confusion, inconsistency, and ignoring or evasion of obviously crucial considerations—that the author's position is untenable. In this connection his heroic efforts, especially in the last two chapters, to deal with the higher values are especially significant and valuable. He attempts to reduce all human purposiveness to the pursuit of "ends" in the sense in which these are achieved by technical procedures, with "social organization merely a means to the ends that men seek" (p. 105); thus the whole problem becomes one of the scientific dis-

4. ". . . The principal problems confronting education are these: . . . [to] inculcate into our population (1) a rudimentary understanding of what is the nature of scientific method as applied to human affairs, and (2) a conviction that this is the only effective approach" (p. 78).

covery of facts and descriptive laws. All else is "art," an absolutely separate domain (cf. p. 234 of this article).

The very clarity and sweeping character of the statement of Lundberg's position ought to make it superfluous to answer it in detail; it will surely suggest cases in which there is obviously much more to the story. Associative life has many values (good and bad) which it is merely absurd to treat as "ends" in any literal meaning of the word. And so also does the individual life, in the sense in which any human life is individual. Are hunting and fishing "merely" means for obtaining quarry? What is the relation between end and means in a game of solitaire? Or in any game, a social conversation, or even a discussion of politics? Or especially in science itself? (We shall have something to say about "truth" as an end and its quest as a means. Has our author not heard the adage about pursuit and possession?) The least reflection on "play" should expose the fantastic oversimplification of a pure means-and-end interpretation of conduct. (Yet the author explicitly lists fun and recreation as ends.)[5] Whether cause and effect means more, even in physical science, is a philosophical problem; while biology, even at the "lowest" level, has to use such concepts as utility, effectiveness, and competition. Every social problem arises out of a combination of harmony and conflict of interests, terms which have no meaning in physical nature. And the more common and obvious problems arise in situations in which both ends and means are well known to all parties concerned; indeed, they arise out of agreement—out of different persons wanting the same thing, whether end or means, of which there is not enough to go around. "Wanting" also has no meaning in relation to physical things, and one could make an indefinite list of other such terms, beginning with "discussion," or "question and answer," or "meaning," hence "communication" (which the scientificist reduces to symbolic behavior).

Apart from the practical damage that may be done by the scientistic propaganda, two theoretical problems justify an extended examination of the argument. The first is posed by the fact that men of superior intellectual powers and equipment write such books, which is surely a social phenomenon of importance and a challenge to investigation. The second is the more vital and still more challenging question of the actual relation between "science" (in some-

5. For that matter, "work" also is not merely the use of means to achieve a given end and still less is the latter merely an empirical uniformity of sequence in events.

thing like the strict meaning of the physical sciences) and other types of intellectual inquiry and still other activities of mind that are involved in any comprehensive, realistic, or fruitful attack on the problems of conduct, human relations, and social action. The main purpose of this review is less to criticize a particular book than to call attention to this latter problem in a way that will make it less likely to be ignored. Naturally, there can be no question of solving it or even of contributing substantially to that result. In the compass of a review, discussion of the main issues must be confined to critical observations interspersed in a summary of the author's treatment.

Since false conceptions regarding ends, motives, values, ideals, and will are viewed as the main obstacle to men's acceptance of the scientific attitude toward social problems, the bulk of our author's space is devoted to refuting such errors. His own conception of these "phenomena" is by no means unambiguous (he completely ignores the phenomenon of error), but in the main it is that already indicated. At the outset, after a few paragraphs on the contrast between the achievements of science in other fields and the unhappy state of social problems, we confront the main question: "Why does not [man] turn in this predicament to the methods which have proved themselves so potent in other fields?" In answer, "The principal reason is simple tradition" (pp. 3–4). But a "second reason" is that "most people feel they already know the answers to problems of human relations" or (after some ridicule of popular moralistic and platitudinous answers) "what we need is not primarily more knowledge but the 'will' to apply what we already know" (p. 6). As to the latter, the author at once remonstrates, "but this will is itself a product of certain conditions," and goes on, "why don't we apply what we know?" In answering—after much sarcasm, assertion, and preaching—he contrasts our lack of education, our paucity of positive knowledge, and the strength of vested and other selfish interests with the harmony of science and idealism. He then turns (in chap. ii, "Can Science Solve Social Problems?") to some consideration of supposed differences between natural and social science. The impossibility of controlled experiment is curtly answered by a reference to astronomy. But the chief alleged "obstacle to a full-fledged natural science of human social phenomena is . . . the presence in the latter of a unique and mysterious something called *motives*" (p. 18). These may corrupt the investigator, but "the danger of biased observation and interpretation is a danger . . . in all science," and in both fields "proper scientific training teaches the ethics of science as well as technical skill and the use of corrective instruments to reduce [errors] to a minimum" (pp. 16, 20; and cf. Sec. III, pp. 20–26).

With respect to the subject matter of social science, the issue is apparently disposed of summarily by defining motive as cause: "The word is used to designate those circumstances to which we find it 'reasonable' to attribute an occurence." While an economic determinist, a Freudian, and an astrologer have other views, "to a scientist, the motives of a stone rolling downhill or of a boy murdering his father are simply the full set of circumstances resulting in either event [and] these conditions are equally subject to scientific investigation in both cases" (p. 19). But the question will not down, and its two phases are discussed through the next two sections—in the latter (Sec. IV) in relation to the notion, or term, "value." "Since valuations or values are empirically observable patterns of behavior, they may be studied as such, by the same general techniques we use to study other behavior" (p. 26). And the argument still goes on throughout most of the book—especially in chapter v, on "The Arts, Literature, and the Spiritual Life in a Scientific World." Here we find equivalent statements on ends, will, tastes, ideals, etc., and even on the behavior of God (pp. 93, 98). The expression "good taste" must be entirely without meaning.

The function of science, specifically in relation to ends, is stated over and over:

. . . What science has done in the fields in which it has been applied and can do regarding human society is precisely this: It can acquaint people reliably with (1) the *possible* alternate courses of action, and (2) the costs and consequences of each course. *Whatever* people do under these circumstances will constitute their "valuing"—their Values. Values represent, therefore, no special or unique problem in the social sciences, as is often asserted. All behavior, human and sub-human, may be regarded as evaluative, and it is as regular and predictable as the behavior of the inanimate world [pp. 99–100; see also p. 29].

Again, ". . . no science tells us *what to do* with the knowledge that constitutes that science" (p. 31); "any scientist who pretends [to the contrary] is a fraud and a menace" (p. 30); and "scientists who contend that they scientifically determine not only the means but the ends of social policy should be exposed as scientific fakers as well as would-be dictators" (p. 32). Moreover, "scientific method as applied to human affairs . . . is the only effective approach" (p. 78 and similarly on pp. 81 and 97). It is true that "the application of scientific knowledge obviously involves value judgments of some sort [but] this problem is equally present in the other sciences" (p. 30).

However, as is not surprising, this position is not always consistently maintained. On page 29, after raising the question of a "special function or obligation [*sic*]" of scientists in determining the ends for which knowledge is to be used, the author states (in substantially the language already quoted) their business as scientists and adds: "Scientists may then *in their capacity as citizens* join with others in advocating one alternative rather than another, as they prefer."[6] Yet we are told explicitly that "science can be valuable in helping men to decide the question of the uses of knowledge" (p. 34). The nearest we come to an explanation of his meaning is perhaps the statement (p. 29) that "the development of the social sciences . . . will doubtless greatly influence the wants, wishes and choices of men," i.e., "to the extent that [the] reputation and prestige [of scientists] is great, and . . . their tastes are shared by the masses of men"; and further, "men will not want impossible or mutually exclusive things." This last would be important if it were true! It is assumed that the scientists themselves will agree in their tastes as to ends, and mutually exclusive things must cover the conflicting wants of different persons and also their conflicting ideals, since all serious social problems involve matters of principle as well as individual wants. We can only submit that, if such unity is ever achieved by intellectual processes, it will not come through the development of "social science" but from a very different kind of knowledge. Its subject matter and content are not to be learned by merely "asking the masses of men what they want" (p. 97) and treating the answers as reliable scientific data. The result must be achieved along the line of the social philosophy of the idealists (Bosanquet, Mackenzie, *et al.*) and their quasi-religious faith in the ultimate harmony of all "real ends."[7] Lundberg expressly admits that

6. The distinction had just previously been made and the question raised of a person's being able to "play [the] distinct roles of scientist and citizen without confusing the two. The answer is that it is being done every day." Illustrations are afforded by the vocation of acting and from science and technology.

We must later have something to say about the behavior of "advocating," mentioned in the quotation in the text. The phrase, "costs and consequences," which is repeatedly used, would doubtless be interpreted as unwanted and wanted consequences.

7. The procedure of M. Polanyi (mentioned in n. 3) reaches much the same conclusion as Lundberg—that social discussion should follow the method of science—but argues in the opposite direction. Minimizing and then disregarding the

"science is not all of life or of knowledge" (p. 14) and that it "is only *one* of the numerous influences that determine an individual's wants and his consequent behavior" (p. 32). Furthermore, "much of what is now called social service will be properly relegated to other equally honorable departments, such as journalism, drama, or general literature" (p. 50). His assumption is that *these* "behavior phenomena" are neither science nor the subject matter of any science and that the findings of their inquiries, as knowledge, belong in another realm (that of art [p. 70]) which has no bearing at all on the problems dealt with by social science.

Since it is "these other, equally honorable departments" (including philosophy) that deal with final ends and purposes, much indeed depends on this assumption. It can be valid under any of several conditions. The specialists in these fields may agree, by a procedure other than science, and be followed by the masses. Or it may not matter whether agreement on values exists or not. Or, combining these two conditions, agreement may be reached (by some non-scientific procedure) to the extent that it practically matters, beginning with agreement on the extent to which agreement matters, for the limit of toleration of differences is a vital part of the social problem.[8] This third view seems to be that taken by historical, nineteenth-century liberalism, with stress on minimizing the need for agreement on ends. Lundberg, as we shall see, adopts a more scientistic position, holding that men must agree through science as to means and are already and always in agreement on values and that this solves that aspect of the problem. Both of the last two notions are clearly false; differences are pronounced and serious, but the major problems arise more out of agreement than out of disagreement on ends, giving rise to conflict over the distribution of means. But by attributing all our difficulties to disagreement over means, Lundberg "logically" justifies his dictum that "the knowledge of how to improve human relations can come only from social science"

---

role of sense observation, manipulation, and inductive reasoning, Polanyi makes natural science itself a process like that of discovering a transcendental reality. This has a certain theoretical as well as "sentimental" appeal, but one must note that it ignores the basic facts. Scientists agree and the masses accept their authority without any coercion, while the opposite is true in the fields of jurisprudence, morals, and philosophy.

8. It might be suggested, though it is not (and it would surely be farfetched), that the necessary agreement on values, which are outside of science, would be produced by the teaching of scientific ethics, a part of "proper scientific training." We should also recognize the possibility that the problem has no solution.

(p. 81)—except for the passages we have quoted in which he seems to say that "knowledge" outside of science also affects behavior.

One more vital proviso should not be overlooked. It is clearly implied and taken for granted that the process of achieving unity is to be non-violent and entirely non-coercive. No effort is made to define coercion or freedom, though the latter word is frequently used. Instead, we are regaled with sarcasm about belief in free will. Perhaps the freedom of the natural sciences should be taken as definition by illustration; and perhaps this freedom itself may be vindicated on purely utilitarian pragmatic grounds of utility to every individual, without a value judgment. One misses any explicit attention to the question. And one cannot help noting that much of the time Lundberg himself is using value judgments, expressed in strong language. He is "advocating," seeking to "convert," as he virtually admits (pp. 29, 99); he is certainly not merely predicting scientifically (historically) what will happen or demonstrating hypothetically what "would" happen under specified conditions ("science" in the usual, non-historical meaning). Nor can one read his book and believe that he regards his "behavior" in writing and publishing it as a piece of instrumental manipulation of the public by himself with a view to his individual purposes and advantages or simply as a detail in the sequence of natural events. He seems to regard (scientific) truth as a value only in the instrumental sense that everyone thinks it useful to everyone to have it ascertained and published; but this attitude is not that which is most common among scientists.

In summary, Lundberg's scientism reduces logically to the following propositions: (1) ends, motives, etc., are *data* merely; they present no problem for social science, hence no problem at all; (2) scientific knowledge alone is required for the prediction and control of social events; and (3) the prediction and control of social events is all that is required for the solution of practical social problems (at least to the extent that this is possible). And we should add that, when all this is made generally known by a proper scientific education, men will be content with what is possible so that, in that crucial sense, the social problem will be solved by the application of scientific method.

However, the author is far from being consistent and unambiguous in stating these three points, and something more must be said about the first in particular—the relation beween science and ends or motives. Adequate knowledge and agreement on ends is by no means always asserted or implied; there is nearly as much indication that they must be ascertained by science, which, if it does not tell men what to want, has at least to tell somebody—"the state" or "administrators"—what the community does and will want (but apparently *not* to tell the men themselves!). At different points in the exposition motives are either identical with behavior or activity (p. 26) or an inseparable part of it (p. 25) or its cause (p. 19). In any case they are to be learned by "observing" behavior, including "verbal behavior" (p. 27) or "symbolic behavior," which includes all the phenomena of communication (pp. 68 f.), and all "thoughts, dreams, imagination, aspirations, worship, etc."—what "has been referred to throughout history by such words as mind, soul, and spirit . . . variously explained throughout the ages." By "purposes" and "ends" we mean "the word pictures that man conjures up from his desires and longings" (p. 96). All doubt about the possibility of scientific determination will be removed by considering the activities of a jury (p. 20), and their "scientific" description runs in terms of such adjectives as "fraudulent, felonious, malicious, etc." Moreover, "scores of instruments are in use today . . . that detect, reduce or measure the bias of our senses and the prejudice of different observers" (p. 21) and also measure and predict "degrees of happiness in marriage, and other equally 'human' eventualities"—opinion, status, social participation, etc. (p. 22). Prediction of election returns by opinion polls is mentioned several times, without the author's saying how far in advance or how accurately[9] or his raising any question about the meaning of measurement or of quantity itself in relation to different sorts of magnitudes. Without at all implying that these procedures have no scientific or practical value, one must challenge the notion that they are to be seriously classed with the observations and measurements of physical science. And the possibility that the social subject matter itself might be moved to do some reciprocal questioning, observing, and inferring, and the probability that this might affect the quality of the reports treated as data, are assumed to be without significance. Besides, there is a strictly objective test: ". . . a thing *has* value or *is* a value when people behave toward it so as to retain or increase their possession of it" (p. 26); if so, why the bother about questioning and reporting? The statement must be assumed to cover all that is true or needful

9. The supposed knockout comparison with the weather, also used a few times, does not seem too happy; our concern is with the differences between nature and human society as scientific subject matter, but limitations of science in the former field are in point.

with respect to such values, for example, as natural beauty and friends.

However, the author's main contention regarding ends—his method of disposing of them as a problem—is that already indicated: they are uniform for all humanity and all history and are already well and generally known. Hence they do not present any kind of problem, scientific or other. "It is disagreement over the means . . . that results in conflict and chaos" (p. 32, and similarly on pp. 99, 100). But the careful reader will note that the agreement is asserted only respecting the "broad general wants," the "principal ends," the "large and broad goals of life," and the substantial meaning must be found in the examples given. These are "physical and social security and some fun"; "physical survival, security, and a livelihood for the individual and for the group . . . group association, activity, and recreational growth, including artistic, religious and spiritual experiences" (p. 98, these last already defined as "word pictures, conjured up"); and "communion with his fellow creatures and with his universe, including his own imaginative creations" (p. 99; quotations condensed and slightly rearranged).

The "ends" named are, indeed, "broad and general," and agreement can be asserted precisely because they are mere abstractions. Logically, the matter might have been simplified still further by sticking to the one word "advantage," which is actually used to define morals or good conduct (pp. 32, 101). There is really, then, but one kind of good conduct, the use of means to achieve advantage, the nature of which is either known to all or can be scientifically ascertained, as can the means (behavior) which will lead to this result; and men cannot do otherwise than to follow these courses of action. Moreover, the means-end relation in conduct is identical with (is nothing but) the cause-effect sequence in inanimate nature. "The ends men *should* pursue are . . . matters of opinion and taste, but opinions and tastes, as such, are also matters of fact" (p. 98), or, more cautiously, "most questions even of taste and ethics in the end turn out to be determined by what people believe to be facts" (p. 99, mostly italics). Finally, as quite logically follows, "taste and . . . choice . . . is the result of all the experience of our species . . . plus all the conditionings of our present surroundings," and "to say that . . . man *should* pursue other ends, simply amounts to saying that man *should* be a different being than he is, that he *should* have had a different evolutionary history . . ." (pp. 98, 99).

One feels embarrassment in posing the obvious question as to whether men *think* that they themselves and others both could and should be more or less different from what they are, without having had a different past or even having different surroundings. If they do not so think, there is no sense in arguing to the contrary; and if they do, they must be in "error," which is usually taken (rightly or wrongly!) to mean something "wrong" and not simply an objective empirical fact, like color or movement or other factually descriptive predicate. The author's whole argument clearly has to apply to the scientist's pursuit of truth. First, the end has to be defined as purely "advantage" and error as disadvantage—and then what becomes of the ethics and idealism of science on which he lays so much stress? And, further, advantage and disadvantage and their "pursuit" have to be defined as merely descriptive properties of a mechanical sequence of events. The alternative is to exclude scientific activity both from human conduct and from natural process (for scientism the same thing) and treat it as an absolutely unique species of subject matter. It is wise of the author, as a debater and propagandist (it is even more embarrassing to refer to his numerous pleas for enormously greater financial support for his "line" of social science), to avoid the question of whether or not science itself, natural or social, is a social phenomenon and a part of the subject matter of social science.[10]

To say that men act with a view to "advantage" is either merely to say that they have objectives—which, incidentally, inanimate things do not, and certainly they do not "pursue" ends implying

---

10. He comes so close as to say: "The fact that the social scientist has always been a part of the social structure is no more a handicap to objective study than is the fact that he is also a part of the physical universe which he studies" (p. 19).

We have seen that he explicitly includes all artistic activity and experience and the "spiritual life" as "symbolic behavior," word pictures, conjured up. And he says that "science, as a method, is a form of human behavior" (pp. 66–67); but this is incidental to the question of the educational department in which it should be taught, and there is no recognition that science may be anything but a course of events subject to prediction and control. We have also pointed out that, in dividing the field of education between science and art, he implies that the latter has no relation to science, as its subject matter or otherwise. If these "other equally honorable departments" yield anything to be called knowledge, that is, more or less "right" answers to real questions, the paragraph in the text above applies to them also.

Again, on p. 71, we find it stated that science and art are "inextricably interlaced at all stages" and "indistinguishable . . . in their higher stages and deeper meanings." But the following sentences merely assert a distinction sufficiently objective to be useful in the lower registers, with no indication as to which merges into the other or the nature of any higher category including both. Whatever the unifying category, it must surely be a value (or simply "value") and again our text applies. (In such cases as this, inconsistency is doubtless more of a virtue than a fault.)

success and failure—or it is again to raise the question of truth and error, the meaning of "real" advantage. It is no answer to, or contribution to the discussion of, any intelligible question about conduct. Actually, there are no "ends" of action,[11] all concrete achievements are looked forward to as milestones and become means as soon or as fast as they are completed. The question is one of the qualities or ingredients of "the good life"; the only one that can be defined in "objective" terms is maximum time-span, and this is not usually considered an unconditional good. Even health is no exception. It is a familiar fact and a primary principle of sociology that men agree more or less, depending on community or similarity of culture, on words designating certain abstract goods such as pleasure or happiness or truth, beauty, and goodness. (Lundberg's lists of ends are quite uncritical.) But they agree hardly at all and change their individual minds most unpredictably on the conditions occasioning their value experiences, which alone can either properly be called "ends" or be handled as scientific data. Even food—which, like other objects of desire, is either means or end by arbitrary choice—is an abstract term; and the particular things so classed—or that will so function—vary enormously with cultures and their changes and with individuals and their moods. Needless to say, this is more and more the case as we ascend into the "higher" values, the instrumental utility of which is often undiscoverable or negative—and they always greatly influence and ultimately dominate the form of satisfaction of the so-called "subsistence needs." Lundberg's attribution of the character of "science" (in the meaning of physics) to such description, classification, and measurement as are possible and such "laws" as are to be found in this field can only be labeled as a "semantic error"—the phrase he uses to explain the "confused thinking . . . offered by current discussions of 'values' and their supposed incompatibility with science" (p. 26). But it must constantly be emphasized that we are not denying the possibility of "science"; it is only its completeness, adequacy, and exclusiveness as a method of solving social problems that are in question. All rational freedom and the higher life are as much dependent on conduct itself being mostly mechanical as they are on a margin of independent internal deter-

---

11. Perhaps we should say "no ends within life," thus excepting "salvation" for another life. In so far as men actually treat that as an objective, they do not look beyond it. Nor do they attempt to characterize the future life; it is "bliss," without problems of any kind, of action or thinking or judgment or will, and without concrete form or content. Lundberg observes (p. 10) that the social structure of heaven is a dictatorship; but it is also complete anarchy—everyone does exactly as he pleases!

mination which makes complete prediction not only impossible (as it is everywhere, even in the best physical laboratory) but also a contradiction in thought.

However, all this has to do with individual conduct and is preliminary to a treatment of genuinely social issues. We must now consider somewhat further Lundberg's begging of the whole question by assuming agreement and completely ignoring conflict of interest of the sort that underlies every social problem. He settles everything by the wisdom of Cheshire-Puss, who, in response to Alice's question as to which way she ought to go from here, replied: "That depends a good deal on where you want to get to":

> Can *science* tell man what *direction* he should go? Yes, if man will tell scientists where he wants to go. *Should* man then do what he collectively *wants* to do? Assuredly, unless you wish to set up a higher source of wisdom and authority than man's collective experience through the ages, interpreted and supplemented by the reliable predictions of scientists as to the costs and consequences of different possible courses of action. To declare ... that man *ought to want* something else than he does want is merely a semantic trick by which the speakers seek to invoke "ethical principles" derived from some source outside of nature in support of what he himself wants man to want [p. 101].

And so on, about universities telling man what to want, the credentials of those who set themselves up as the authority, man as a "child of nature," etc.

It should not be necessary to point out the evasions and absurdities (or the imputation of evil motives) in this; but it evidently is necessary—if it will do any good! Apart from the "if" clause, which should suggest philosophical but obvious questions, we note that "man" is used collectively to beg the question of agreement and (logically still more important) that "man" is sharply set over against both the "scientists" and all others who "presume" to set themselves up as a higher authority, which they claim to derive from a source outside nature and experience. "Man" is a part of nature, but scientists, in particular, are not a part of "man." "Nature" means just what Lundberg wants to include, to support his own propaganda for science, i.e., for scientists. "Trick" (i.e., deception) is a characteristic of this part of nature, as is "wanting" some other part to "want" (and to believe) one thing rather than another and also "advocating" "preference" (p. 29) and "trying" to "convert one another," while "insisting" on "conformity" to "mores" that are "accepted" and "enforced" (p. 99). Yet scientific description of their behavior (by a part of the part in question) is all that is to be intelligently said about man, the class of objects that does and suffers all these things. The statement that individuals or minorities, or even majorities, may indeed disagree with the goals which their culture as a whole pursues but that such questions of taste and temperament may be left to them, as nearly as is compatible with community standards (p. 99), is supposed to raise no question as to who is doing what, to whom, or why. And possible "compromise or defeat of the more ultimate or desirable goals . . . is a question of fact" (*ibid.*).[12]

Finally, any careful reader should note that in all Lundberg's lists of wants ("what men actually want"), they are assumed to be purely individual. He astutely avoids all mention of such things as power, prestige, relative status, and winning versus losing in any form of contest or competition where "advantage" is necessarily disadvantage to someone else. And he is likewise oblivious of the conflicts that grow out of agreement—wanting the same things which are limited in supply or things that are products of the same indirect and limited means—and of similar conflicts over who is to bear the "costs" to which he constantly refers, in relation to whose wants are to be gratified, though such problems are nowhere more conspicuous than in "science" itself and "education."[13]

We should not give the impression that our author, in advocating

12. All this nonsense is inherently a part of the pragmatic moral and social philosophy; Lundberg may be a little less cautious in his statement than Dewey is, but quotations essentially the same in meaning permeate the latter's book, *Liberalism and Social Action*, and other works. "Pragmatism" is the name current in America and "utilitarianism" in England, while elsewhere in Europe "positivism" or "logical positivism" is more familiar. Adherents generally describe the position as "empirical" and "naturalistic." But does "nature" describe, explain, theorize, and dispute? Yet this is the philosophy on the basis of which modern liberalism was ostensibly developed.

13. Economics is the social science most concerned with wants and costs and is of especial interest to most who will read this review. As far as noted in careful and repeated reading of Lundberg's book, economics (apart from financial support of social science) is referred to just once. The passage is interesting: "A competent economist or political scientist should be able to devise, for example, a tax program for a given country which will fall in whatever desired degrees upon each of the income groups of the area concerned. Social scientists should be able to state also what will be the effect of the application of this program upon income, investments, consumption, production, and the outcome of the next election" (p. 31). This clearly disposes of the whole problem of taxation—"for example"! But, while we are quoting, the problem of education (another example, generously offered) is similarly finished off in the same paragraph: "In the same way, competent sociologists, educators, or psychologists should be able to advise a parent as to the most convenient way of converting a son into an Al Capone or into an approved citizen, according to which is desired."

"science" as the "only effective approach" to social problems—the "only source of knowledge of how to improve human relations"— avoids all reference to the crucial problem of the relation between controller and controlled (*quis custodet custodes?*). His main concern is to show that the scientists themselves will be harmless, having no power over the use to be made of the knowledge which they provide. We have seen above (p. 231) how emphatically the negative point is made and also (p. 231) that "scientific ethics" (a result of "proper scientific training") will prevent scientists from having any "bias," any interest that may conflict with finding and stating the objective truth. But this is not the whole story, and the reference to "training" suggests a glance at what the author says about education, which may be viewed as the heart of the problem of authority and control; for no fact is more familiar historically, and particularly in the light of current history, than the vast power of a despotism to "condition" the bulk of a population (the few heretical exceptions are easily "liquidated" with the enthusiastic approval of the masses) to believe and to want virtually anything or, in general, to make them devotedly loyal to itself, believing what it promulgates as truth and unquestioningly obedient to its command.[14] And, accordingly, control over education is the first and the key objective of every despotism, political or ecclesiastical (they are all combinations of both forms). It is quite true, as our author says (p. 100), that "the dictator does not fly in the face of the most generally accepted underlying mores of his people"; but this fact sets no limitation on the power of one who knows under what conditions wants, will, ideals, etc., arise and how to control these conditions.

On education, our account can be quite brief. Practically all that we are told about it is contained in the passage already quoted (n. 13 of this article) about the ability of science to advise parents how to make a son "into an Al Capone or into an approved citizen, according to what is desired." The long chapter on "Education in a Scientific Age" (chap. iv) consists almost entirely of assertion as to what education, organized around modern science as its unifying discipline, "could" do and preaching as to what it "should" be like.[15]

14. How far this is done by the use of "scientific method," taught by scientists, is another question; if space allowed, some consideration of this would be highly relevant to the general issue.

15. The first section of this chapter is typical sarcasm contrasting science with the "good time moralizing" that is enjoyed by Americans in particular: "men and nations *shouldn't* behave in certain ways, therefore . . . they *won't* . . . if we

In other chapters our author comes closer to explicit grappling with the power problem, and certain features of his conception of the proper political order are discernible. We quote most of a paragraph which admits the necessity of government[16] and indicates his attitude toward it:

> Even when the alternate possible courses [of action] have been laid before a community and the costs and consequences of each have been pointed out, there will still be differences of opinion because of different tastes and temperaments as to which course we should pursue. This must be decided, as it has always been decided, by whatever method of consensus happens to be accepted and accredited, or at least happens to be operative, in the group. These methods vary all the way from purest democracy, through the various types of aristocracy and authority, to so-called absolute dictatorships. . . .
>
> For myself, I happen to prefer the democratic method [and] I accordingly rejoice . . . in the development of instruments for opinion and attitude measurement which, if properly applied, could perhaps restore the vitality of the relatively pure democracy which has fallen into considerable disrepute because of the obsolete technology through which it seeks to function. If future generations develop still other mechanisms of achieving community, I certainly will not insist that they blindly adhere to the techniques to which I am habituated.

Government, then, is not a social problem; in this field whatever happens is "right" or inevitable, which is the same thing for all practical purposes.

In his concluding chapter (chiefly a tirade against the United Nations setup) our author is slightly more specific. "What is to be gained by organization unless administrators *know what to do*, including how to secure . . . support for action which can be shown to be adapted to the ends sought?" (p. 112). "Administrators," then, are a third class, placed in opposition both to "scientists" and to "man" or "the community"; but their position is left as unclear as the question is interesting. They are the ones who are to know what to do and to have the knowledge, and whatever else it takes, to se-

---

exhort them enough." The second section raises the question, "What, then, *should* be the content? . . ." (our italics); and the rest of the chapter is taken up with general and hortatory statements of opinion about present-day "defects" and how to remedy them, answers to "objections," etc.

16. The necessity is inconsistent with, and implicitly qualifies, the view that agreement on ends already exists, that agreement on means will be established by science, and that the result leaves no social problem unsolved. Any conception of means and ends in conduct is inconsistent with the more strictly scientistic view of ends simply as behavior to be scientifically described, making end and means meaningless terms.

cure support for their measures. We are apparently supposed to believe that "scientific ethics" will be a part of their "proper training"
also and that they will see and follow an absolute distinction between means and ends and will only *find* the ends—either by "ask-
[ing] the masses of men what they want" (p. 97) or by asking the
scientists—while enforcing use of the means which the scientists
make known to them. Such enforcement is their sole function. Between administrators and scientists there is to be a neat and perfect
division of labor, into which "man" the citizen also fits, in the role
of docilely doing what he is told, i.e., what "science" tells administrators is good for him. Neither the scientists nor the administrators
will take any active interest in the doings of the other group—what
is done with knowledge or what knowledge is sought and provided.
There will be perfect accord within each class and between classes
on a thousand points where common sense sees obvious clashes of
interest. It must be established by the mores or by some inscrutable
power, directly or perhaps through "proper training," inculcating
"scientific ethics."[17]

Freedom and power are most fully dealt with in chapter iii, "The
Transition to Science in Human Relations," beginning with Section
III, on the costs to be incurred. Naturally, the first cost is giving up
moralizing and sentimentalizing about society and its problems. It
"would probably deprive us in large measure of the luxury of indignation . . . as regards social events." An example is our recent
"great emotional vapor-bath directed at certain European movements and leaders. Such indignation ministers to deep-seated, jungle-
fed sentiments of justice, virtue," etc., and is later (scientifically?)
described as "frothing at the mouth." The second cost is abandoning
or redefining "concepts like freedom, democracy, liberty, independence, aggression, discrimination, free speech, self-determination,"
and others, which "have never been realistically analyzed by most
people." And the third is abandonment of "cherished *ideologies*, resembling . . . their theological predecessors" (pp. 43–45). A sneering
derogation of democracy, with indirect praise of contrasting forms,
is repeatedly expressed. Again, Lundberg personally happens to like
it, "with all its absurdities," but the scientific significance of his at-
tachment may be, in fact, to show his "unfitness to live in a changing world" (p. 46). At a later point (p. 52) it is indeed recognized,

17. One might suggest "God," but Lundberg assures us that "God is clearly a
being with remarkably and demonstrably regular habits" and that he (Lundberg) can predict His will and choices, like those of men, "by exactly the same
techniques I use to predict other natural phenomena" (p. 93).

in an indirect way, that liberty is a value on its own account, a "desired result," and apparently worth some costs; but "result" and "costs" must be objectively defined and the connection demonstrated. And the analysis of such concepts as freedom and democracy, already referred to, is "sure to seem like an attack upon these cherished symbols and the romantic state of affairs for which they stand" (p. 44).

The one concrete case considered is the freedom of science, and the tenor is to pooh-pooh the idea of a positive connection between this and political freedom:

The favorite cliché . . . that "science can flourish only in freedom" . . . is a beautiful phrase, but unfortunately . . . the historical fact is that science has gone forward under a great variety of forms of government, and conversely . . . has been suppressed and frustrated by each of the same types, including democracy. The first truly popular democratic government in Europe, namely, the French Revolution [*sic*], declared itself to have "no use for scientists" and proceeded to behead Lavoisier, the father of modern chemistry.

And some American states have passed laws against teaching evolution. The author himself would, he assures us, condemn attacks on science and "freedom," wherever they occur. Is it "scientific" to condemn, or merely to describe such attacks and the conditions under which they arise or go on?

The difference between democracy and dictatorship seems to be unimportant, but, in any case, we need have no fear of the latter as a consequence of social science. The proof is that "dictatorship . . . has not accompanied the rise of the physical sciences" (p. 30). The ordinary citizen, who now accepts rather blindly the authority of physical scientists, will merely adopt "a similar attitude toward the conclusions of social scientists," although this "is suspected of being authoritarian, as indeed it probably is." But:

A lot of nonsense has been spoken and written about authority in recent years. We need to recognize that it is not authority we need fear but incompetent and unwisely constituted authority. When we undertake to insist on the same criteria of authority in the social as in the physical sciences, no one will worry about the delegation of that authority, any more than he worries about the physician's authority. All persons who presume to speak with authority will be expected to submit credentials of training and character of the type that physicians and other professionals now submit, and *to the state*, at that . . . [and] whether they purport to speak for God or nature. The state may in turn *delegate* the function of formulating and administering these requirements back into the hands of the members of the profession concerned . . . [while] maintaining the ultimate authority in the hands of the community's accredited governmental agency. . . . [To] find this idea authoritarian, fascist and what not [is] name-calling . . . an attempt to distract attention from something one is afraid to examine [pp. 51–52].

And early in the book we are warned to "beware against making fetishes of words like Fascism, Communism, and Democracy" (p. 10).

One feels estopped from serious criticism of such a social philosophy and social order, as much because of its inherent and palpable absurdity as because pointing out the obvious would be name-calling and making fetishes of words. To this latter "argument" the too obvious rebuttal is the *tu quoque*, meant as objectively as possible, plus the very serious observation that, beyond a certain point, human and social phenomena cannot be described in terms free from all flavor of approval and disapproval. One may use a definition of "thief" from a dictionary of legal terms instead of the word itself, but the meaning will be the same, and it will not be primarily an empirical description of behavior and of its "consequences." Use of the word "costs" is a surrender of the position, since it is a teleological and not an empirical-behavioristic term; it implies either some end assumed as given or a superindividual norm that is "objective" but in a sense utterly different from the data of sense observation. Nor are purely individual ends or wants (mere taste, in contrast with good taste—or, for that matter, opinion in contrast with fact) on a par with sense data. Internal mental activity, not manifested at all in external behavior of any kind—or, worse still, falsely represented, either through error or intentionally—is an essential part of the "conditions" under which wants and behavior arise. Motives are in part analogous to force in mechanics, but only in part. Forces are known only by inference from observed and measured effects, hence the two must correspond; but for motives we have numerous and subtle sources of information, and they give conflicting and certainly inaccurate reports. The motives of the observer are an essential part of the data, and these are very inaccurately known, and that to a negligible extent through sense observation; cancel them out, and, instead of securing objectivity, a major premise of inference is destroyed. Further, a premise of natural science is that observation and publication do not change the material observed, and in human relations this is false.

The heart of the matter is that the scientist and scientific behavior are themselves social phenomena, and, while they are physical phenomena too, the scientist cannot regard or treat them as merely and purely physical or mechanistic. Empirical prediction of an experiment and its result is self-contradictory; if that can be done in advance, it is not an experiment and will not be carried out. No scientist would think of predicting empirically the course of events in his own laboratory or that of any other scientist who is really investigating. There must be a one-sided relation between an explorer and his material and even more obviously between a controller and the matter controlled. If two persons predict each other's behavior and act on their predictions, each will falsify the prediction of the other. And, finally, to the extent that an individual does "predict and control" the behavior of others, he operates on the basis of coercion or deceit, and these concepts have no meaning for the relation between men and inert natural objects. (In fact, deceit is always a factor in coercion and especially when it is so effective that the subject thinks his action is a free choice.) The social scientist who seeks a real understanding and effective social action cannot ignore relations of mutuality of interest between himself and his subject matter and between the units which make up the latter. He cannot be a "solipsist" (however logically satisfying it might be), regarding all other human beings as belonging to a wholly different order of being than himself, beings who merely respond mechanically to situations that can be accurately observed, described, and measured from without; for he "knows" that these others also raise and answer questions, more or less rightly or wrongly, while he legitimately assumes that mere physical objects do not (though neither proposition can be strictly proved).

For a genuine understanding of social phenomena and problems we "obviously" have to use the methods and concepts of various sciences, physical, biological, and "psychological" in a broad interpretation; but, in addition, we have to enter other universes of discourse. Whether "adaptive response" can be interpreted mechanistically is a disputed question; but human beings engage in *rational manipulation*, which certainly involves *more* than either or both. And, apart from various forms of quasi-mechanical interaction and one-sided "control" among themselves, they to some extent reach a consensus through discussion, which cannot be conceived in terms either of mechanics or of the use of given means to achieve given ends. Ends are also in part problematic; and discourse which recognizes them as such cannot make sense without reference to norms, "values," which are more than individual wants, as the latter are more than empirical facts.

IV

XI

The Role of Principles in Economics and Politics[1]

THE more than generous words of introduction by the chairman may suggest or illustrate the underlying theme of my remarks to follow—the conflict of values. Needless to say, the value qualities of an introduction lie in the fields of morals and aesthetics. No one would think of applying the category of truth. And as to utility, the "function" of an introduction seems to be, by a little amiable and gracefully stated prevarication, to add to the embarrassment of the speaker—if he has enough modesty or candor in self-appraisal to be subject to embarrassment. I say this, not to return unkindness for kindness, but for the serious purpose stated of illustrating what I believe to be a profoundly important principle in connection with principles; and I wish I had more time than I shall be able to take, to consider in particular the conflict between truth and other values, specifically in a liberal ethic and culture.

Let me add that I am modest and candid enough to be "plenty" embarrassed already. It is not only my inadequacy to the occasion and dislike of disappointing an audience such as this. The occasion comes to me at a time when members of our profession cease, by the usual official standards, to be useful and are pensioned off—decently and quietly laid on the shelf. Standing at this vantage point and surveying the history of our society, of west European civilization, and of the world, during the generation and more in which I, with colleagues in economics and other branches of what is called social science, have been diligently "improving" that society and the world, I find little cause for jubilation or enhancement of self-esteem. And if I turn to view the standing of my profession in the world, or that of my special branch of it, dealing with principles or "theory" in the profession as a whole, I get no more comfort from what I see. So, I have proposed for the address, which custom demands on this occasion, a bit of general stocktaking. Such an endeavor is itself reasonably in accord with custom, if somewhat

1. Presidential address delivered at the Sixty-third Annual Meeting of the American Economic Association, Chicago, December 28, 1950. Reprinted by permission from the *American Economic Review*, Vol. XLI, No. 1 (March, 1951).

strange for a "learned society," and I hope it is a custom not dis-
honored in the observance. Custom also allows the speaker, perhaps
especially one of the age of this incumbent, to take a somewhat personal or reminiscent tone and to verge toward the character of a
sermon rather than that of science or scholarship.

My embarrassment not only at standing before this audience but
in all teaching and writing about economic principles is not new, as
its source is not. I have been increasingly moved to wonder whether
my job is a job or a racket, whether economists, and particularly
economic theorists, may not be in the position that Cicero, citing
Cato, ascribed to the augurs of Rome—that they should cover their
faces or burst into laughter when they met on the street. Thus, for
reasons which I hope to develop briefly, my interest has of late
tended to shift from the problems of economic theory, or what
seem to be its proper concerns, to the question of why people so
generally, and the learned elite in particular, as they express themselves in various ways, choose nonsense instead of sense and shake
the dust from their feet at us. And also, why the theorist is so commonly "in the doghouse" among economists, as classified by academic faculty lists and books and articles in learned journals carrying the word "economic" in their titles.

I also note that the period of my career as an economist has been
marked by a series of "movements"—I will not say fads—in economic writing and teaching, consisting largely of attacks on traditional
views of the nature and function of economics, in which the term
"orthodoxy" commonly appears as a "cuss word," an epithet of
reproach. The critics, aggressors, have more or less explicitly advocated the abolition of an economics of economic principles and its
replacement by almost anything or everything else, other principles
if they can be found—psychological, historical, statistical, political,
or ethical—or no principles at all but factual description of some
sector of social-human phenomena called "economic" for reasons
not clear to me. I cannot comment in detail on these fashions in
thinking. The latest "new economics," and in my opinion rather the
worst for fallacious doctrine and pernicious consequences, is that
launched by the late John Maynard (Lord) Keynes, who for a dec-
ade succeeded in carrying economic thinking well back to the dark
age; but of late this wave of the future has happily been passing.

This same period of history has also seen a growing disregard for
free economic institutions in public policy, increasing resort to legislative and bureaucratic interference and control, the growth of

pressure groups employing both political and "direct" action to get what they want, and with all this the debasement of the state itself, completely in much of the European world, from free forms to ruthless despotism. It is surely legitimate to ask whether there is some connection between the movement of economic thinking and that of political change.

Now all thinking involves "principles" in some sense, at least the formation of concepts and fitting of concrete data to concepts through propositions. Surveying the quality of economic thinking in matters of policy which seemingly tends to win out, one faces the unpleasant question whether, if people will not think more or less correctly, it is good for them to think at all. Perhaps it might be better to go back to the good old days when men believed and did what they were told by hoary tradition and constituted authority. For so the great mass always lived, prior to the advent of our historically unique west-European civilization a couple of centuries ago. Perhaps the "principle" of authoritarian dictatorship is right after all—or inevitable, which for practical purposes comes to the same thing—as large groups even in this country insist and preach. And I do not mean only the Communist party and its sympathizers; there are others, far more numerous, who are among its most vociferous opponents. For one totalitarian party will naturally hate another with different leaders and slogans far worse than they will hate those who stand for freedom.

My doubts and discouragement—for there is no reason to avoid such words, since I propose here to place truth ahead of other values —are not new. It has long been my habit to mention to classes the sinister import of such intellectual phenomena as protectionism in foreign economic policy; and the perpetual popular demand for making capital cheap by manufacturing money; and for creating a demand for labor by enforcing all sorts of inefficiency, waste, and even destruction. The free traders, as has been said, win the debates but the protectionists win the elections; and it makes little difference in our policy which party wins, the avowed protectionists or the professed free traders. Inflation is of course to be brought on as a more pleasant alternative to taxation and then suppressed by law and police action. Try to get people to see that if the value of money has been depreciated by, say, 45 per cent, any price, charge, or tax that has not risen in money terms by over 80 per cent has actually been reduced. If the rulers of democracy, the demos, will not heed simple arithmetic, what is the use of talking and writing about problems which really are problems—not to mention developing higher mathematical formulas in which the "given" magnitudes must be largely guessed at. Why engage in public discussion at all, unless one is content with what seems to be our role to serve as an antidote to the poison being disseminated by other social scientists, even economists? Is it not insulting one's own intelligence?

The serious fact is that the bulk of the really important things that economics has to teach are things that people would see for themselves if they were willing to see. And it is hard to believe in the utility of trying to teach what men refuse to learn or even seriously listen to. What point is there in propagating sound economic principles if the electorate is set to have the country run on the principle that the objective in trade is to get rid of as much as possible and get as little as possible in return, if they will not see that imports are either paid for by exports, as a method of producing the imported goods more efficiently, or else are received for nothing, or if they hold that economy consists in having as many workers as possible assigned to a given task instead of the fewest who are able to perform it? Of late I have a new and depressing example of popular economic thinking, in the policy of arbitrary price-fixing. Can there be any use in explaining, if it is needful to explain, that fixing a price below the free-market level will create a shortage and one above it a surplus? But the public oh's and ah's and yips and yaps at the shortage of residential housing and surpluses of eggs and potatoes as if these things presented problems any more than getting one's footgear soiled by deliberately walking in the mud. And let me observe that rent freezing, for example, occurs not at all merely because tenants have more votes than landlords. It reflects a state of mind, a mode of reasoning, even more discouraging than blindness through self-interest—like protectionism among our middle western farmers.

One must grant that some critics of rationalistic economics seem to have something in their contention that theories based on the assumption that men are reasoning beings run contrary to facts. But, from the standpoint of policy, the question is, will they be more reasonable in more sweeping political action, considering that it is absurd governmental policies which lead to the criticism in the first place? However, one notes that protectionism and "featherbedding" of organized workers and even monetary inflation are not (not often) carried to the logical point at which all exchange and specialization through exchange would stop or all accumulated resources be eaten up. Explanation of policy might conceivably get farther if we did take a more psychological tack and instead of reasoning logically, ask why men believe and practice nonsense but in general act so much less irrationally than they argue—and what follows from that. Presumably our lucubrations must have *some* relation to the public interest if we are to expect public support; but why they pay us for it anyway is one of the deep economic mysteries, one might say another striking example of popular economic irrationality. However, any politician can always find an "economist" to indorse any position or policy he sees fit to advocate, and perhaps this is the proper function of our "science" in a democracy.

Let me say here that I feel like apologizing for the negativistic and even complaining tone of my remarks so far—for there is no transgression more unforgivable than refusing to be "optimistic" and "constructive." But I started out by mentioning the conflict of values and especially that between truth and other values and have said that on this occasion I propose to give a considerable preference to truth over other standards. It is an advantage of getting old, which I believe even Cicero overlooked in his great apology for age. A certain independence goes with getting to a point where one will hardly be hunting a job or running for office or (probably) even courting the ladies. One may then indulge in the luxury of a moderate amount of candor, even of calling a spade a spade. And unpleasant truth—and truth is likely to be unpleasant or we should not place so much stress on optimism—may be useful, up to a point. I would not carry it too far, but occasionally, and in homeopathic doses, as it were. I am reminded of a deep philosophical observation made by a high politico in a speech some years ago, here in Chicago I believe, as reported by T. V. Smith: "The time has come to take the bull by the tail and look the situation square in the face." It has occurred to me that one of the interesting "facts of life" is that the expression itself refers to things so ugly or unpleasant that they are to be kept out of sight or explicit mention. If time allowed, I should like to follow this out with some "research" into the reasons why our professional stock in trade is referred to as "the dismal science." At any rate, I do wish to stress the importance of negative conclusions, particularly in relation to action, the advisability of *not* doing things that will make matters worse, and the fact that principles of economics do have in a high degree this unromantic sort of value. And perhaps this applies to knowledge in general. A humorist once popular in this country stated my favorite "principle" in education: "It ain't ignorance that does the most damage, its knowin' so derned much that ain't so."

I also spoke earlier of philosophizing, or preaching, in contrast with more objective discourse. A sermon should have a text, and I have found a suitable one in the gospel according to "Saint" the Marquis de Talleyrand-Périgord: The only good principle is to have no principles (*le seule bon principe est de n'en avoir aucun*). Talleyrand, to be sure, is not regularly listed among the evangelists. But he was in fact a bishop in the Church, and another churchman, of the civilized eighteenth-century French pattern, the abbot Galiani, had earlier stated the same creed. And, anyhow, the saying suits my purpose as a text. It is, no doubt, usually enjoyed and dismissed as a witty cynicism; but I propose to treat it quite seriously, as a starting point. Not literally, I admit. It is an epigram; and an epigram has been defined as a half-truth so stated as to be especially annoying to those who believe in the other half. I wish to stress both halves, the value of principles as well as their limitations. Accordingly, I must reword the text into one of rather the opposite literal import. The right principle is to respect all the principles, take them fully into account, and then use *good judgment* as to how far to follow one or another in the case in hand. All principles are false, because all are true—in a sense and to a degree; hence, none is true in a sense and to a degree which would deny to others a similarly qualified truth. There is always a principle, plausible and even sound within limits, to justify any possible course of action and, of course, the opposite one. The truly right course is a matter of the best compromise or the best or "least worst" combination of good and evil. As in cookery, and in economic theory, it calls for enough and not too much, far enough and not too far, in any direction. Morever, the ingredients of policy are always imponderable, hence there can be no principle, no formula, for the best compromise. That laws must be stated in sentences partly accounts for the familiar "principle," "the law is an ass." And if people don't have good judgment, or won't use it, it is "'just too bad,'" for themselves and for others over whom they have power.

After so much by way of "preliminary," I am at last ready for some consideration of economic principles. These have, or surely ought to have, two kinds of significance: in explaining what does happen and in providing guidance for bringing about what is thought desirable or what ought to happen. In the first role they assimilate to principles of science; in the second, they raise questions of political principle, since action must be primarily political, and both economic and political principles are inseparable from ethics. Political principles are of course affected by the same ambiguity, they both explain and direct, and this is also true in a sense of the ethical. The problem is complicated by the tangled relation between the two concerns, explanation and critical evaluation; for these also are inseparable, yet are finally contradictory. A complete explanation shows why an event is inevitable, given the antecedent circumstances; hence it excludes purposive control. Here I propose, after a brief reminder of what the main economic principles are and what they mean, to consider them in the light of three questions: their value or usefulness, their limitations, and the possible alternatives—all with respect to explanation and guidance of action. I need hardly say that all these topics raise the deepest philosophical issues and that only a few general and superficial observations, selected rather arbitrarily or at haphazard, are possible here. But let me note at once that Talleyrand was referring to moral principles in connection with political action, and it is with respect to these in particular that I wish to sound an emphatic warning. The most pernicious and abominable principle of all, though it has been stated and preached by the highest authorities, ecclesiastical and lay (from Athanasius to Kant), is the principle of acting on moral principles—"do right though the world perish." That is—as will be found to be true of moral principles generally—false and pernicious if it is taken to mean anything in particular, anything beyond the best compromise, the best combination of good and bad, and in both means and ends, where the problem has the means-end form.

Economic principles are simply the more general implications of the single principle of freedom, individual and social, i.e., free association, in a certain sphere of activity. The sphere is that of economizing, i.e., conduct in which quantitative means are used to achieve quantitative ends, or rather provisional ends, goods and services quantitatively comparable as means to a general end, also quantifiable. But economics deals only with the apportionment of means among the provisional ends or the proportioning of these, leaving to engineering and kindred studies the all-or-none choices among technical processes. The general end has no good and accepted name; it may be called economic well-being if it is recognized that both terms require definition. It is simply the common denominator necessarily implied in comparisons between uses of means. Acceptance of the principle of freedom makes it superfluous to define the end, and the less that is specified about it the better. The provisionally final ends, as noted, are the impersonal goods and services desired and sought, produced and consumed, at any time and place. However, we must not fail to include additional means or resources, produced with some fraction of those in existence at a given time; maintenance of these, including all replacements, is of course part of the production of the flow of consumable things.

The free association in question is exchange in markets, an instrumentality necessary to specialized production and distribution of the joint result. The meaning of economics in the traditional or orthodox sense is the analysis of this system of co-operation in the production and distribution of impersonal goods. "Competition" has no necessary or proper place in the organization and its use to describe the free choice by each co-operator is a linguistic accident calamitous for understanding. All "personal" association, by contrast, involves power, and personal values are not subject to exchange. The form of purchase and sale of friendliness or enmity is viewed as immoral, though there is much pretense both ways—as in most human relations. Exchange or its terms may be much influenced by personal considerations (really mixed with giving) and we actually in large measure exchange dinner parties, various presents, etc., as well as disfavors. (One reason why a science of human behavior, in the literal sense, is impossible is that, in contrast with physical objects, our behavior is so saturated with varied make-believe and deception not clearly separable from the "realities.") A special and very important form of exchange occurs when one person places his economic capacity under the direction of another, on terms fixed by agreement —the principle of "entrepreneurship." Such direction is a distinctive service in that it cannot be measured until after the arrangement is liquidated, hence cannot be treated as a means of production or "capitalized" as can be done with other services, including the personal type, so far as contracts can be enforced.

The "perfect" market (miscalled perfectly competitive) is unreal but conceptually necessary. It is the embodiment of complete freedom. There are no power relations, since everyone has a choice among a number of equally good alternatives. The freedom in question centers in the right of each to be the judge of his own values and of the use of his own means to achieve them. There is no implication of selfishness or any other judgment of the moral quality or artistic taste reflected in any want or act. We usually speak of "individual" freedom, but it applies to any group acting as a unit. The family, "represented" by its "head," is the usual minimum unit, and there are other units in unlimited number and variety. Wants and resources are treated simply as "given" attributes of any individual or other unit; "technology" must either be included among resources or added as a third given—the latter is the more useful procedure. On the average, an economic subject's own person, with all its capacities, is the chief means under his control and is in the majority of cases nearly his only resource. Differences between personal capacities and external "property" are the creation of the legal system and would be absent under a slave economy. The virtual outlawing of enforcible contracts for personal services creates a serious disadvantage for one whose resources are in the personal form; for he cannot freely "realize" future value by sale or pledge and is consequently dependent on a continuous market as well as continuity in the capacity itself. But the benefits of freedom are presumably thought greater than the evil.

The principle of freedom is apparently accepted in modern civilization—consequently called "liberal"—on three or four grounds, which overlap somewhat. First, and most commonly cited, it is instrumental to the realization of other ends accepted as rightful. Modern thought locates value in the individual rather than making him an instrument to the purposes of the state or its ruler. And it is assumed that the normal adult person is ordinarily a better judge of his own interests, values, or well-being than any agent of society (bureaucrat) given authority over him is likely to be. Second, freedom itself is a thing men want, and have a right to, even possibly at the cost of a formally better management of one's affairs by an overlord of any kind; the normal person prefers within wide limits to "make his own mistakes." Third, it is a "value," a thing the individual ought to want, even ought to have if he may not choose it, a part of the modern ideal of the dignity of the person. Thus the laws of liberal states do not allow men to sell themselves (or their children) into "involuntary servitude," even if they so choose, though everyone is free from day to day to place himself or his property under the direction of another, on terms satisfactory to both parties. This is the entrepreneurial relation, which is in a real sense the central feature of the modern free economy. Finally, there is a fourth, "pragmatic" reason for extending the scope of freedom; policing is costly to the public authority and coercion itself needs to be economized.

From the standpoint of explaining actual behavior, one can only submit that people want to economize and that their efforts to make resources go further are more or less successful; also that correct apportionment of resources among uses is a way of economizing, as are specialization through exchange of products and the organization of effort under specialized direction. A large sector of individual and social behavior is then more or less fully "explained" by these principles. How far they go, and what other principles or unsystematic occurrences may have to be considered, I obviously cannot take up in detail here.

Certainly economic principles are subject to sweeping limitations as to their explanatory value. They tell us nothing about concrete economic facts, what wants people have, what goods are produced and exchanged, what resources and techniques are employed, what distribution takes place. The justification of treating these data in a purely abstract way is the significance of theory for policy, and I shall come back to that. Further, it is easy for a critic to "riddle" the principle of abstract rationality. No one thinks, I hope, that consumers consciously strive to maximize satisfaction, well-being, or whatever it be, by acting in relation to a known function connecting the state in question with measurable quantities of things available at given prices. Effort to get the maximum return in money for productive services seems more realistic, but the view that production is purely in order to have consumption, unaffected by interests of its own, is clearly indefensible. Yet comparisons between uses of means are made and apportionments effected; and the logical principles inherent in these acts are useful for interpretation even if they do not accurately picture the conscious motives. It suffices that men largely behave "as if" they were trying to conform to the principles. These have great value in the prediction of effects of changes, effects both on and through price movements, changes that happen or are contrived. And the alternative, which is statistics on a behavioristic basis, is subject to much the same limitations, rooted in the vagueness and instability of motives. Certainly the main effort in statistical economics, the prediction of changes in business conditions, has not produced results justifying much elation.

More detailed consideration would carry us into the question of the possibilities and limitations of a natural or positive science of human conduct. Many limitations are plain to see, and they are related to the essential fact, which is that such a science is not what we need; indeed, the idea is an absurdity. For, if even two people predict one another's behavior and act on their predictions, both predictions will be falsified and the activities of both parties misdirected. From the standpoint of explanation alone, motives correspond to forces in mechanics. These too are unobserved, metaphysical; we read them into the phenomena for interpretation, because our minds work that way. Forces, however, are known and measured only by their effects, hence always correspond exactly with the latter. But we have other information about human motives, and "know" indisputably that they do not correspond closely with results, that the connection is affected in all degrees by error of numerous kinds. Particularly, where motivation takes the form of using means to achieve ends, either may be more or less "wrong," and the two errors are only vaguely separable. In this field, knowledge is so vague and evidence so conflicting that no one can tell with any accuracy at all, even afterwards, to what degree any action is really economic. Still further, we know that the goods and services produced, traded, and consumed do not correspond to final or real wants. These are largely not individual, as the theory requires, but inhere in social relations, such as "keeping up with the Joneses," and "getting ahead of the Joneses"; or they are symbolic, even deliberately "set up," as in play, to make action interesting and yield the feeling of success or victory—thus reversing the means-end relation assumed in economics. Or the motive is no particular result but mere gratification of curiosity as to what the result will be. And all these symbolic relations are extremely unstable and change unpredictably.

Since a fetish of "scientific method" in the study of society is one of the two most pernicious forms of romantic folly that are current among the educated, the theme ought to be developed at a length which is impossible here. (The other "folly," which will receive more attention presently, as my main theme, is the idea that devotion to moral principles offers the solution of social problems.) "Science," in the meaning of the natural sciences, can of course do something toward both explaining and directing social events; and nothing is further from my purpose here than any belittling of the importance of ethics. What I insist upon is an understanding of the meaning and limitations of simple or statable principles in both areas. In the naïve form in which both doctrines, scientism and moralism, are usually preached, both are antithetical to the principle or ideal of freedom; they imply, and if taken seriously would lead to, absolute authoritarianism. The notion that evils are due to sin works out, as European history makes clear, in having the right people (as shown by their being in power) enforce their orthodoxy on all by burning or otherwise liquidating the heretics, schismatics, and infidels, as occasion demands, though mainly by effective indoctrination and conditioning for submissiveness before the age of responsibility. The principle has merely been taken over by the Marxists from historical ecclesiastical Christianity, with unimportant changes in moral or political content, though with sweeping but practically irrelevant change in the professed underlying metaphysic. As to a "science" of human conduct, I have mentioned some difficulties, notably that one of the most distinctive traits of man is make-believe, hypocrisy, concealment, dissimulation, deception. He is the clothes-wearing animal, but the false exterior he gives to his body is nothing to that put on by his mind. My evangelist, Talleyrand, also remarked that speech is the medium by which men disguise their thoughts. The "real wants" or wishes, referred to before, run largely in pairs of opposites; besides conformity and distinction we find familiarity and novelty or fixity and change, adventure and security, and so on. Mostly they have no specific content and anything that happens or is done will fit one or the other of some pair. Such principles cannot explain any concrete occurrence; this was the obvious weakness of the theory of "instincts" that was the groundwork of a "psychology" very popular some years ago.

Another obstreperous feature of human phenomena is that men have "attitudes" toward law as such, both descriptive and imperative law, and both positive and negative attitudes. If there is a law, either a uniformity or a command, and someone finds it and publishes it, one of the first results is a general impulse to violate it. Man is a "contrary critter"—in contrast with the conformism of physical nature. And on the other hand, men love to make laws for their own sake, to conform for a while, until tired of it, then break them and make new ones. Much of the apparent uniformity of behavior is such ritual. And there may be substantive reasons for non-conformity or for temporary conformity that ultimately causes disruption of the pattern. A familiar example is boom and depression in various prices and in general prices—the purchasing power of money. An accepted prediction of change will cause the change predicted, for a time, then an inevitable reversal. It is true that many generalizations can be made about men and about all known societies. Professor Murdock has listed some dozens of them. But they are of a general, abstract type. All men have a language—but what language? And what will they say in it or with it? And so with numerous institutions. Every society has a technology which "works" up to a point, keeps people alive; but in spite of the conformity of the physical world to uniform natural laws, the fact tells us virtually nothing significant as to what to expect in the way of concrete "economic" behavior, corresponding to the prediction of planetary orbits, eclipses, etc., or the outcome of physical operations. (But if a physical operation is experimental, problem-solving, prediction of the result or the course of the operation itself is a self-contradiction.) All peoples and most individuals have some religion. But a careful student, Professor Lowie, finds it impossible to give a general definition of the word, and the dictionary definitions, vague as they are, do not cover actual usage. The simple fact is that we commonly recognize and describe human behavior forms as expressions of some feeling, intent, belief, not as bare acts. And our terms often contain an inseparable value judgment as well; there is no specific intent, not to mention a specific act, of murder or theft.

All this about the abstract and interpretive character of economic theory or principles has little to do with their significance. That is because their main value is connected with policy determination, under the fundamental ethical principle of freedom. Assuming that men have a right to want and strive to get whatever they do want, and to have the tastes and "higher" values they do have, so long as their conduct does not infringe the equal rights of others, the business of the economics of principles, of utility, productivity, and price, is to explain that, and how, the organization through buying and selling enables everyone to do whatever he tries to do (whether rational or not, as judged by anyone else) many times more effectively than would be possible if each used his own means in a self-sufficient economic life. Everyone is free, as a Crusoe is free, and also enjoys the nearly boundless gain in the effectiveness of action possible through organization. In fact, the individual's range of choice is extended in a new dimension beyond that of Crusoe; he can produce anything he pleases, or make any specific contribution to production, and independently consume anything or any combination produced by anyone anywhere in the economy. No other possible method of organization will afford this twofold freedom. And anyone is also free to stay out of the system and live his own self-sufficient life, so far as he cares to stand the loss in efficiency—which usually in fact would rapidly become too great to be borne. And all are free to give and receive goods or counsel and to co-operate on any terms other than those set by the market which they, the parties concerned, may agree in preferring on moral grounds or for any reason. Distribution, what the individual (family unit) gets out of it all, is also in principle the same as with a Crusoe; it is what he produces. That is, what he—the productive "capacity" he furnishes—adds to total output, which is the only meaning the product of a unit can have when production is a joint activity. In fact, the "imputation" process under market competition is valid in the sense in which any single causes produce an effect where causes act jointly, as they always do. It is the *difference* caused by the single contribution, as isolated by the mathematical operation of partial differentiation. (Consumption is usually treated, not very accurately, as unorganized.)

Stating all this at length makes me feel that I ought to apologize to you and to myself; for it is really at the level of truism and triviality. Of course there are "assumptions": that free association implies mutual advantage and that freely chosen advantage to individuals is "good," in contrast with obedience or ascetic self-denial or self-torture (as men professed to believe even in Europe only a few centuries ago). It is assumed that, in general, normal adults are rational enough to be trusted to manage their own affairs and decent enough to allow others to do the same; but this means only in comparison with the dictates of some human authority, political or ecclesiastical, chosen in whatever way, who might be in a position to order them around. The ethic of liberal civilization holds (I repeat) both that men want to be free and have a right to be and that they ought to be free, even if they themselves feel that their affairs might possibly be technically better managed for them as slaves by some possible master. Of course even these assumptions in an extreme version are made only for the purposes of theory; everyone admits that in practice governments have to set some limits to individual freedom and freedom of association and to perform many functions on behalf of the community as a whole. If only economics could really teach people the simple and obvious fact, which most of them already know but refuse to accept, that anyone producing for exchange is producing for himself, as much as a Crusoe, but merely a thousand times more effectively because he does it indirectly by producing for the needs of others. If this were realized, it would surely put an end to all the insane or diabolical revolutionary propaganda and most of the stupid criticisms of the "capitalist system" that menace our free institutions. Why it is necessary to teach this, and accordingly so hard—if not useless—to try, is the major real social problem. I can give it little consideration here. But I must note an apparent "innate disposition" in men to think that somebody is getting the better of them, that they are working for somebody else, even where it is, if possible, more absurd than the idea of the wage-worker that he is working to make profits for some greedy capitalist. Doesn't the student regularly talk about working for his professor, and even the patient avers that he is coerced by his doctor, whom he hires and fires and even defies at will—except for the natural consequences? The much abused "profit system" is of course merely a pattern of co-operation, on the terms most satisfactory to the parties concerned, or the only terms they can agree upon. "Property" has intrinsically nothing to do with it; it may be and is the same where only labor services are involved at all.

I wish I had time to follow up in particular the relation between doctor and patient. The similarities and differences as compared with, say, the relationships of an industrial corporation, should be interesting, even instructive. Two or three obvious facts which need emphasis must be barely mentioned. The doctor in whose hands one places one's self as a "case" will inevitably have much power, variously and precariously limited by moral, legal, and other restrictions and compulsions. The only real freedom the patient can have is the right and opportunity to choose and change at will his doctor. And the significance of this is limited, since in the nature of things the patient cannot act very intelligently in the matter. He would himself have to possess the specialized knowledge of the medical profession, and much more, in order to appraise it in others. But the case of individual patient and individual doctor (or other professional counselor) is simple in comparison with the problem presented by the vast and highly organized productive units required for the exploitation of modern technology. Here centralized direction is imperative anyway, apart from specialized competence in the directive function. Hence the final word of the candid economist to the public must be—don't expect too much in the way of freedom or justice, along with the immeasurable increase in technical efficiency that results from these two facts of modern civilization, special competence and centralized direction. In particular, don't expect too much of "the state"; be very critical in appraising the prospects for good and for harm to result before calling on "Leviathan" and giving him power. In the scope of this address, this, the most vital conclusion, must be stated rather than argued; but it remains true that the chief reliance of the "employee" must be freedom of choice among employers, unsatisfactory though it is, as in the case of the patient and the doctors.

Given the principle of freedom, as active freedom of association, the notion of scientific control of society is a palpable contradiction. (It applies in varying degree in the treatment of defectives, young children, and criminals.) For a dictator, the problem would be formally parallel to that of scientific technology; but, even in that case, the content of control would be utterly different. For, unless he could competely drug or hypnotize and so eliminate the minds and wills of his subject-slaves, the autocrat proprietor of a society would have to rule *through* those minds and wills. Hence the operation would employ such techniques as persuasion or coercion, suggestion, cajolery, flattery, and, above all, deception—which is at the heart of what is called "force" in human relations—and also, inevitably, some real discussion. But these things have no meaning for the relations between purposive human beings and the inert objects of nature where scientific technique is literally applicable. (The higher animals, notably in domestication, present an intermediate situation which must here be ignored.) In a democracy the notion of control is not merely unethical, it is excluded, *ipso facto*. The self-contradiction of a number of persons mutually predicting one another's behavior and acting on their predictions has already been pointed out, and that of mutual control is even more obviously absurd. The problem of democracy is to establish a *consensus*, by genuine discussion, with intellectual appeal to superindividual norms. Mere expression of individual desires is not discussion and can only exacerbate conflict of interests and intensify the problem, not tend toward solution in all-around agreement. Objective norms belong to a third level of reality, distinct from and above individual desire or end and means, as the category of the instrumental is different from and "above" mechanical sequence or cause and effect. And judgments about norms and ideals are affected by a different category of error, though the facts that norms are objects of desire and that "means and end" parallels "cause and effect" make clear analysis impossible.

Genuine "free" discussion is a difficult thing to deal with conceptually and more difficult to realize in practice. The problem presents two aspects: first, agreement on the range in which agreement itself is considered necessary, as marked off from individual freedom and diversity, and second, the specific content of uniformity in its sector. On any considerable scale, discussion itself must be organized; and this organization presents practically the same problems as the matter to be dealt with, specifically the limitation of freedom by rules and authority in order to secure the greatest possible freedom and the performance of function.

The supreme and inestimable merit of the exchange mechanism is that it enables a vast number of people to co-operate in the use of means to achieve ends as far as their interests are mutual, without arguing or in any way agreeing about either the ends or the methods of achieving them. It is the "obvious and simple system of natural liberty." The principle of freedom, where it is applicable, takes other values out of the field of social action. In contrast, agreement on terms of co-operation through discussion is hard and always threatens to become impossible, even to degenerate into a fight, not merely the failure of co-operation and loss of its advantages. The only agreement called for in market relations is acceptance of the one essentially negative ethical principle, that the units are not to prey upon one another through coercion or fraud.

This picture of the open market, free-enterprise organization must sound very one-sided, and it is one-sided. Presumably no competent mind has ever believed in it exclusively. If there have been real anarchists, they were not economists. And the society pictured by the pure, idealized theory of the market economy is, or would be, one held together by the single moral principle just stated. This is entirely proper as a postulate for theoretical analysis at a certain stage of abstraction. But the idea that freedom, or any single principle, contains the solution, or the best solution, of social problems, is of course unrealistic and is directly contrary to the thesis of this paper, as stated at the outset. Exaggeration or overemphasis of the significance of freedom to the neglect of other principles was the great error of the liberal age, and is partly responsible for the reaction we now witness, which threatens extinction of freedom and of all defensible values. It should go without saying that freedom alone would not produce an approximation to the conditions required for a market itself, the freest possible market. And modern economists have not thought otherwise. The accusation that Adam Smith, for example, believed in a universal harmony of interests among men is merely one discouraging example of what passes widely in learned circles for history and discussion. At a minimum, rules must be made and enforced by some agency representing the whole market collectively; and the policing must be paid for on a principle other than direct individual payment for service received. And, at most, as I have emphasized, the market deals only in impersonal values. To realize its ideal character, the system would have to be operated through vending machines, avoiding personal contact between the parties to exchange. At this point, I turn to more detailed, though brief and inadequate, notice of the limitations of freedom from the standpoint of policy or of freedom as a policy. This will be followed by an even briefer glance at the alternatives and the final practical problem making up the classical three parts of the argument.

There is a paradox about the general problem of economic organization. One can state a case which sounds much like an "airtight" justification of market freedom or laissez faire. But if it is easy to "riddle" the notion of means-end rationality as an explanatory principle, this is still more true of the apologetic for reliance on the free market as an ideal social policy. We also encounter a logical paradox in the concept of freedom. On the one hand, it is not discussable, being the presupposition of discussion, and freedom in conduct is inseparable from that in communication. Yet we are brought up short by a glance at our own history. For it is only in the small island of our own modern (post-Enlightenment) west-European culture that the axiom is accepted; in history as a whole, including rather especially European history in the preceding epochs, political or economic liberty, and, even more, religious-moral-intellectual freedom, was emphatically rejected on principle, if it was ever contemplated as a possibility. The aristocratic, slave-holding town-republics of ancient times hardly call for mention as exceptions, though we can learn from their experience and discussion because some problems of democracy arise within any ruling class (unless it is an established hierarchy headed by an absolute authority like Hitler, the Pope, or Stalin, with effective provision for the succession). The rise of the strange phenomenon of modern liberalism is undoubtedly to be explained in part as a reaction against the peculiar dogmatism, intolerance, and obscurantism of medieval "Christian" Europe. But much of the former spirit is with us yet; and the superposition of an ethic of extreme freedom and individual rights on an extreme authoritarianism of obedience and duties based on status is surely a chief source of the moral-intellectual confusion of our age, of which we hear so much (and so much nonsense). And a kind of pendular principle in history no doubt helps to account for the new turnabout which has carried so much of the world back to despotism.

My own view of the social-economic policy is not greatly concerned with the notion of treating the individual satisfaction-function as a welfare-function and proceeding to the notion of a social maximum in terms of some relation between individual maxima. It is too clearly indefensible to treat "happiness" or the "good life" for the individual as a definable end to be achieved by a definite technique; and even more indefensible to view the objective of social-economic policy in terms of the amount and distribution of measurable impersonal goods and services. Wealth and poverty are terribly important things, but that view of their significance seems to me an absurd oversimplification. Freedom itself, as a value per se, is far more important. In "economic" life, in the ordinary empirical reference, the motivation of competitive sport plays a role at least as great as the endeavor to secure gratifications mechanically dependent on quantitative consumption. Some business efficiency expert is said to have advised reforming football by having all the men play on the same side, instead of half pushing against the other half. The real problem centers, of course, in the fact that activity has both characters; it is a game, but one in which the most vital substantive goods, comfort and life itself, are stakes, inseparably combined with victory and defeat and their bauble-symbols. The social problem is to make the best possible rules for this complex and paradoxical game, which everyone is compelled to play. And it must go on almost without interruption, and it is impossible to play a game and discuss the rules at the same time. The intellectual problem involved in rule-making is different in kind from that of play itself, and neither—it is important to note—has much relation to scientific technology, or means-end rationality, nor to our traditional religious-ethical principle of charity. For, when charity comes into a game, the game goes out; though, in relation to the other aspect of the process, the production and distribution of goods considered intrinsically useful, it does have a part to play. I may suggest that the ethic really believed in and reasonably practiced by the modern man centers in sportsmanship and the related principle of workmanship.

Even with much and costly social action, there can be no very close approximation to the theoretical perfect market, particularly in one important area, the labor market. This fact does not at all justify most of the action being taken in that field, by unions or by government; in general, the argument against price control and other interference is made stronger, not weaker, by the "imperfect competition" which is used as a defense for it. And the action we

see is designed to make the market still more imperfect and to benefit a select stratum already comparatively well off, at the expense of
their weaker brethren. The effects cannot be traced and measured
in detail, but it is a safe "principle" that in a power contest the
weakest get the worst of it. The chief "mechanical" defects in the
market system arise less out of "frictions" than out of speculative
situations. When in order to act rationally each must first know or
guess at what everyone else will do, the result is complicated cyclical tendencies; in particular, speculation in the future value of
money gives rise to "the business cycle," sometimes an actual social
disaster. Monopoly is another evil, though the public misconceives
its nature and grossly exaggerates the extent and power of business
monopolies. A majority of producers and dealers have some short-
run monopoly position; but, in general, monopoly is temporary and
functional, on the same principle as patent rights. Protective duties
foster monopoly; but where monopoly really bites is in the legal
brigandage of organized wage-earners and farmers. The business interest itself is far more dangerous to free society through political
action as a pressure group; but it stands no chance in competition
with voting masses "agitated" and organized for power and plunder
—all the worse for their self-righteous motivation. Obviously, anything like nationwide collective bargaining and striking is coercion
of the country, not of any opposed economic interest; and, as noted,
the heaviest cost falls on other "workers," especially those still
weaker. (Perhaps I should use a more polite word; but I said I would
exploit the privilege of age to put truth ahead of manners; and what
does anyone, including the "honest brigand" want but his "rights,"
to be judge of his own case and have coercive power to enforce his
own verdict?)

Far more important than all the mechanical imperfections of
"market competition" (the real ones, not created by stupid or un-
wise public action) are limitations of the principle of economic freedom inherent in unalterable conditions of life and associative action.
Our economic ills are not due to the failure of competition; on the
contrary, the result of perfect functioning of the system would be
socially quite intolerable. The free market, with reasonable help
from state authority, can make tolerable provision for the economic
co-operation of individuals and other "units," so far as it is "co-
operation" and so far as their interests are mutual. By the same argument it cannot solve any other problems, and there are many other
and grave problems that insistently call for solution. So in other

fields: free association will solve the problems "up to a point," but not completely or by itself. Social problems are not only hard but finally insoluble. Yet many of them will inevitably get some kind of "treatment"; it is a question of better or worse, or of making things better, more or less, or making them worse than before, even to downright disaster. As I remember hearing "Tommy" Adams say in a classroom, we must not call any problems insoluble which must be solved in some way and for which some solutions are better, or worse, than others.

The most serious limitations of the free-market economy, and major problems set by it, arise from the fact that it takes the "units," individuals, families, etc., as "given," which is entirely unrealistic. In the economic aspect specifically, it "assumes" given "wants, resources, and technique," in possession of each and all. The market is an agency of co-operation between such given units; it is no agency for improving tastes (wants) or manners or especially for conferring productive capacity to meet wants or needs; it will not redistribute capacity, and hence product, to accord better than the realities do with any norm of ideal justice. Business relations clearly do work to dissolve clannishness and dogmatic allegiances and to promote tolerance and a degree of generosity. But in the distribution of economic resources atomistic motivation tends powerfully toward cumulatively increasing inequality. For all productive capacity—whether owned "property" or personal qualities—is essentially "capital," a joint creation of pre-existing capacity (or the result of "accident"). And those who already have more capacity are always in a better position to acquire still more, with the same effort and sacrifice. This applies about as much to personal capacity as to property, though the latter is a more convenient way of passing on "unearned" advantage to heirs or successors. It is a gross injustice—by one of several conflicting norms of justice generally accepted in liberal society. But it is also the main reliance for the motivation of accumulation in all forms, hence of progress, all forms of which are directly or indirectly dependent on means and their economical use. And the tendency goes on beyond the individual life, from generation to generation, through the family and transmission of advantages. It is modified but hardly mitigated, and certainly not simplified, by the large element of "luck" in human affairs. Any serious effort to interfere with the process would weaken the family in other connections, and, if it were replaced by some other primary group, the anti-equalitarian tendency might still be as strong.

No doubt we all agree that extremes of wealth and poverty are unjust—especially when they do not correspond with personal effort or sacrifice—and are bad in other ways. The question is, what can we do about it? Can the rules of the economic game be so changed that the winnings, symbolic and real (and the former are not much inferior in importance), will accord better with some accepted or defensible criterion of justice? And can it be done without wrecking the game itself, as a game, and as a producer of the fruits on which we all live? The intricate conflict of values here cannot be spelled out in detail—freedom with order, efficiency and progress, interesting activity, but especially freedom versus justice. The ancient provision against misery was to stress as sacred the obligations of family and neighborhood, and "charity," almsgiving, by those having an excess over "needs." But in the main, men were told and conditioned to believe that somehow everything is really for the best, and the evils of life have to be borne with patience and fortitude. Almsgiving tended to mean supporting the clergy and endowing religious foundations, while an uncertain fraction went to relieve poverty (real or feigned) and that did an uncertain amount of good —certainly it made little impression on poverty as a whole. Modern society has largely shifted the load of relief from the family and local group, which can no longer so well bear it, or be made to, and centralized it more and more on the national government through progressive income and inheritance taxation. A vast improvement has come about, chiefly through assuring to poor children support and some equipment for earning a livelihood, with family limitation offsetting improved sanitation and medical care. This of course does not meet either ideal requirements or the popular demand—perhaps even social necessity—considering, again, the children, now future citizen-voters as well as producers of more children and soldiers. But specialists seem to agree that taxation, for peace uses, can be pushed further very gradually at best, if the practical limit has not already been approached, at least for a government that is not to employ powers incompatible with basic freedoms. So what? I have no answer to that one, especially for the crucial matter of how far society can allow free production of children and agree to support them "decently" and of necessity their parents along with them. But the classes that produce babies can outvote those that prefer "substance and culture" to large families, particularly if the latter are soft-hearted and encourage them to demand "justice." Moreover, the prolific can muster the larger armies, and perhaps the tougher too, where the distinction conforms to national areas; and it is here that the conflict between freedom and equalitarian justice now is the great world menace.

With no pretense that my message is a cheering one, I can only, in the interest of what seems to me plain truth, go on to emphasize the difficulties of our problems and the danger of action that will make things worse instead of better. As is now evident, the "liberal" nineteenth century, following the rationalistic eighteenth, was wrong in its view that mere individual liberty, religious-intellectual, political, and economic, would yield well-being and happiness. It did indeed accomplish wonders, supplemented by the kind of state action accepted by its original advocates. And people seem much more actively dissatisfied than before. J. S. Mill's *Principles of Political Economy* and Marx and Engels' *Communist Manifesto* appeared almost simultaneously in the middle of the "wonderful century," wonderful especially for the common man. But Mill was very critical of the institution of property; and the Manifesto called on the workers of the world to unite for the violent overthrow of all pre-existing social order, because "you have nothing to lose but your chains." Madness, criminal madness, of course; but how many of the bright and educated have fallen for and preached it, in democratic countries where the masses are well off beyond historical comparison! And it has become the accepted political creed in the largest nations of the Old World, who now threaten us so dangerously with "liberation" in accord with its tenets. Is it human nature to be more dissatisfied the better off one is? I shall not venture an answer to that one, either.

All I can do is to indicate the nature of the problem of free society, as I see it, point out some false leads and some things that "have to be," "or else." I do not predict; it may be a case like Uncle Remus' rabbit that was "bleeged to climb a tree" to get away from a dog. If free society is to exist, the electorate must be informed and must have and use economic and political intelligence and, of course, possess the moral qualities actually needful. On the intelligence factor I cannot take time to say more. I hope I have said enough to show that the problem is not of the kind so successfully attacked by natural science and technology in the interest of control by man over the natural environment. It must be "social" intelligence, of the general sort exemplified in the discussion by a group of the problem of improving a game—but with complications due to the vast scale of national and world society and the complex of conflicting interests and ideals involved. For help as to intelligence, we now instinctively turn to institutional education. This can certainly impart information, up to varying individual limits, and schools have also been successful enough in increasing knowledge—some say too successful—and the somewhat opposed functions of transmission and revision might perhaps be better co-ordinated. But does education make people intelligent? As to certain "intellectual skills," no doubt it does, again up to varying limits. But as to good sense, the "gumption" required to select and reject between sound measures and crude economic nostrums, such as I mentioned at the outset, the arbitrary interference with freedom of trade, fixing prices by fiat, and preaching revolution, the evidence is not encouraging. The "smart" and the educated seem to fall for these as readily as the man in the street. Indeed it often appears that the result of costly training is to make people more ingenious in thinking up and defending indefensible theories. The crackpots of all kinds and degrees are not recruited from the dumbbell or ignoramus classes. Even outside the "moral sciences," it is not these who spend their lives squaring the circle and inventing perpetual-motion machines.

What schools can do on the side of moral qualities is another question. But first let me say here what I have long believed, that the crucial problem in our whole intellectual-spiritual life, our culture, is the relations between the great values, perhaps especially truth and goodness or knowledge and virtue. I have time only for these and to note the relative neglect of the third member of the trio, beauty and taste—taste that is good or bad, in contrast with "mere" taste—and the even more neglected role of play or fun, entirely left out of the good life in our Hebrew-Puritan tradition. You will recall that Socrates and Plato thought that virtue is knowledge (meaning reasoned knowledge, like mathematics, not science) in opposition to the Christian (Pauline) view, that we know the good but choose the evil. (But Aristotle at least partly disagreed with Plato, and a famous saying of Ovid sides with Paul.) My point is that I see the main task of education in our age as training to separate believing and believing-in from liking for other reasons, at the crudest level, to distinguish sound from sense and, in general, truth from aesthetic or moral or any "romantic" attraction. In any case, indoctrination is a vicious trap, and a liberal must wish it were impossible. The first test of a free society is that it teach its youth to question and criticize and form opinions only by weighing evidence

—and to admit ignorance where there is no evidence—instead of implanting eternal and immutable truth, with abject submission to the inevitable authoritative interpreter, by some prescriptive right. And, on the other side, it is an equally pernicious idea that by education a society can lift itself by its bootstraps. Who is to educate the educators? Only some absolute authority, manifestly. And control of education is the first aim of the totalitarian. His ideal is a priesthood as the custodian of Truth, "conditioning" each generation in helpless infancy to unquestioning belief and making them go through life like little children.

One of the hardest lessons which in my opinion our democracy has to learn is to make necessary reservations about much of our ethical tradition, propagated under religious or church auspices. It should be superfluous to point out that this is an inheritance from an age when virtue in the common man was thought by everyone to consist precisely in the acceptance and submission I just spoke of— conformity to a sacred law and obedience to consecrated authority, Holy Mother Church and Holy Father King. What our Sunday-school moral adages mean is simply the command to be good children and mind Momma and Poppa. They sound well, and their sentiment has a place; but if we ask what they mean, from the standpoint of democratic citizenship, they are simply irrelevant. When they were proclaimed, the idea that the ordinary man (not to mention the woman) should make and unmake the laws and literally hire and fire the rulers would have provoked only loathing and terror, if it had been dreamed of as a possibility. Even the Golden Rule, to treat others as you would be treated, is also epigram. First, it should of course be as the other himself would be treated or as "you" would be in his place and with him in yours. But for the slave master, what the slave would want would be to change places: "Let me be master and you be slave" —which would be no improvement in the system. But such is the romantic view of God: one who puts down the mighty from their seats and exalts the lowly, who fills the poor with good things, but the rich he sends empty away. Well, turn about may be fair play, but again we get no light on how to improve the social order. Taking slavery or any institutional framework as given, humane behavior is laudable. And that is exactly what our religious ethic did and does; it takes the established order of things as given, in fact as divinely ordained: "Let every soul be subject unto the higher powers. For there is no power but of God: the powers that be are ordained of God" (Rom. 13:1). And of course this explicitly included subservience of wives to their husbands. The only exception recorded is the right of the propagandist of the "true faith" to preach in defiance of the authorities (Acts 5:29).

Again, as always (in accord with my theme) there is another side. Liberalism can be equally naïve and as given to empty words. No adult in his right mind ever believed that men are born free and equal—except for that complete and in that sense equal helplessness for which freedom is without meaning. The socialists and communists have called religion the opiate of the masses, and in a broad historical sense that is correct. But two other truths have not been so clear to either side in the controversy. First, some pacifier, reconciler, or escape was necessary in a society that accepted the "static" philosophy of life that actually was accepted everywhere prior to the "awakening" in western Europe in the seventeenth and eighteenth centuries. Then were born the ideas of freedom and of progress in and through knowledge and intelligent action under free cooperative association. For man is a romantic animal; and until a people is prepared to make changes by intelligent agreement, supernatural sanctions are required to make them accept what is established and not criticize or try to change it. The second fact is that—disregarding the question of how much intellectual maturity west-European peoples had attained by the age of the Enlightenment—it is certain on general grounds that the basic framework of social order must always be accepted custom, interpreted and applied by agents having a large amount of power. The possible amount and speed of free and intelligent social change will always be quite narrowly limited. This is particularly true if intelligent change is taken to mean change in the direction of the ideals of justice and freedom, justice implying some kind of fundamental equality—and other values generally accepted in our modern liberal world view. As I would like to show at greater length than is possible here, no close approach to realization of those ideals is within the realm of possibility. Consequently, men will always require, as a condition for maintaining any high civilization at all, some "opiate" or some effective agent to prevent their demanding their rights. The only alternative to belief in supernatural sanctions of an existing system quite far from just is that intelligence shall be fully aware of its own narrow limitations and be supplemented by a high order of tolerance and self-sacrifice, the patient acceptance of the best all-round choice among evils. Especially, as the world is built, the chances of loss are overwhelmingly greater than the chances of gain in any effort to escape the ills we have by flying to others that we know not of. Since order is the absolute requisite of civilized life, we must stick to the order that is, until there is a reasonable agreement on changes that will be on balance beneficial.

The balance will always be hard to strike and entirely a matter of judgment, not of formula, a balance between principles that conflict, while each claims to be absolute. The danger now, in the world and in the West, is that freedom will be thrown away for a promise or hope of justice but with an actual result of neither justice nor freedom, and very likely the suicide of civilization in war without rules. The world could be heading toward a new age of essentially religious wars, ideological wars. Historically this would be nothing new, except for its scale and for the destructiveness of modern military technology. Otherwise, Europe is reverting to form. For as I have said, communism, in its social program or pretensions, is largely a revival of historical ecclesiastical Christianity, with the church more effectively merged in one all-powerful state. From the downfall of the Roman imperium to the age of liberalism, Europe lived under one or more dogmatic, intolerant, persecuting, and violently proselyting religions—claiming possession of the formula for salvation, they could not be or do otherwise—and much of the time in a state of war between two or more such religions. In Christianity, surely, we find the supreme "irony of history": that an original teaching centered ethically in humility, meekness, self-denial, and self-sacrifice became organized into corporations whose dignitaries have hardly been matched for arrogant grasping, using, and flaunting of power and wealth and for insistence on prerogative to the borderline of worship. One turns to Dostoevski's famous speech of the Grand Inquisitor for any adequate portrayal of this situation and its sinister indications of the nature of human nature.

The plea of communism, like that of Christianity, is justice, under absolute authority, ignoring freedom. (The former does extol progress, and progress through science, both of which Christianity despised; by the same argument, communism is overtly less devoted to law and tradition, more openly claims the right to ignore or break the law.) For liberalism, the primary value is freedom, self-limited by laws made by the community, ideally by general assent, in practice by representatives elected by a voting majority—one of its dangers. The laws of a liberal state will also be general, non-specific, but in a sense quite different from the Golden Rule or Law of Universal Love. The familiar figure is "rules of the road," in contrast with instructions where and when and how to travel, whether arbitrary or conformable to a traditional practice. But such freedom must be sweepingly limited by measures, not only of a "police" character in a broad sense, but also designed to equip the individual and family for social life by implanting wants and tastes in general conformity with the culture and endowing each with a minimum of productive capacity (or ultimately with final goods) without which freedom is a form empty of content. To take these units as "given" is flagrantly contrary to essential facts of life and means ignoring the major social problem. It is along this line that eighteenth- and nineteenth-century liberalism went to an extreme that has provoked a reaction which threatens to engulf all freedom, and justice too, in the modern conception of it, if not to destroy civilization. Liberal states have been engaged, however, through their short life, in correcting this imbalance between freedom and justice; more intelligence and better judgment is our need, rather than any radical departure in method.

The prime requisite is simply critical intelligence. And it may well appear as if the race at large hates this type of effort, naturally, instinctively. Anyhow, we have been conditioned in the opposite direction virtually throughout history, at least until the first breaking-away from the ideals of conformity and submission to sacred law and authority during the past few centuries. The real heart of modern liberalism is a radical change: a virtual inversion in the conception of truth and believing, a transfer from a moral-religious to an intellectual-moral basis. What the world really needs to learn from science, for handling social problems, is not its techniques but its moral code. In the religious age, truth was absolute and belief a matter of right and wrong, hence naturally to be controlled by reward and punishment. For liberalism, truth is always provisional and rests on the "best" evidence—incidentally, not on logical demonstration, but that is a long story. Right belief was a virtue, finally the condition of eternal salvation. The principle was stated, particularly with reference to our own religious tradition, by Lord Bacon: "The more absurd and incredible any divine mystery is, the greater honor we do to God in believing it" (and in similar terms by Tertullian, around 200 A.D.). Liberal moral values fit the same description as the liberal conception of truth; not virtue versus vice, but the best possible at any time and place. This means that the object of devotion and pursuit is not ends but ideals, progressively redefined as they are progressively realized, and always with the mode and spirit of pursuit and definition—freedom, but under critical direction, not caprice —as the most essential value.

A further consequence is that liberalism is fact-facing above all. It does not pretend that existing economic conditions are just but recognizes that justice can be approached but never attained, and freedom likewise and any other social ideal in its ideal form. It just is not that kind of world. It is childish if not hypocritical to preach that all discord is harmony not understood, that "in erring reason's spite, One truth is clear, whatever is, is right," or, accordingly, that omnipotent goodness and omniscience rule the world. As T. H. Huxley said, the ways of the cosmos are not our ways. Rather it is man's work to remake the world, as far and as fast as he can, according to his sentiments and ideals, about which the cosmos gives no evidence of the least concern—and to be careful not to defeat the whole project by trying to go too far or too fast with it. Also, to enjoy what goodness and beauty he can find, without letting these appreciations confuse and corrupt his judgments of truth. Any of my students or former students in the audience will please forgive me for repeating here a statement I often quote, from Clarence Darrow, characterizing divine justice. Said he, "God made one man a genius and the other a fool—which always seemed to me a raw thing for God to do—to the genius." Of course, it is a raw thing for both of them, but the world *is* like that, and we must take it or leave it. Nor is much freedom possible in any social order, and notably in the large-scale organizations, efficient and yet constantly changing, that are required to exploit modern technology. You're in the army now, even in peacetime, especially in the mass-production industries. You can only be reasonably free to elect some other work, in view of the "net advantages." As to justice, other things are distributed even less in accord with merit than wealth and income, and we can do little against the monstrous vicissitudes and caprices of the natural world. To secure any form of social justice, we should have to begin with a much more equitable distribution of parents and more remote ancestors and manifold other circumstances that largely determine the character of one's life long before birth. And even when one reaches the fullest responsibility, it is possible to have but a fraction of the knowledge necessary for really intelligent action. As to "happiness," it is easy to agree with Darrow, and Meredith, and many more, that the idiot or, as Whitman puts it, the animals, have the best of it. But *that* happiness, at least, is not what makes human life worth while.

We must, as I have suggested, be good sports, enjoy the game whether we win or lose, not cheat even to win, and not even be too sore when the opponent wins by a little cheating. And we must try, all along, gradually to improve the rules as well as to obey and help enforce them. The main injunctions that can be given are negative, especially not to go too fast, not to oversimplify, not to grasp at easy solutions for hard problems. I think the greatest danger is that suggested by my text—a "moralistic" approach, attributing social evil to sin, with the implication of cure by liquidating somebody, or at least firing some scapegoat, and seeking a savior. People are not bad, in the main, but they are ignorant and do not understand. They have not been taught to approach problems in terms of knowing and understanding but to obey some ancient rule, as interpreted by those in power, or follow some new prophet. Democracy calls for leadership, but that does not mean finding the right man or party and giving him or them irresponsible power. We surely know what a dictator will do, once in power; he will, indeed, use "science" to make everyone be good and do right.

I have used up my time without saying much about the alternatives to the free economy; but that would be an endless task, and also one for a corps of experts. Let me repeat that how people expect to cure the social ills by a radical shift from business to democratic politics is a question for which I see no answer except in terms of the psychology of romantic prejudice and screwy thinking. Most of the evils inherent in the market organization plainly inhere still more in political campaigning, legislative debates, and administration, perhaps even judicial trials. Especially the tendency to centralization and concentration of power—which can only go so far until voting and political discussion will be empty forms, if the boss allows them to go on at all. Yet freedom is not enough; it was carried too far, and more and more political action is called for, though it is dangerous; if only it can be in the main right action or not too far wrong! Democratic action is hard. It means government by discussion, and the organization of discussion itself, as I said before, involves the main problems. Not much intercommunication is even theoretically possible. As the world is built, the cards are heavily stacked in favor of centralization. Even in one direction, communication is bad enough; among economists, for instance, the typical reply to a criticism is, "But I didn't say that." I myself have been made a bad example for views I supposed I was arguing against all through the years. As to intercommunication—even with two persons there is an insoluble problem of dividing the time for both between speaking and listening, and it is said to give rise sometimes to friction, even causing dissolution of the holy marriage bond. With larger numbers, the limitation increases rapidly, in I know not what form of compound progression. One person can, indeed, be heard by a considerable number and, with mechanical aids now available, by "the world," as well as reached by print—if so disposed. But, though no prophet, I will predict that no invention will ever enable one to listen or attend to more than one, other at a time or to "send" and "receive" communications at the same time.

To conclude: There was a time, no doubt, when society needed to be awakened to the possibility of remedying evils and stirred to action, mostly negative action, in establishing freedom, but some positive action too. Now, we have found not only that mere individual freedom is not enough but that its excess can have disastrous consequences. And a reaction has set in, so that people have too much faith in positive action, of the nature of passing laws and employing policemen, and the opposite warning is needed. At least so I hold; perhaps it is a prejudice—how can one tell?—but I mistrust reformers. When a man or group asks for "power to do good," my impulse is to say, "Oh yeah, who ever wanted power for any other reason, and what have they done when they got it? So I instinctively want to cancel the last three words, leaving simply, "I want power"; that is easy to believe. And a further confession: I am reluctant to believe in doing good with power anyhow. With William James, I incline to the side of "the slow and silent forces," slow as in all conscience they are—and though time is fleeting.

There is much more that should be said, but certainly not on this occasion. When I started this, I knew, from experience, that I'd never finish it. Life seems to consist of "unfinished business." And, having already imposed on you too long, without waiting for the peremptory order that is given to naughty corporations, I simply cease and desist.

XII

Free Society: Its Basic Nature and Problem[1]

FOLLOWING a venerable precedent, which has become rather hackneyed usage, we may begin by observing that "man is a political animal." But it is more in keeping with modern ideas and knowledge to say a "social" animal; and we must immediately add that social "animal" is misleading, for it is the differences between human and animal societies that especially need to be emphasized. The only highly organized non-human societies of separate organisms are those of certain "colonial" insects, which are based on a physical (anatomical and physiological) specialization not found in man. Their patterns of behavior and of social order are fixed by instinct, which is also true of the crudely organized "herds" or other groups among the higher mammalian species. The notion of pure mechanism, without intelligence, cannot be strictly accurate, even for ants and termites, but it must be close to the truth; in the absence of speech, there can hardly be any "thinking," properly so named, or anything whatever of group deliberation. The social animals do not feel conflict between the interests of individuals or between individual and group interests, and do not solve, or confront, group problems.

Man is as completely social as a termite in being unable to live at all outside a group of considerable size and of complex yet fairly stable structure (even a Crusoe is no real exception); but the reasons and the accompanying phenomena are utterly different. Human evolution did not start from a highly socialized animal; man and the insects represent the culmination of two different lines that separated far down in primitive marine life. "Our" line was socialized for the most part long after the final achievement of the physical basis of a high intelligence and after other profound physical changes, notably in the reproductive system, that occurred between the highest known animals and *homo*. Of these physical changes, excluding brain size and general form, no record is likely ever to be found, as they affected only the ephemeral flesh, not the bony structure or any durable artifacts. Very little if any human behavior is biologically in-

1. Reprinted by permission from the *Philosophical Review*, Vol. LVII, No. 1 (January, 1948).

herited in a pattern at once definite enough and complex enough to be properly called an instinct. Man's original nature has been dissolved and diluted into vague urges or "drives," whose specific manifestations are acquired after birth by learning, in one form or another. They are "cultural" in the anthropological sense of custom, mores, or institutions, i.e., derived from the community in which the individual grows up—not necessarily that in which he is born. The patterns are subject to modification by individual experience, and the activities traceable to particular drives have become overlapping and more or less interchangeable. They change gradually by the process of unconscious drift (spontaneous variation and selection), with invention at a minimum until very recent times. On the other hand, such "culture" is scarcely found among animals; some exception may be made for the birds, which are not in the evolutionary sequence leading to man (and which, interestingly, are the only animals that can even be taught to imitate speech).

We can imagine social life operating entirely on this principle of custom and conditioning. It is as mechanical as instinct, but has the biological advantage of a flexibility and adaptability greater than the accidents of gene mutation. But we have no knowledge of any actual society of this simple kind. In the most primitive human society, at least three other principles are operative, all more or less connected with intelligence (in the instrumental sense). The most ancient seems to be authority or leadership. In addition, there is informal or conversational discussion, not rationally directed but undoubtedly contributing to modification, by drift, both of language itself—the basic and typical institution—and of attitudes and overt behavior. Finally, among men there is always some formal deliberation, with explicit formulation of issues and "discussion," leading to agreement on a conclusion—or, if this fails, either to compulsion or to disintegration of the group. The mores never function by themselves, for human nature is antisocial as well as social; intelligence seems to be inherently individualistic, conceiving of ends and modes of their pursuit in forms that involve conscious conflict with other units. Consequently, usages or protolaws are not merely scientific principles but are also laws in the higher sense of being felt as imperative, and they always require enforcement by various sanctions. It seems impossible to think of man as not characterized by these traits or to call by that name any creature that is without them.[2]

2. Interrelationships among these several social principles are almost infinitely various. It would be of the greatest interest and value to know something of the

The reference to sanctions suggests the fact that whatever arrangements are established in human society they seem practically always to be "sanctified" by *religion,* an elaborate and various institutional phenomenon almost as important as language, and like it much more important than any concrete usage or custom. (Naturally, religion itself is peculiarly conservative, resistant to drift; but it is subject to more or less considerable mutation through the agency of "prophets.") It normally includes much ritual, partly of the nature of play, but of varying supposed potency over supernatural powers, conciliatory or coercive, and over natural events and the efficacy of various acts. In addition to a quasi-religious reverence for their customs as such, primitive peoples believe in occult forces and invisible powers—totems, ghosts of ancestors, and other spirits, living in the objects and phenomena of nature or hovering about the tribal habitat. These are concerned with rewards and punishments (operating in this world) to enforce conformity to custom and obedience to authority, serving to counteract the antisocial tendencies of man as an instrumentally intelligent being. Fear alone may be effective, or there may be action by special authorities or the general mob. For innate human nature apparently includes an urge to force others to conform, or to extirpate those who do not, as well as both a love of ritual for its own sake and an impulse to break any law,

---

evolution and historical development of the complex, particularly the development of speech and the differentiation within the primitive harem herd (said to be characteristic of the anthropoid apes) of fairly definite and stable *families.* If we only knew how protomen learned to talk and what they said, especially the relation between imparting useful information and emotional expression! Speech may well have begun with love song or inspirational "oratory"; and ballad history, lament, and jest are doubtless older than logical discourse. Again, sex relations and family life, within a large organized group, would seem to be the crucial point at which mores and authority replaced instinct; and they are basic for the higher emotional life and for all civilized, hence all human, social order.

Recent study of animal groups suggests for protohuman society a large role of authority in the brutal form of "dominance," established by fighting—for food, for sex (among the males), and for dominance itself or prestige. It is not a nice process, by our moral and aesthetic standards, but that is characteristic of nature's methods. It would be effective in bringing to the top intelligence, courage, and other leadership qualities, and whether our gentler ways are as effective, or effective enough, is a question still to be answered by history. Savage peoples now living are organized predominantly through *mores* (customary law), along with all sorts of leadership forms, themselves customary, or *ad hoc* devices. What we know of the beginnings of civilization indicate a tendency toward authority and status inherited in family lines, but hereditary monarchy is always vulnerable to family decadence, intrigue, and insurrection. High civilization has also shown a tendency to general moral decadence, and it is certainly open to doubt whether our own will prove an exception to the rule.

with a craving for sociability and for power and more specific selfish desires.

The philosophic basis of any soundly descriptive or useful discussion of man and society must be recognition of a complex and subtle *pluralism* of fundamental categories. The most important fact about man is that he is at the same time a number of kinds of being, which are not only different but in theory mutually incompatible. He seems to be the product of "emergent evolution," in which many new traits have been successively superimposed upon an extending series without, in the main, eliminating the earlier. First, of course, he is a physicochemical mechanism. And it cannot be proved experimentally that any of the laws describing the behavior of non-living matter are inoperative or operate in any special or peculiar way in the human body, though, unless there is some exception, these laws should exhaustively account for all that a man is or does (including the writing, and the reading, of this essay!). Second, he is a biological organism, in which, again, the main facts and processes of other life, plant and animal, are exemplified. Scientists generally reject the idea that anything is involved in life beyond physics and chemistry; but even the botanist, dealing with unconscious life, cannot talk sense without using teleological terms such as will or urge to live and reproduce, adaptation, struggle, competition, economy.

As to the emergence of novelty, the sharpest break in continuity seems to be the appearance of consciousness. However, its more primitive manifestations and the relations of its different aspects— awareness, feeling, intelligence, and will—are so uncertain that no clear lines can be drawn. It is impossible to doubt the existence of a complex conscious life in the higher animals, but no tolerably definite account can be given below the level of men, who communicate by speech. Within the range of human life, anthropologists speak of savage, barbarian, and civilized, emphasizing the breaks that come with writing, the use of metals, and other technical achievements. Several of these steps represent considerable and fairly sudden advances. But for our purposes, and within the compass of a brief sketch, the discontinuities that seem to call for recognition, after the appearance of animal life, are two. The first marks the advent of primitive human society, based on the principles already described, but with intelligence virtually inoperative (suppressed) in the social order (our third level). The final discontinuity is that which ushers in the fourth level, modern free or democratic civilization. The essential change is the replacement of sanctified custom and authority, socially inherited and transmitted through cultural conditioning, by the still-experimental attempt to base social order on secular rationality—"government by discussion," in the words of Lord Bryce's famous definition of democracy.

At the third level, that of premodern man, the emergence involved more supersession than was true at the earlier break, from the physicochemical process to life or consciousness. The principle of instinct was largely replaced by the other types of action pattern already considered—mores, authority, and lower forms of intelligence. Various combinations of these superbiological social forms characterize the cultures or civilizations of world history, including prehistory, prior to the advent of free society, as an ideal and more or less an achievement. Not only did biological evolution cease long before the dawn of history; more important still, human development has to be discussed in terms of new purposive directions or ends as well as new processes. The changes we refer to as "progress," even before this was consciously recognized and pursued, are described in relation to qualitative differences and norms, which bear no clear relation to the apparent intention of nature—mere quantitative increase of life—and often seem to clash with the latter. On the whole, human life must have been more efficient than the lower forms, as shown by its actual increase at their expense or through their control and utilization. But, prior to modern times, civilized society has evinced increasing instability of organization, apparently due to a tendency of individualistic intelligence to break out of institutional and authoritarian—and intelligent moral—control and become predatory or even to turn explicitly against life and pronounce it an evil. In consequence, cultures, if not the peoples as biological entities (that have become primarily bearers of culture), have typically flourished for a time only to become decadent and disappear or be absorbed in a new development from a more primitive start. (But each new wave has typically risen higher than the preceding.) In this process a large role has of course been played by organized war, a phenomenon nearly or quite peculiar to man and an activity in which he has been somewhat especially inclined to use intelligence.

The final great "emergence" and, so far as we know, the last (unless some form of totalitarianism turns out to be really the "wave of the future") is modern free society—the setting of the problems we are concerned to characterize. Practically speaking, it is a phenomenon of the past few centuries in the history of west-European civilization. The development occurred through the diffusion of power in a new wave of development achieved as usual through consolidation and centralization, but with important differences. The Renaissance was actually much more the birth of a new and historically unique civilization than the rebirth of the Greco-Roman civilization that became decadent over a millennium earlier. The crucial differences centered in the place and role of religion, its relation to politics, and back of that to intellectual and economic life. The prime key to understanding what happened is the fact that in the period of decadence of the classical world, Europe had taken over Christianity, a new universal (i.e., dogmatically and violently intolerant) religion, a blend of Judaism with elements of contending mystery cults of the period, plus an infusion of Greek philosophy, all by this time "organized" on an imperial-authoritarian pattern. In other words, the key to postclassical European history lies in the twin notions of orthodoxy and heresy (distinguished from personal and political loyalty), the heresy issue nearly (not quite) always a clash between rival orthodoxies. Of course all religions have taught that morality, law, and order depend on religion, and all true morality on acceptance of that particular one, and many of the protagonists have sincerely believed both doctrines; and, of course also, the leaders in all the contests, on both sides, have stood to gain or lose heavily in power and perquisites of power, which have been objects of desire to most human beings always and in all circumstances. And of course (finally, and the real heart of the matter) all orthodoxies are *in principle* adhered to and supported uncritically, irrationally. As Lord Bacon said, "The more absurd and incredible any divine mystery is, the greater honor we do to God in believing it."

The great result of several centuries of war of the most terrible kind, of "treasons, stratagems and spoils," was the birth of liberty. But few indeed of the contestants or perpetrators wanted liberty or thought it good or possible; they wanted—and in a sense believed in —their own power and formal right to coerce all who disagreed. The twin ferments of change were the growth of science and the economic interest, the desire to get ahead in terms not only of wealth but of political power, social position, and culture. What human ends, good or bad, are not dependent more or less directly upon material means, in spite of all the nonsense talked and written about materialism and the economic motive? But of these two factors, the one logically if not historically prior is science. For the crucial fact is the freedom of the mind; if thought and expression are free, freedom of action and of association follow inevitably. The historical and moral relation in the sociological sense is far from simple, because the distinctive and crucial feature of the modern scientific movement is a close tie-up with practice, again not merely in technology but in warfare, medicine, and the fine arts. In earlier times, the crafts had been traditional and science extremely aristocratic and snobbish. The modern relationship to commerce and industry involved a new respect for the ordinary affairs of men, for work, and for ordinary men themselves.

As a matter of course, too, the basic freedom and the faith and respect that it presupposes imply political democracy, of which the formation of public opinion by discussion open to the participation of all is the essential part. Representative machinery is a corollary as the only way of assuring that government will do things the mass of the people want done and will not do things they oppose. Further, it just as inevitably implies the open market as the main general form of economic organizaion. One of the major "discoveries" of the revolutionary age, the Enlightenment or Age of Reason, into which the Renaissance inevitably merged, was the self-evidence of a harmony of interests in *free* relationships, excluding force and fraud and presupposing mutual respect for the freedom and the competence of the other party. Previously, the best minds had held the absurd notion that any gain by one trader must mean an equal loss by the other. It is quite false to allege, as is so commonly done, that the new economics of laissez faire rested on an assumption of a "natural harmony of interests" apart from this condition of mutual respect for one another's rights, and, if this should not be rendered voluntarily, its enforcement by whatever legal and political measures might prove to be required. It is unfortunate, though natural in view of the historical development, that the term "laissez faire" became distinctively attached to economic freedom. It means simply "freedom," and was supposed to apply as a matter of course to all individual and associative life. By this time the burning issue of religion was in abeyance, through loss of interest, in favor of politics, trade and industry, science and culture, and other concerns (good or bad) of this world.

In economic life itself there was no implication of restriction of ends to "lower" wants or to any particular category. Moreover, men would be free to co-operate on any terms other than those fixed by the open market, to whatever extent they might agree on such terms as more equitable or preferable for any reason. This explicitly covered used of the state as an organ of co-operation, provided only that it restricted itself to such public works and other functions as would command general agreement, i.e., require a minimum of coercion. Logically, the extent of the sphere of state action might be indefinitely large, even to socialism in any form that would use the open market as a general framework; this proviso is necessary because the market is the one possible form of organization that permits of individual freedom in consumption and production, including provision for the future.

The establishment of freedom, rooted in the liberation of the mind from traditional dogma and mythology, enforced by ecclesiastical and political authority, is the greatest revolution of all time or since the dawn of conscious life. Stated in abstract terms, the doctrine and program are very appealing. And for a time the change seemed to be fully justified by its fruits. Free science and free enterprise, with general cultural freedom, led to much the most rapid advance yet seen, not merely in the conquest of nature by mind and the harnessing of the forces of nature to the purposes of man, but in humanitarianism, the unification of the world's peoples, and the diffusion of the advantages of civilized life among the populations of the advanced nations, and among others as fast as they were able to join in the movement. But only for a time, and no one would now make the period very long. The liberation had not gone far toward completion (if the notion can be given tolerably definite meaning) before evils forced themselves on the public attention, and evils affecting the lower classes, not those who had lost a position of special privilege through the change. The close of the Revolutionary epoch (so-called from rather overdramatized political events in British North America and in France) saw the beginnings of violent criticism of the new individualism, of socialistic propaganda, and of measures making the state more responsible for the life and well-being of the weaker members of society. And it is a notable fact that in the same year, 1848, still in the first half of the nineteenth century, were published the *Principles of Political Economy* of J. S. Mill and the *Communist Manifesto* of Marx and Engels. The nature and significance of this coincidence does not need to be spelled out here; nor does any reader need to be reminded of the later course of events leading in the twentieth century to world wars and the relapse of much of the European world into totalitarianism, with ominous portents for the future even of formal democracy in the small part of it that remains nominally committed to what a short generation ago was liberalism but is now called conservative (if not reactionary) social doctrine.

The causality of this astounding counterrevolution, or yearning for counterrevolution—rooted in a feeling not that the ideals of free society were wrong but that historical liberalism has made a mockery of them—is the mystery that cries for explanation. A little candid inquiry will show that the graver moral and intellectual problems of a free society have not been faced or even stated. This is in part because of a Pollyanna optimism on the part of the more articulate classes that is natural to a period of rapid progress, together with an innate aversion to hard thinking (and the problems are forbiddingly hard); the tendency to oversimplification and wish thinking is an obvious trait of human nature, which in general is more romantic than it is rational. But it remains true that in essential ways the liberal movement went wrong, partly because of the failure to think out its problems, hence in ways more or less subject to correction, but especially because it generated expectations and implied promises impossible of fulfilment. This again was partly for the same reason, a moral failure to face problems. Partly it was because of the limited competence of human intelligence, its proneness to err and blunder in ways that later become evident or are even discerned at once by minds especially competent or favorably placed for seeing pertinent facts and escaping prejudices that are part of the reason others do not see them. From this point of view, the failure of several generations of liberal education to get the articulate and influential strata of the public to understand the mechanics of free enterprise and its merits, and the relation of natural science to the various levels of value problems, is indeed discouraging. But further, it is clearly of the nature of life and thought insistently to pose questions that are insoluble by minds of any kind or any degree of competence that we can imagine.

As has been suggested above, the movement of revulsion and revolt arose first in connection with the "free" economic order, the open-market organization, including that specialization of responsibility and risk in the hands of entrepreneurs, which gives it the name, "enterprise economy." Some denunciation of freedom in natural science and demand for curbs have arisen, but they have come later and have only currently become strong enough to prompt any serious effort to bring about action to this end, and only in connection with the wartime development of methods for releasing the incredibly destructive powers of intra-atomic energy (with some disposition to include biological weapons of war). Accordingly, we turn our attention first to the problem of economic organization, postponing to the next section the few remarks that may be offered with respect to science and intellectual freedom.[3]

It must be briefly remarked that the economic problem is far from being fundamental in the sense that is generally taken for granted. No conceivable economic reform would by itself go far to achieve general social contentment or probably even peace. Motives that cannot reasonably be called economic are more important causes of war than any that can be so classed. If the gift of some Aladdin's lamp were to give all men power to satisfy all cravings dependent on the use of means (but without power over other persons!), it is quite certain that in the absence of other equally revolutionary changes in man's nature discontent and social friction, animosity and conflict, would be increased and not diminished and in ultimate essentials would hardly be changed in form. Games and even arguments (on any subject) have to be policed, as well as markets! Even casual conversation has a tendency to run into altercation and then into a fight. But this sketch must be limited to the issues in the economic and intellectual life (in the fairly narrow meaning of science and closely related activities), ignoring play, sociability, cultural pursuits, and sex and family relations, all of which are intrinsically at least as important.

In our consideration of economics we are concerned with the political policy of laissez faire, i.e., simply *free* co-operation or mutual consent in all joint activity in the use of any means to achieve any end. (The categories of end and means, hence that of economy, cannot be given any really satisfactory definition.) The policy rests on the ethical principle of freedom, the *right* of any person to choose his own ends and to pursue them in his own way, and, as an obvious corollary, the *duty* or moral obligation of each to respect the same right in others. The "science" (if it should be called such) of economics (here, economic theory) is relative to this policy and this ethic. Its function is to show by analysis of market competition how freedom of exchange works out automatically (without central control) to an organization of production and distribution on a national and world scale, to show the kind of system that results under speci-

3. It goes without saying that the tradition of orthodoxy in religion is still very much alive in the Western world; also, that any church in the Semitic-Christian tradition that is strong enough to do so will (logically must) struggle to control intellectual, social, and private life.

fied conditions, and to show the results of interference in specified ways by the state or other agencies. (Market competition presupposes purely impersonal behavior; hence involves no "competition" in the common meaning of rivalry.) The analysis shows how, under the conditions necessary for its existence, this organization achieves *efficiency* in the utilization of resources and *justice* in the distribution of the joint product, efficiency being defined by the ends chosen by individuals and justice by the principle of equality in relations of reciprocity, giving each the product contributed to the total by its own performance ("what a man soweth that shall he also reap"). But, as we have seen, any "higher" form of justice is provided for by freedom to co-operate on any other terms or through any other form of organization on which the parties may agree.[4]

In the face of the theoretical appeal of the principle of free enterprise, and its period of conspicuous and recognized success, and the non-comprehension and incompetence of the general public in relation to it, with the resulting stupidity of much of the criticism to which it has been subjected, there still are theoretical and practical considerations that weaken and go far toward destroying the case in its favor. As the theory of the system has been more fully worked out in the light of criticism and of experience, in the generations since Smith's *Wealth of Nations* was published in 1776, more and more implicit assumptions have been brought to light, conditions more or less contrary to fact, that must be fulfilled if the working of the system is to be such as can be ethically approved. Many of these conditions could be established only by social action going far beyond the laissez faire ideal of policing against force and fraud, even in the broadest definition of terms that have no objective or precise meaning; others could never be established by any human means. The issue, which may be stated before going further and should be kept in mind from here on, centers in the fact that social

4. Full scope is allowed for life devoted to contemplation or ascetic ideals, subject only to the condition of self-support or voluntary support by others. As a matter of historical fact, of course, the whole movement for freedom was an incident of a revolution in the mores that discredited idleness or parasitism and all submissiveness and credulity, in favor of activity, independence, and responsible self-assertion. The good life came to be conceived in terms of ends achieved through intelligent use of means (the meaning of "economy") and especially in terms of *progress* through the accumulation of resources and knowledge, and growth of taste. But this is not logically essential. What is essential (after recognition that important truth can be discovered by critical investigation) is the gradual discovery that there is a presumption of mutual advantage in all free association, resting on a new faith in human intelligence and morality, which replaced the dogma of original sin.

action means "politics" of some variety, conducted by the same frail human nature that performs with such unsatisfactory results in economic relations. This fact raises doubts as to whether the remedy may not involve the same evils, in a form as bad or worse, or others intrinsically worse. The romantic character of political power and the psychological law that distance lends enchantment create a systematic temptation to imagine a political system as much or more idealized in comparison with probable reality than the most extreme conception of open-market economic order ever was. Incidentally, our inherited religious tradition has always treated the position and powers of rulers as sacred (without suggesting the rule of law, other than the "Law of God," necessarily interpreted by rulers themselves) and has regarded as sinful the use or quest of economic power, if not its possession.

Relative to this issue, another and even harder truth must imperatively be kept in mind. There are different principles of justice and right which conflict among themselves, at least in application to the stern facts of life where alone they have practical meaning. Such conflicts between basic values often underlie the alternative evils mentioned above. The pluralism of human nature culminates in an ethical pluralism, also the product of emergent evolution. It is easy to condemn a social arrangement because it runs counter to some ideal and to indorse another which would or might avoid or lessen that particular evil, without duly considering effects which the change would actually have upon the achievement of other values quite as important. A large part of the social problem centers just here. Especially, freedom and progress, the distinctive values of modern civilization, conflict with the older ones of order and security but of course do not invalidate and supersede them; and there seems to be no principle of compromise that can be stated in words and that is of much help in making concrete political decisions. Men must be keenly aware of the problems and use judgment and be tolerant and patient! They must accept the inevitability of gradualness, while striving for possible improvement. Taking moral principles too seriously may be as bad as not taking them seriously enough.[5]

In our present compass it is possible only to present a list of the

5. The conflict between representatives of these two tendencies is one of the most serious in politics, as the issue itself is one of the deepest in the moral life. Moral absolutism makes discussion impossible, and the situation is indefinitely aggravated when religious absolutism is superadded, as it tends to be. It is the essence of religious belief that all discussion and all questioning of "the truth" is wicked, truth meaning my truth, which is never based on critical examination.

main grounds for criticizing the free-enterprise organization, grounds which are valid in terms of some ideal, whether or not they are finally valid on balance. First, a rough dichotomy; some of the defects have to do with the mechanics of the system, as it actually operates, "human nature being as it is," in contrast with the assumption of (instrumentally) rational behavior. Others center in ethical principles in relation to unalterable social facts and raise questions regarding the factual as well as the ethical presuppositions of the individualism which is the basis of historical liberalism. Under the head of mechanics, the weakness that is practically and theoretically most serious is the tendency of economic activity to go in waves of expansion and contraction, both in a particular industry relative to others and, especially, in production on the whole—the business cycle. A condition of boom alternates with one of depression, the latter bringing disastrous unemployment and suffering. These symptoms are an expression of an essential weakness in all social relations based on individual freedom. All human conduct is more or less speculative, and when it is directed toward change and improvement it is more so. But when activity is individualistically organized, a far more speculative element is introduced, since what it is rational for any individual to do depends on what others will do, and there is theoretically no solution except to reach a mutual understanding and establish a consensus in advance. Such a result calls for political action of a sort that must largely nullify the principle of individual freedom. The intricacies of the resulting economic and political problem are the subject of intense controversy among specialists and of a voluminous literature.

The only other mechanical problem that can be mentioned here is the familiar one of monopoly. About this we can say only that it is both badly misunderstood and grossly exaggerated in the popular mind. Much monopoly in the technical meaning is not only inevitable in a free and progressive economy; it must be called positively good. The principle is illustrated by the deliberate granting of monopoly power in the patenting of inventions, and a great deal of other monopoly is essentially of the same nature, a stimulus to devising and introducing useful innovations. But much is not, and it is a serious problem to differentiate between the good and the bad (both features are present in the patent system itself) and to make and enforce regulations to secure the best possible balance.

More serious, at least in a philosophical sense, are the evils of the second class, involving social-ethical problems. Only the most essential facts can be noted here. Economic freedom means freedom to use means to achieve ends; the means include one's own personal capacities and external materials and instruments, which one owns or controls—either is useless without the other and both are uselesss without knowledge of technical processes. Freedom is empty without *power,* and its effective content depends both on the possession of power (in all these forms) and on what the individual actually wants to do with power. But both power and wants or tastes come to the individual chiefly through the processes of the society in which he lives, especially by inheritance, biological and cultural, and through the family. Thus social policy cannot possiby treat the individual as a datum in any of these respects, since he is in fact largely the creation of social action. Hence the main social problem becomes that of the kind of individuals, or persons, and primary groups that are to be created. The family is much more real as a social unit than the individual and itself exists only in a hierarchy of larger communities.

The economic problem that lies nearest the surface arises out of the unequal distribution of productive capacity. The large if not predominant role of inheritance (not of property alone, as commonly assumed, but equally of capital in the form of personal qualities) runs counter to individualistic conceptions of justice, even of a fair competition, not to mention more idealistic standards. The role of luck must be considered in relation to fair and interesting sport and the distribution of prize money. Because both property and personal capacity are so largely historical creations—neither given by nature nor produced by individual effort—there is a tendency for inequality to increase cumulatively. Those who at any time have more are in that much better position to acquire still more. Through the family, and other institutions, this goes on beyond the individual life. And it should be stressed—because it is generally ignored—that this tendency applies not only to personal capacities but to taste and appreciation, to all culture, which is humanly more important than means of gratification.

Finally, some mention must be made of the limitations of the whole economistic view of life and conduct—the view, that is, in terms of the use of means to achieve ends. There really are no "ends" in any final sense—they are rather milestones on the way ahead and these become means as fast as they are achieved—and the qualities of good and bad belong about as much to means as to ends in any right use of the terms. In play, for example, the end-means relation is largely reversed; the objectives are unreal; they are set up arbitrarily to make the activity interesting. In fact, both economic and political relations have about as much the character of play, of competitive sport, as that of satisfying wants that can be regarded as real. And the notion of economy has very limited application to any explorative or problem-solving or creative activity, where there is no end that can be defined or measured in advance.

As the writer is only too keenly aware, all that has been said in this section sheds little light on the question of what is to be done; it only calls attention, and that inadequately, to the complexities of the problem set by individual freedom in economic activity and relationships. But we must turn to the deeper problem of individual freedom in intellectual pursuits. Here again only a few general observations can be offered. We must ignore what would naturally be the first question, the vitally important economic problem of the "support" of cultural and creative life. We have already pointed out that the whole modern movement of liberation was on one side a doubly indirect consequence of the growth of interest in natural science. On one hand, science was bound up with technology, hence economics, which as a direct interest was the other main ferment; and, on the other hand, the issue overtly argued and fought over in the transitional centuries was tolerance for sectarian religious differences. This has little in common with intellectual freedom rightly conceived, which came out of the struggle as an unintended result. The freedom of natural science itself today is, of necessity, only partial, the role of arbitrary power large; and large also is the role in the minds of scientists themselves of numerous interests much less exalted than the self-sacrificing or wholly unselfish pursuit and dissemination of "pure" truth. Yet, comparatively, science is free, and its freedom rests on the general acceptance by its votaries of a rather high and austere ethical ideal. Its phenomenal success has offered a strong temptation to students of the human, historical, or moral disciplines to adopt or imitate its procedure, or pretend to do so, and to clamor for the application of the scientific method to social problems. And there has been much yielding to this temptation. But that is just what it is, and our last few paragraphs must consist of an attempt to expose the error as one of the most depressing signs respecting the capacity of modern man—the best minds—to solve by thinking the problems that now probably have to be solved in that way if any civilized life is to continue on earth. For, critical thinking once started, there seems to be no way quietly to turn it off (all over the world at once) and revert to older bases of order.

To begin with, natural science in the study of nature itself raises problems far more serious than it solves. Its success lies in yielding *power*, and it has made it plain that man is not really fit to be trusted with much power, individually or collectively. If only he were just an instrumentally intelligent animal, he would use power in subduing nature to the support of more and more healthy human beings, biologically speaking, and the matter would be fairly simple. But, as we have noted, the development of intelligence is associated with the proliferation of new ends or purposes not embodied in particular definable ends. Perhaps the worst case is the erection of power itself into an end—outright dominance over other persons—or pseudo ends that are symbols of power, their concrete form being a historical accident. The real import of economic issues is greatly reduced by the fact that our wants are so largely rooted in a desire to be like other people or to be different in some way that is a sign of superiority. Each wants to have more of anything, little matter what, of which there is not enough to satisfy everyone.

Moreover, man soon developed ideas of "beauty" or, in general, *quality* of life and its impedimenta that he calls "higher values," the pursuit of which clashes with the "lower" requisites of life itself. With the progress of civilization his tastes become more expensive, without apparent limit, and lead to aristocratic scorn for the means and activities that must support alike the higher and lower pursuits. How far and when the higher values are really higher, or really values at all, and not mere symbols conferring distinction, is a question earnestly and heatedly discussed, without much progress toward agreement on the answer. They certainly contain a large admixture of the second element. And they certainly derive very largely from the particular culture in which they happen to be recognized; hence the issues in social conflict run into the ranking of cultures, where argument is especially difficult and dangerous. The burning and menacing problems of the modern world arise largely in this connection and by no means only in international relations.

To the student, viewing the scene with Olympian detachment, as well as to the publicist or statesman directly up against issues of peace or war, life or death, the problem presents two related aspects, one general, the other more specific. The obvious general problem is whether men have the capacity to resolve conflicts of values by discussion—meaning in any other way than the "natural" one of fighting it out to the final test of who survives, or what, if anybody or anything with any claim to human concern. (We cannot here develop the close connection between the warfare of nations or alliances and of classes formed on one or another line; machinery exists for limiting fighting between individuals—relatively unimportant anyway.) Now it is a presupposition of any discussion—as more than an ephemeral amusement, a more or less amiable contest tending less or more toward resort to force—that the natural solution must be repudiated absolutely; for we all agree that might does not make right. But agreement on that point does not mean agreement on a peaceful alternative to fighting.

The more specific question is the role of scientific method in relation to value problems, and what has been briefly said on the general question logically disposes of this one. For the scientific solution *is* simply the natural one just suggested, the test of force and survival. Carried into discussion of human conflicts, the categories and procedures of science become self-contradictory and self-destructive. Science here means one of two things—which, incidentally, have been strangely confused in the history of liberal thought. It may mean adopting the Olympian point of view of "watch what happens and explain it," without moving to do anything about it. Or it may mean attempting control. But that means somebody controlling something—logically (in this connection) with everybody controlling everybody else! And in practice it must mean an unpredictable scramble and fight for control. In any case, we are back to the "grim arbitrament of war," of some sort, on some scale. And, incidentally, or rather fundamentally, the much advocated and attempted procedure of "preaching," either moral idealism or metaphysics, is from the scientific point of view the same thing over again. It is either a phenomenon to be explained or the use of a particular technique—the one the user thinks will work—and leads at once to the same impasse. In fact, the attempt of everyone to convert everyone else could not proceed far on the basis of such gentle arguments as the spoken or written word.

Even the "pure" science program of merely watching, describing, and explaining could not possibly be carried out unless all scientists —self-selected as a group—were to organize themselves into a party dictatorship and secure the absolute control that is necessary over any subject matter if it is to be studied effectively. Even astronomy and geology do not get far without using the results of laboratory experimentation. Newton's discovery of gravitation rested on Galileo's study of falling bodies. And the sciences of man, in so far as they are sciences, depend on observation of the results of manipulation, especially in medicine (physical and mental), also in politics and other administrative activities, and increasingly in the psychological laboratory. Not much knowledge of man is to be had—or especially to be applied—without his consent and co-operation, which presupposes that consensus upon values which is the main problem. Any attempt at use of the unqualified procedures of natural science in solving problems of human relations is just another name for a struggle for power, ultimately a completely lawless one. Something not too remote from scientific procedure is available in enforcing a given law, hence in conection with the problems of premodern society. But the essence of free society is that it deliberately attempts to change and improve established practice; hence it must find norms somewhere outside the factual space-time world.

Science, pure or pragmatic, is *not* the answer and has no clue to the answer to the essential problems of free society. Unless, that is, they are to be solved by war, which is the only observational and manipulative criterion of values, and we hate to admit that it is any real test of values at all. The various sciences, natural as well as social, have a very great deal to tell us about man and society; it is no service to the doctrine of spiritual freedom to pretend that we are not *mostly* mechanism, physical, cultural, and perhaps psychic. Yet finally we must understand ourselves and each other and act intelligently in relation to both, in other terms altogether. A simple and conclusive proof, by illustration, is the fact that the scientist cannot apply his science to his own distinctive behavior or that of another scientist. If the course and result of an experiment or investigation can be predicted in advance, it is no longer a problem and the project will not be carried out. Science can produce fairly conclusive evidence that man is merely a mechanism, that scientific description and explanation can answer all questions about him that can be intelligently asked. But the fact remains that man raises the question and marshals and appraises the evidence; and mechanism does not have these capacities or traits.

With this chiefly negative result, inadequately grounded and sketchily set forth, limits of space and the difficulty of the constructive side of the problem compel us to be content here, admittedly at the point where the subject begins to get really interesting.

Index

Index

i

PHOENIX BOOKS

PHOENIX BOOKS

PHOENIX BOOKS

PHOENIX SCIENCE SERIES